CHAPTER ONE

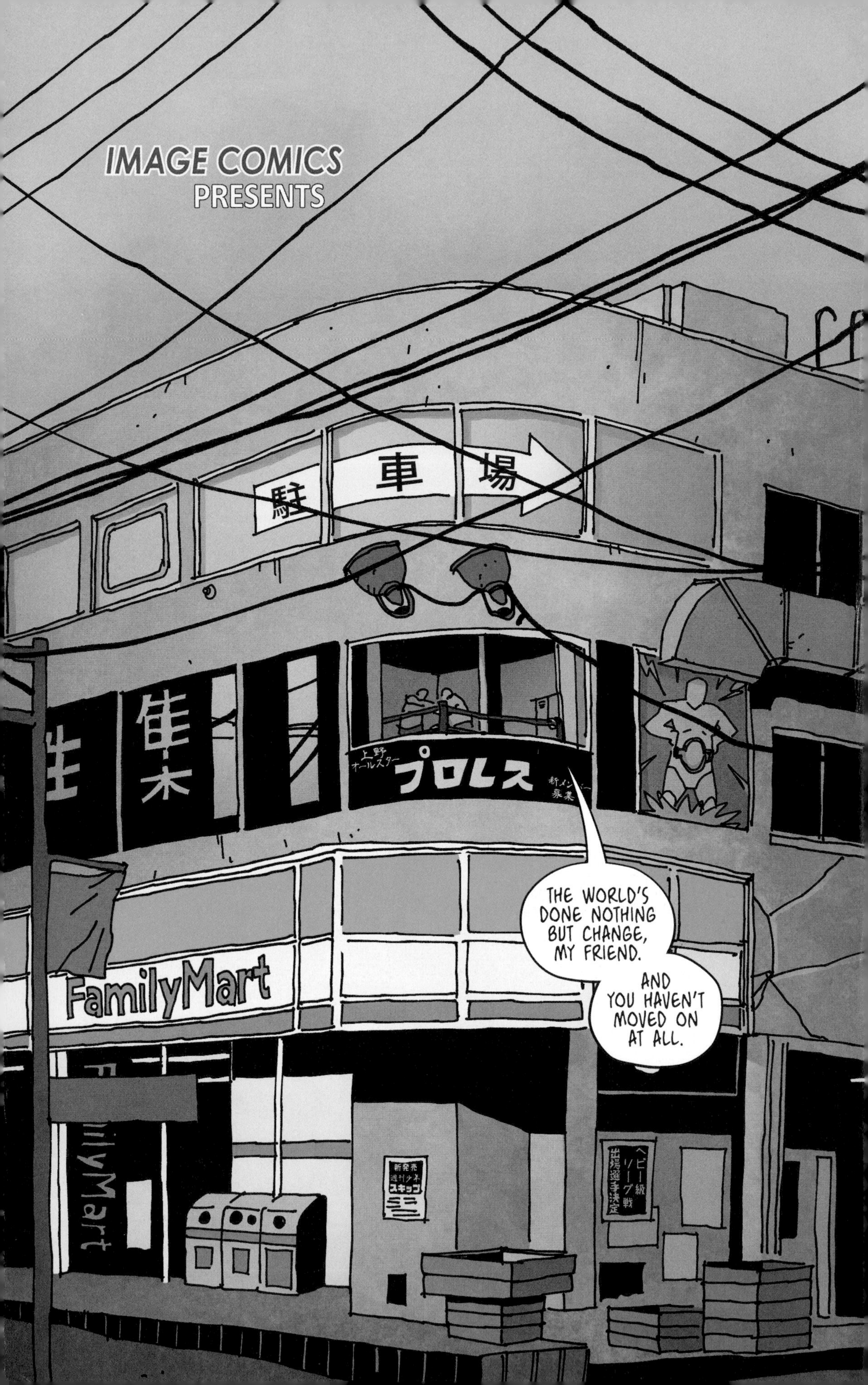
IMAGE COMICS
PRESENTS
駐車場
上野
オールスター
プロレス
新メンバー
募集
FamilyMart
THE WORLD'S DONE NOTHING BUT CHANGE, MY FRIEND.
AND YOU HAVEN'T MOVED ON AT ALL.
新発売
週刊少年
スキップ
ヘビー級
リーグ戦
出場選手決定

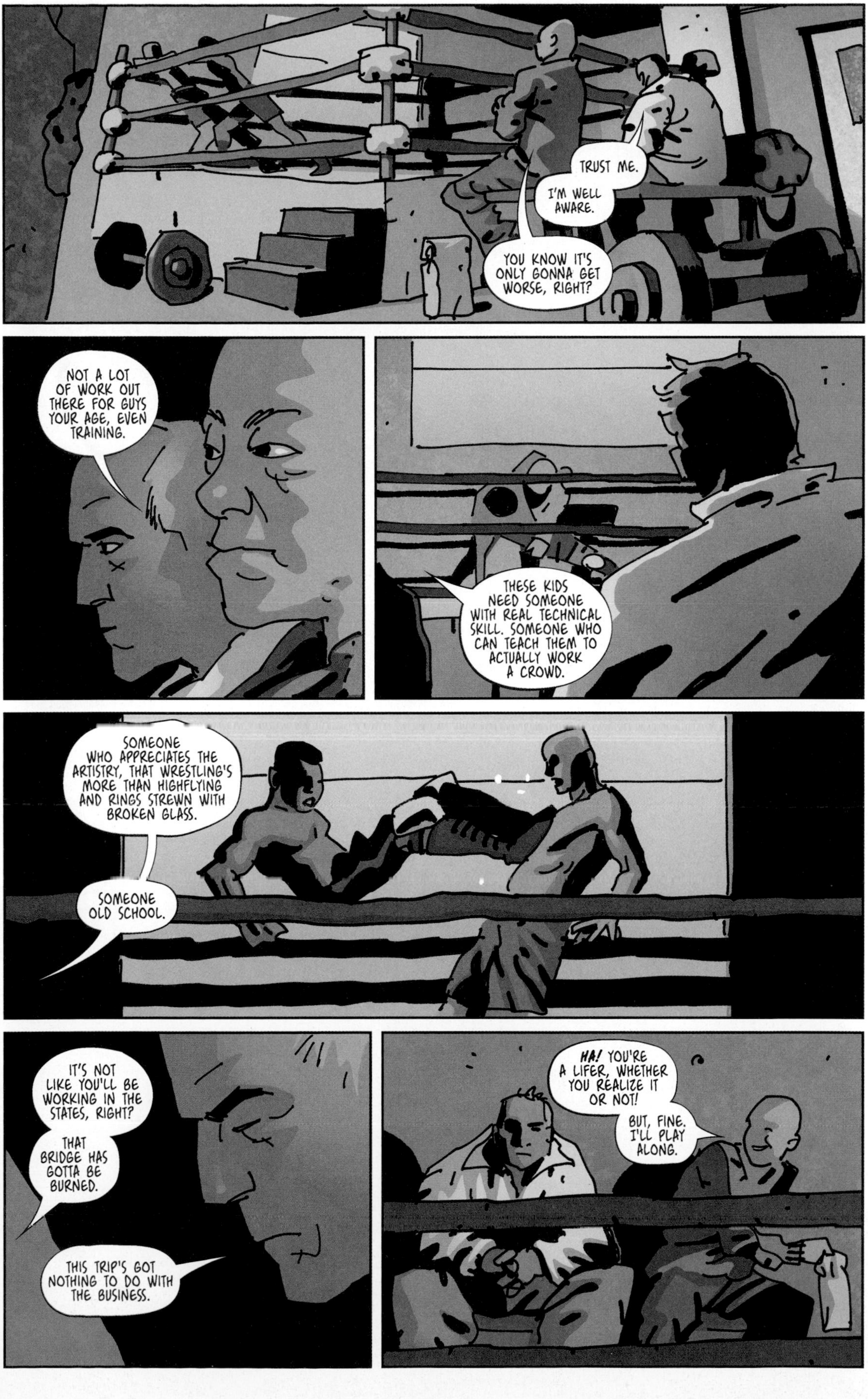
TRUST ME.
I'M WELL AWARE.
YOU KNOW IT'S ONLY GONNA GET WORSE, RIGHT?
NOT A LOT OF WORK OUT THERE FOR GUYS YOUR AGE, EVEN TRAINING.
THESE KIDS NEED SOMEONE WITH REAL TECHNICAL SKILL. SOMEONE WHO CAN TEACH THEM TO ACTUALLY WORK A CROWD.
SOMEONE WHO APPRECIATES THE ARTISTRY, THAT WRESTLING'S MORE THAN HIGHFLYING AND RINGS STREWN WITH BROKEN GLASS.
SOMEONE OLD SCHOOL.
IT'S NOT LIKE YOU'LL BE WORKING IN THE STATES, RIGHT?
THAT BRIDGE HAS GOTTA BE BURNED.
THIS TRIP'S GOT NOTHING TO DO WITH THE BUSINESS.
HA! YOU'RE A LIFER, WHETHER YOU REALIZE IT OR NOT!
BUT, FINE. I'LL PLAY ALONG.

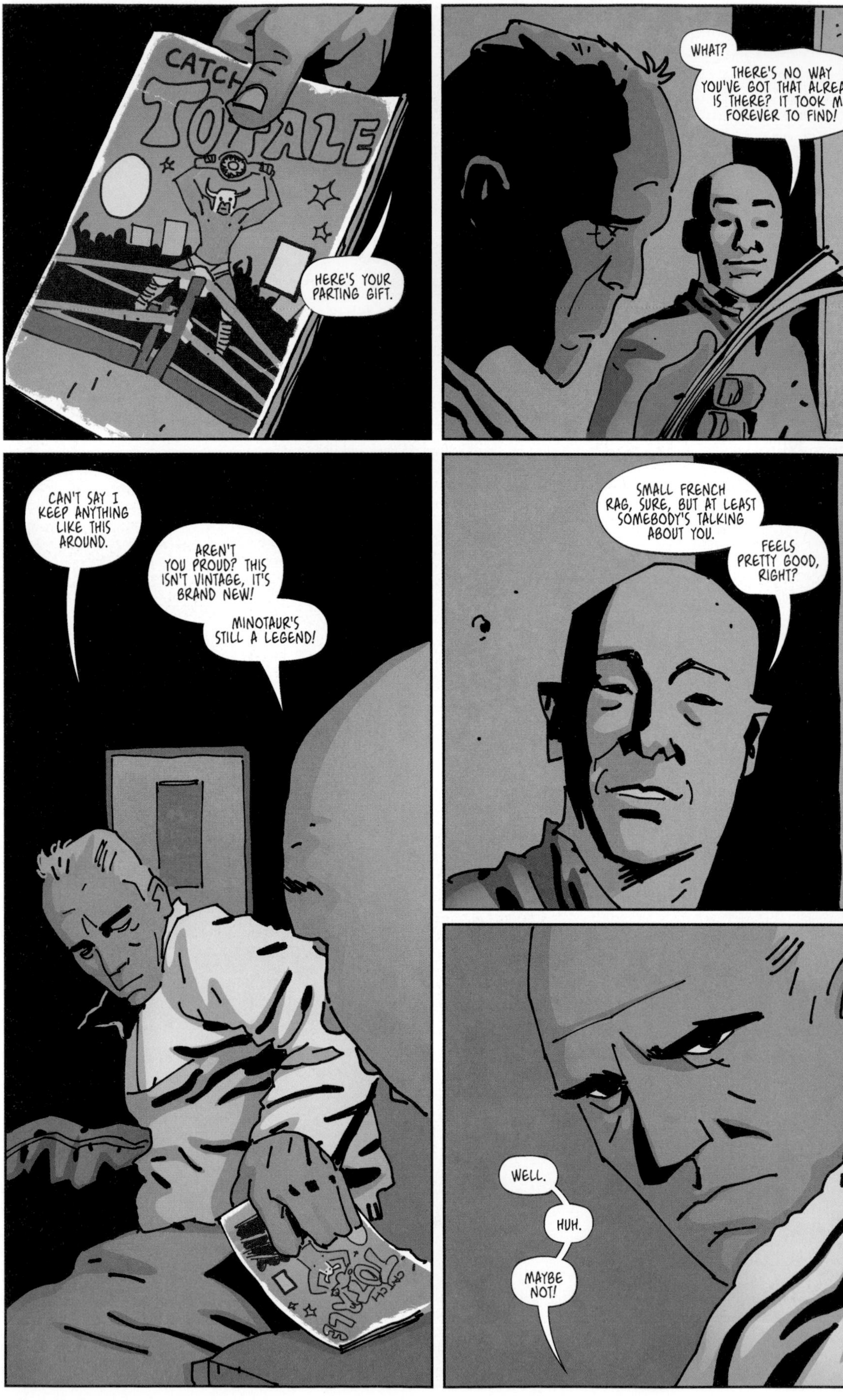
CATCH TOTALE
HERE'S YOUR PARTING GIFT.
WHAT?
THERE'S NO WAY YOU'VE GOT THAT ALREADY, IS THERE? IT TOOK ME FOREVER TO FIND!
CAN'T SAY I KEEP ANYTHING LIKE THIS AROUND.
AREN'T YOU PROUD? THIS ISN'T VINTAGE, IT'S BRAND NEW!
MINOTAUR'S STILL A LEGEND!
SMALL FRENCH RAG, SURE, BUT AT LEAST SOMEBODY'S TALKING ABOUT YOU.
FEELS PRETTY GOOD, RIGHT?
WELL.
HUH.
MAYBE NOT!

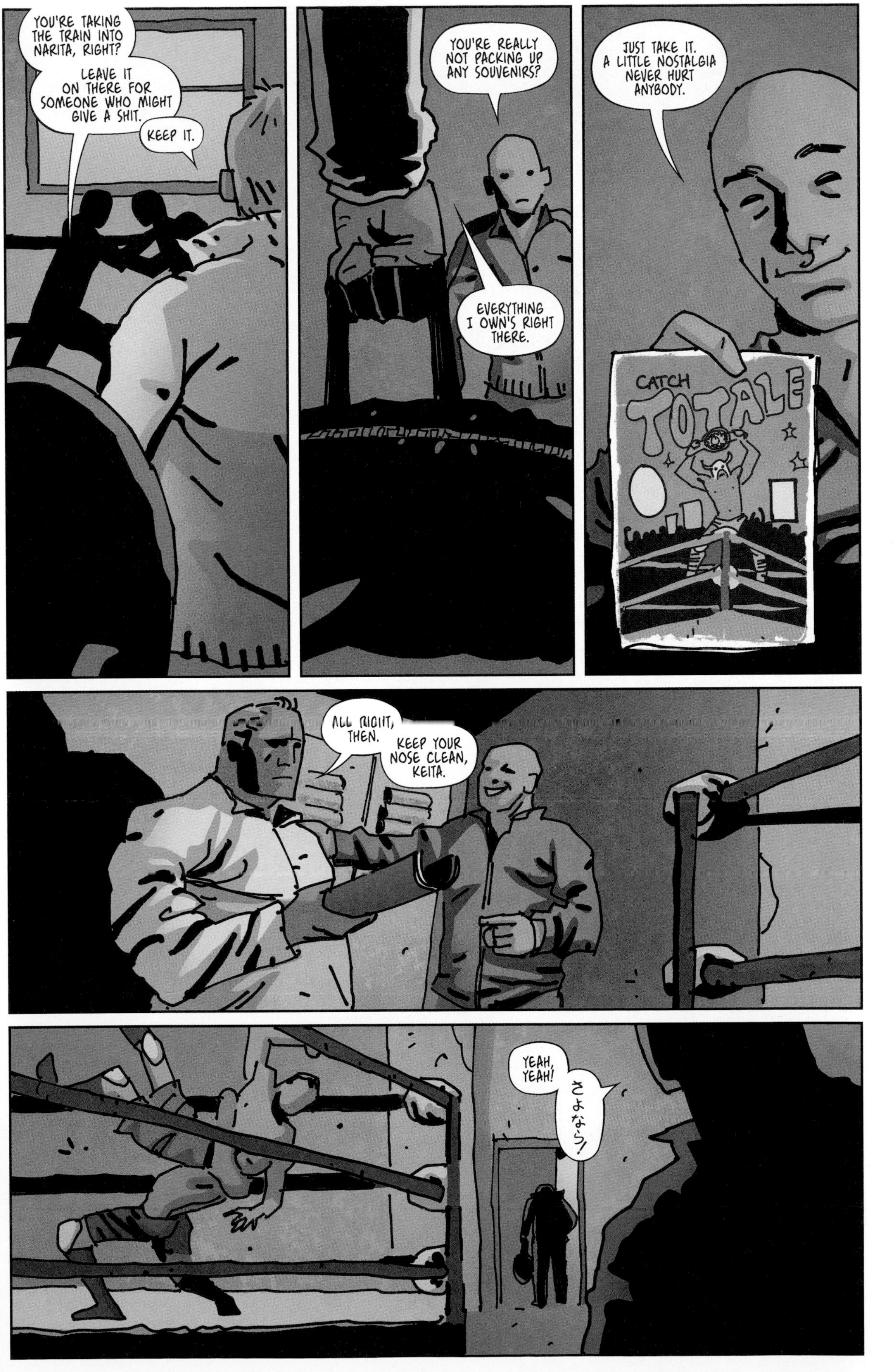
YOU'RE TAKING THE TRAIN INTO NARITA, RIGHT?
LEAVE IT ON THERE FOR SOMEONE WHO MIGHT GIVE A SHIT.
KEEP IT.
YOU'RE REALLY NOT PACKING UP ANY SOUVENIRS?
EVERYTHING I OWN'S RIGHT THERE.
JUST TAKE IT. A LITTLE NOSTALGIA NEVER HURT ANYBODY.
CATCH
TOTALE
ALL RIGHT, THEN.
KEEP YOUR NOSE CLEAN, KEITA.
YEAH, YEAH!
さよなら!

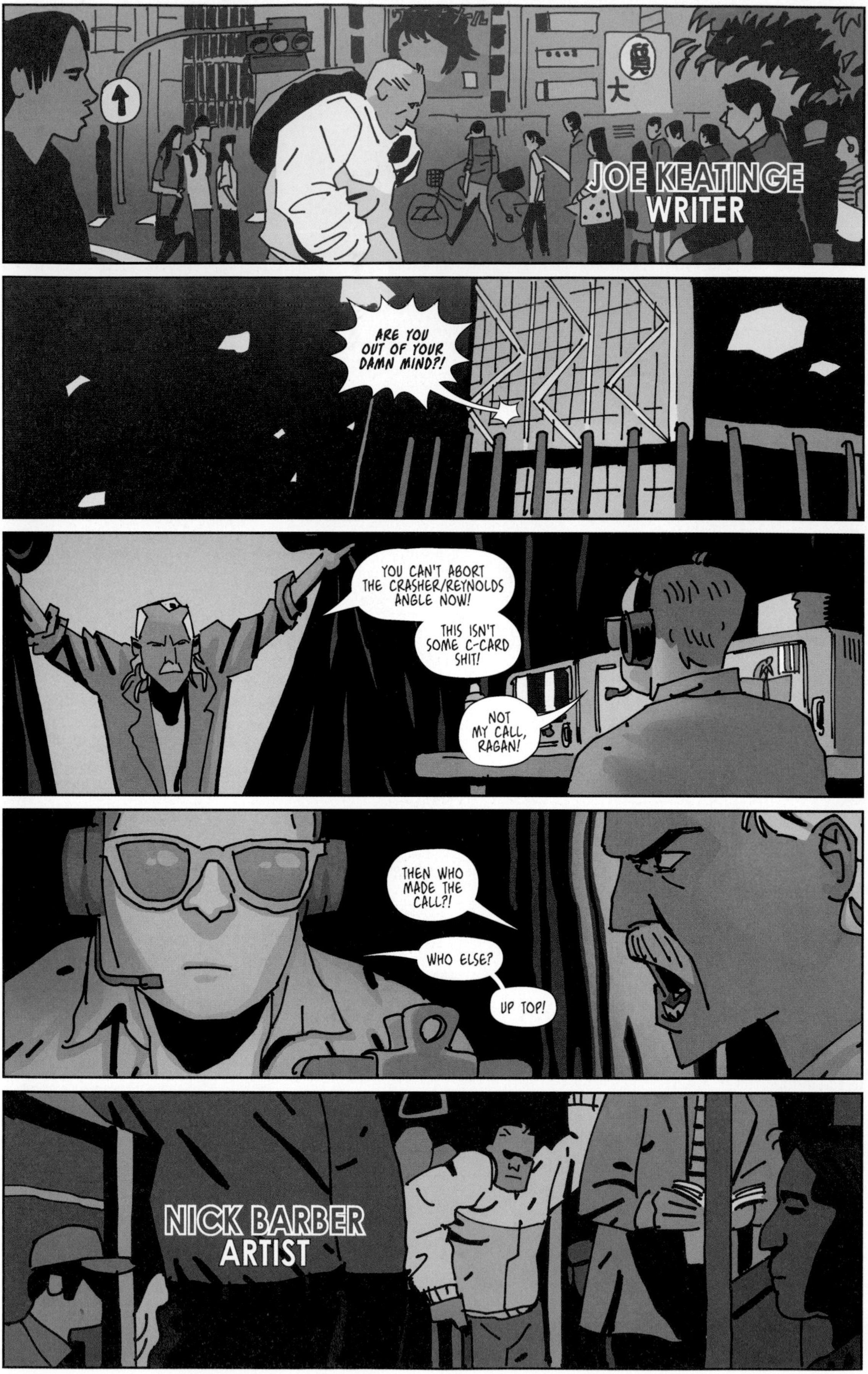
JOE KEATINGE
WRITER
ARE YOU OUT OF YOUR DAMN MIND?!
YOU CAN'T ABORT THE CRASHER/REYNOLDS ANGLE NOW!
THIS ISN'T SOME C-CARD SHIT!
NOT MY CALL, RAGAN!
THEN WHO MADE THE CALL?!
WHO ELSE?
UP TOP!
NICK BARBER
ARTIST

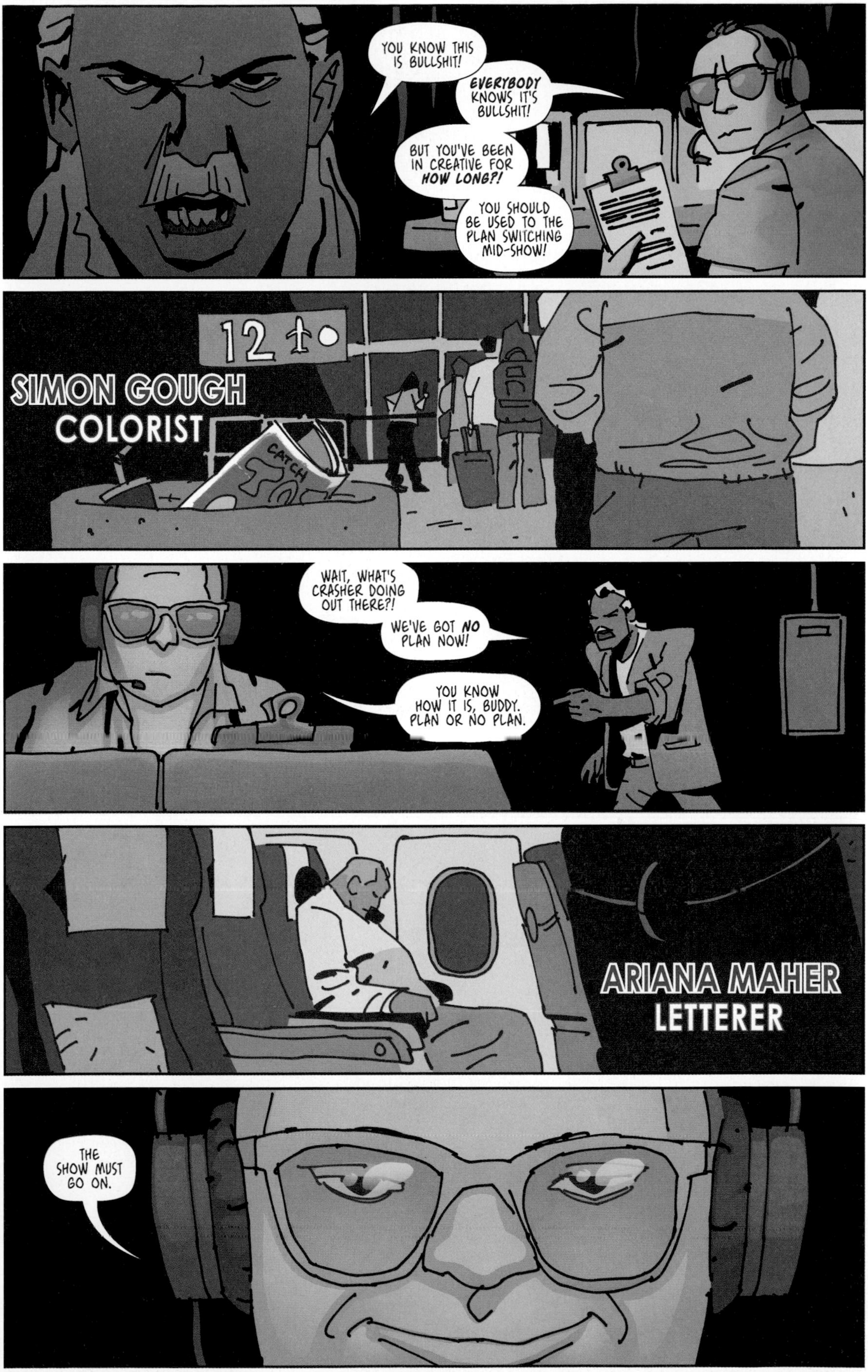
YOU KNOW THIS IS BULLSHIT!
EVERYBODY KNOWS IT'S BULLSHIT!
BUT YOU'VE BEEN IN CREATIVE FOR HOW LONG?!
YOU SHOULD BE USED TO THE PLAN SWITCHING MID-SHOW!
12
SIMON GOUGH
COLORIST
CATCH
WAIT, WHAT'S CRASHER DOING OUT THERE?!
WE'VE GOT NO PLAN NOW!
YOU KNOW HOW IT IS, BUDDY. PLAN OR NO PLAN.
ARIANA MAHER
LETTERER
THE SHOW MUST GO ON.

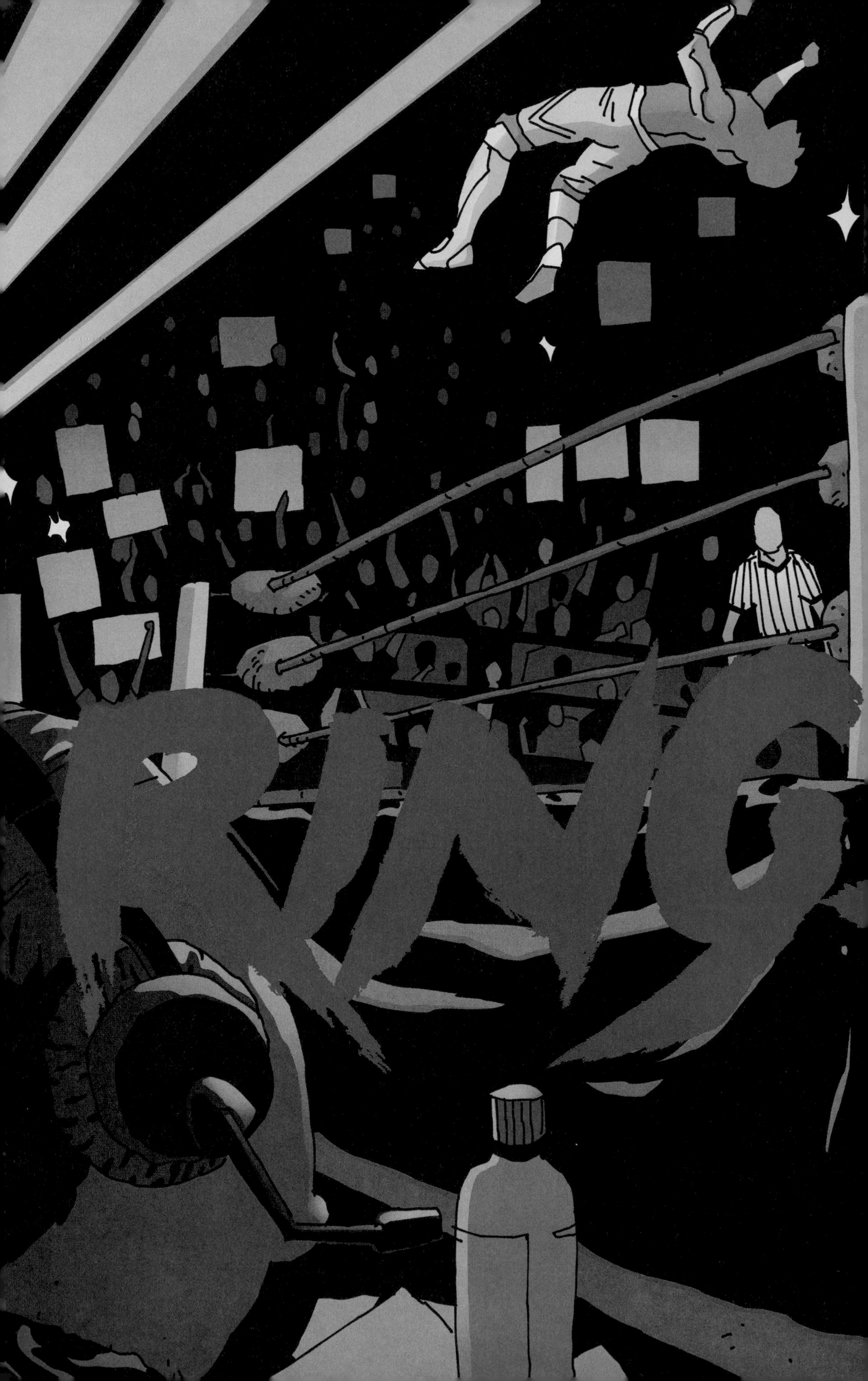
RING

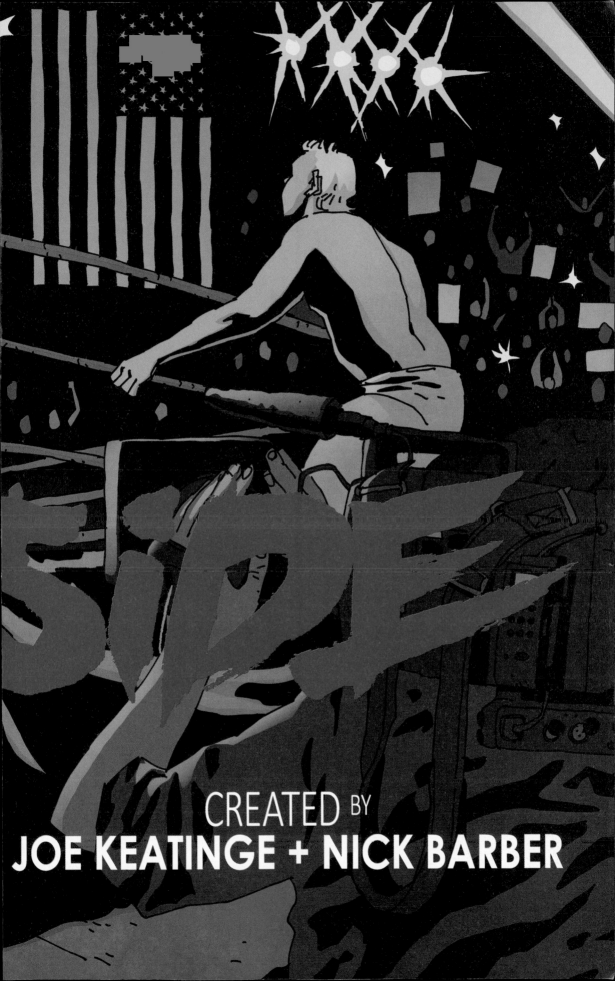

CREATED BY
JOE KEATINGE + NICK BARBER

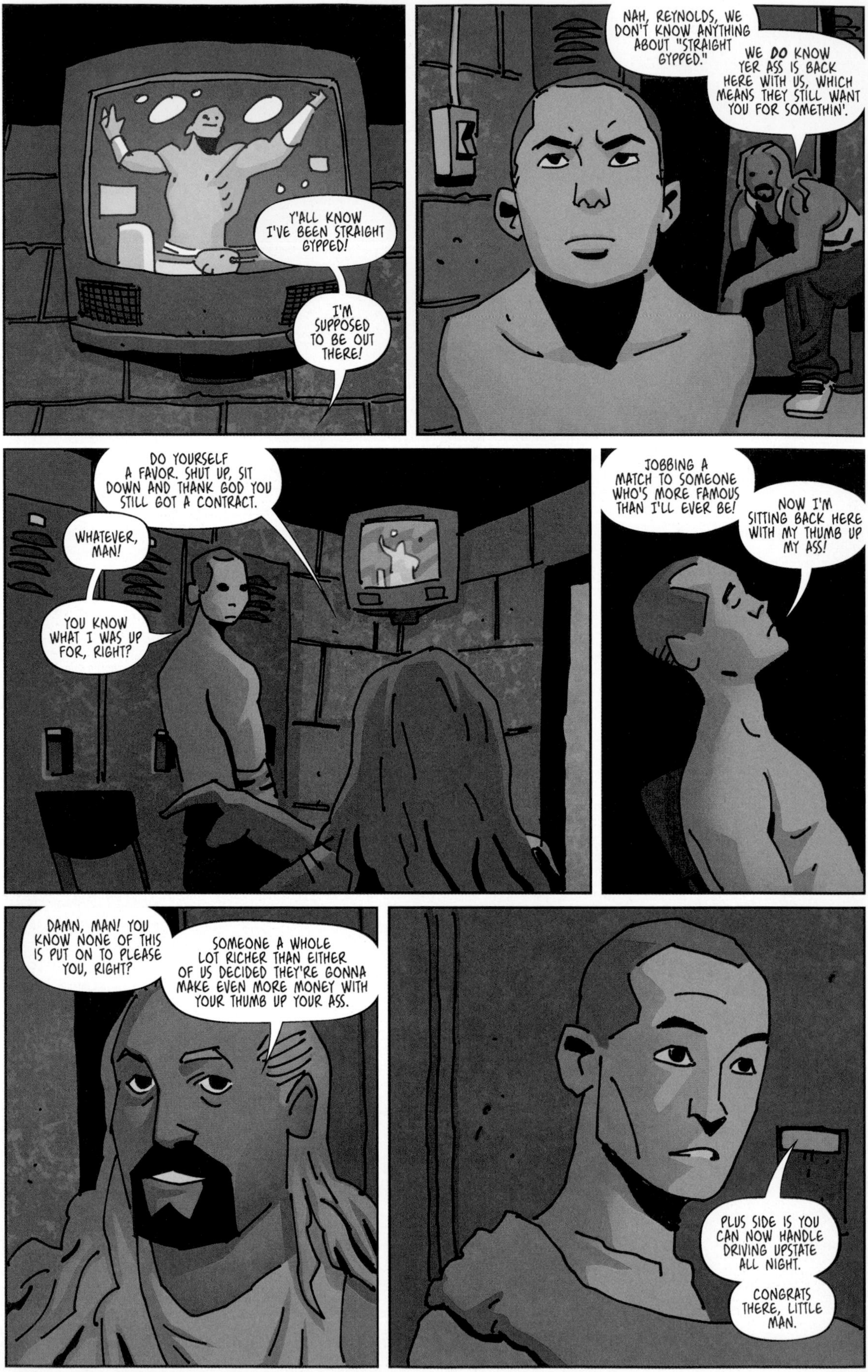
Y'ALL KNOW I'VE BEEN STRAIGHT GYPPED!
I'M SUPPOSED TO BE OUT THERE!
NAH, REYNOLDS, WE DON'T KNOW ANYTHING ABOUT "STRAIGHT GYPPED."
WE **DO** KNOW YER ASS IS BACK HERE WITH US, WHICH MEANS THEY STILL WANT YOU FOR SOMETHIN'.
DO YOURSELF A FAVOR. SHUT UP, SIT DOWN AND THANK GOD YOU STILL GOT A CONTRACT.
WHATEVER, MAN!
YOU KNOW WHAT I WAS UP FOR, RIGHT?
JOBBING A MATCH TO SOMEONE WHO'S MORE FAMOUS THAN I'LL EVER BE!
NOW I'M SITTING BACK HERE WITH MY THUMB UP MY ASS!
DAMN, MAN! YOU KNOW NONE OF THIS IS PUT ON TO PLEASE YOU, RIGHT?
SOMEONE A WHOLE LOT RICHER THAN EITHER OF US DECIDED THEY'RE GONNA MAKE EVEN MORE MONEY WITH YOUR THUMB UP YOUR ASS.
PLUS SIDE IS YOU CAN NOW HANDLE DRIVING UPSTATE ALL NIGHT.
CONGRATS THERE, LITTLE MAN.

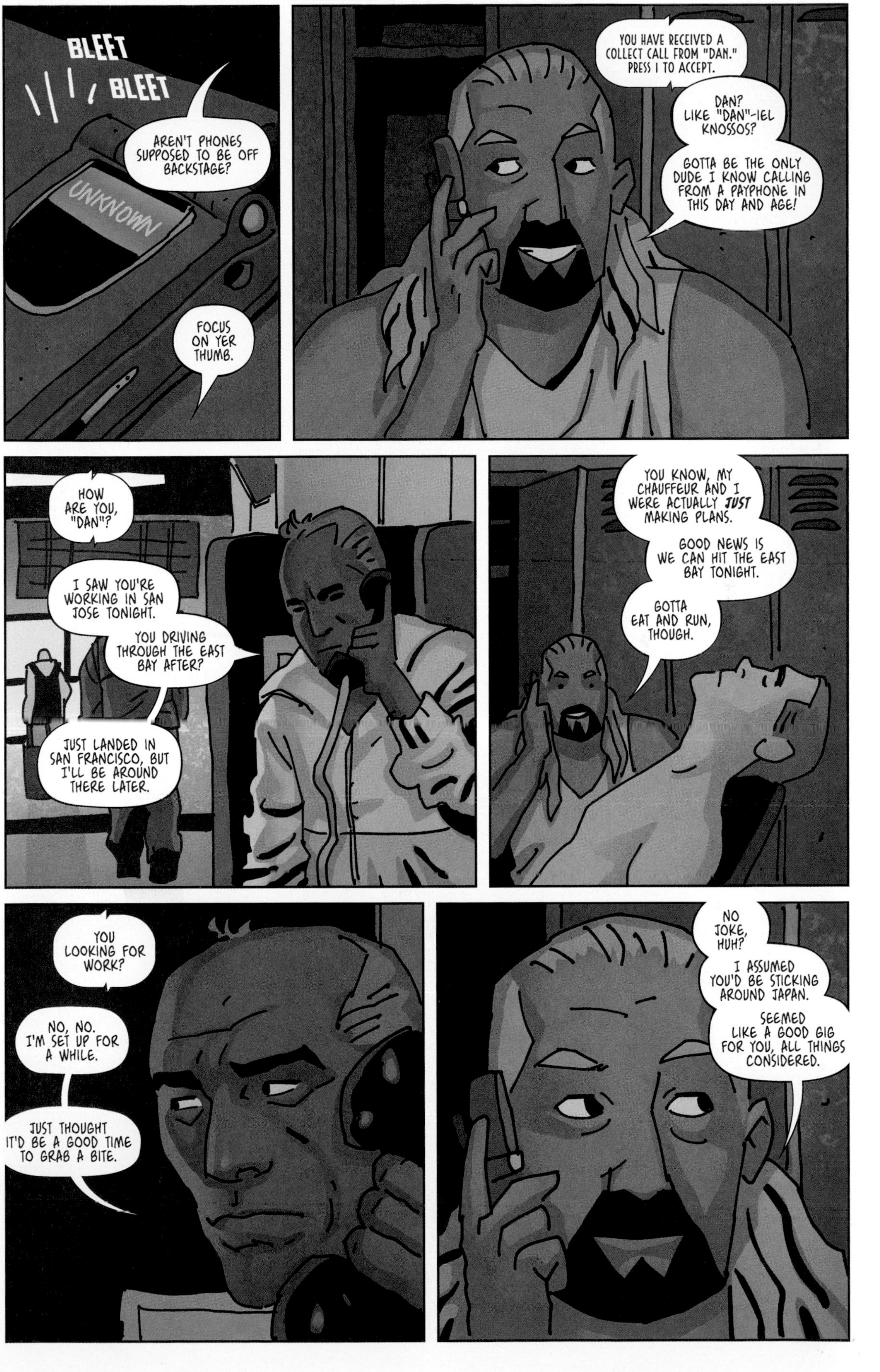
BLEET
BLEET
UNKNOWN
AREN'T PHONES SUPPOSED TO BE OFF BACKSTAGE?
FOCUS ON YER THUMB.
YOU HAVE RECEIVED A COLLECT CALL FROM "DAN." PRESS 1 TO ACCEPT.
DAN? LIKE "DAN"-IEL KNOSSOS?
GOTTA BE THE ONLY DUDE I KNOW CALLING FROM A PAYPHONE IN THIS DAY AND AGE!
HOW ARE YOU, "DAN"?
I SAW YOU'RE WORKING IN SAN JOSE TONIGHT.
YOU DRIVING THROUGH THE EAST BAY AFTER?
JUST LANDED IN SAN FRANCISCO, BUT I'LL BE AROUND THERE LATER.
YOU KNOW, MY CHAUFFEUR AND I WERE ACTUALLY *JUST* MAKING PLANS.
GOOD NEWS IS WE CAN HIT THE EAST BAY TONIGHT.
GOTTA EAT AND RUN, THOUGH.
YOU LOOKING FOR WORK?
NO, NO. I'M SET UP FOR A WHILE.
JUST THOUGHT IT'D BE A GOOD TIME TO GRAB A BITE.
NO JOKE, HUH?
I ASSUMED YOU'D BE STICKING AROUND JAPAN.
SEEMED LIKE A GOOD GIG FOR YOU, ALL THINGS CONSIDERED.

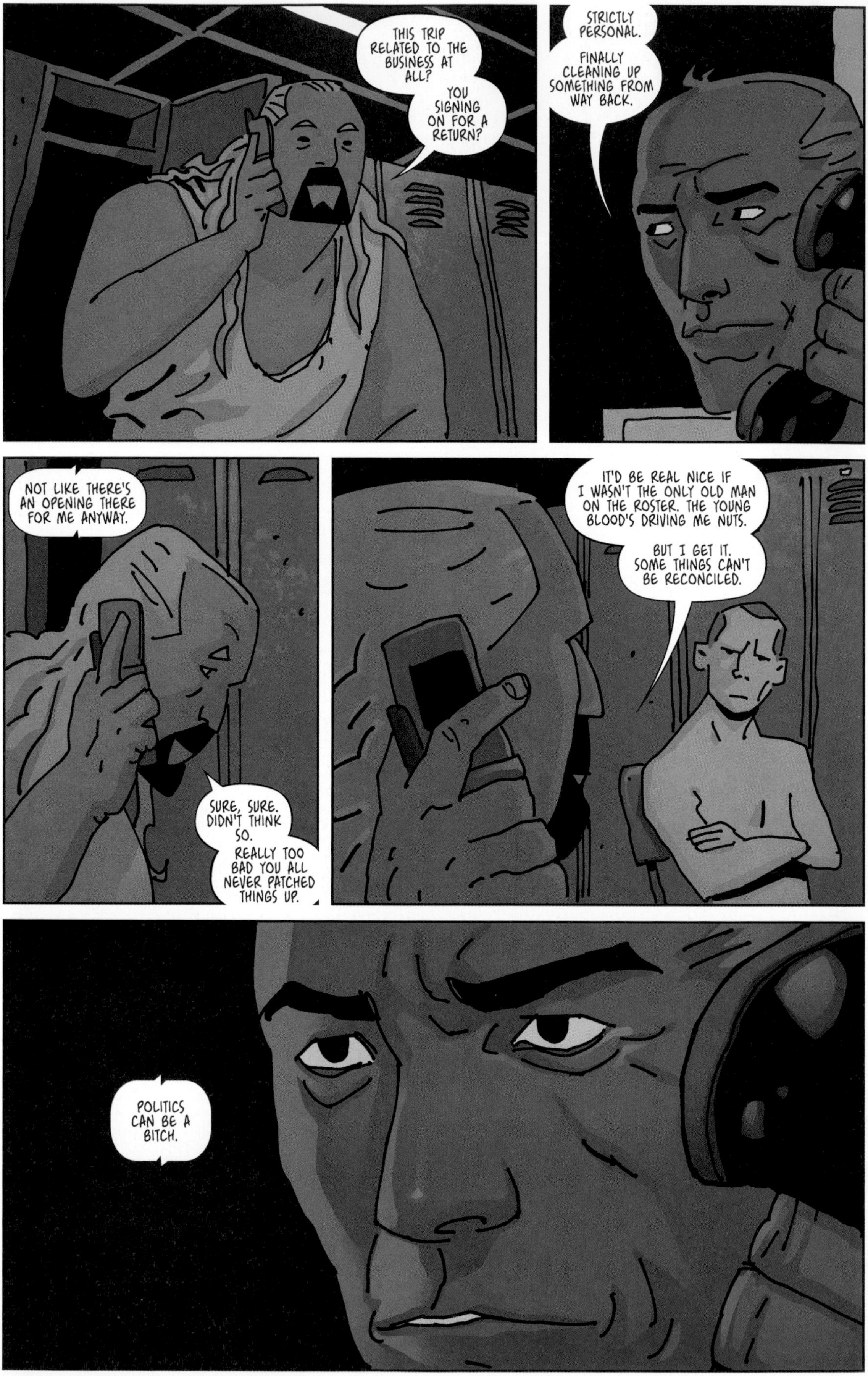
THIS TRIP RELATED TO THE BUSINESS AT ALL?
YOU SIGNING ON FOR A RETURN?
STRICTLY PERSONAL.
FINALLY CLEANING UP SOMETHING FROM WAY BACK.
NOT LIKE THERE'S AN OPENING THERE FOR ME ANYWAY.
SURE, SURE. DIDN'T THINK SO.
REALLY TOO BAD YOU ALL NEVER PATCHED THINGS UP.
IT'D BE REAL NICE IF I WASN'T THE ONLY OLD MAN ON THE ROSTER. THE YOUNG BLOOD'S DRIVING ME NUTS.
BUT I GET IT. SOME THINGS CAN'T BE RECONCILED.
POLITICS CAN BE A BITCH.

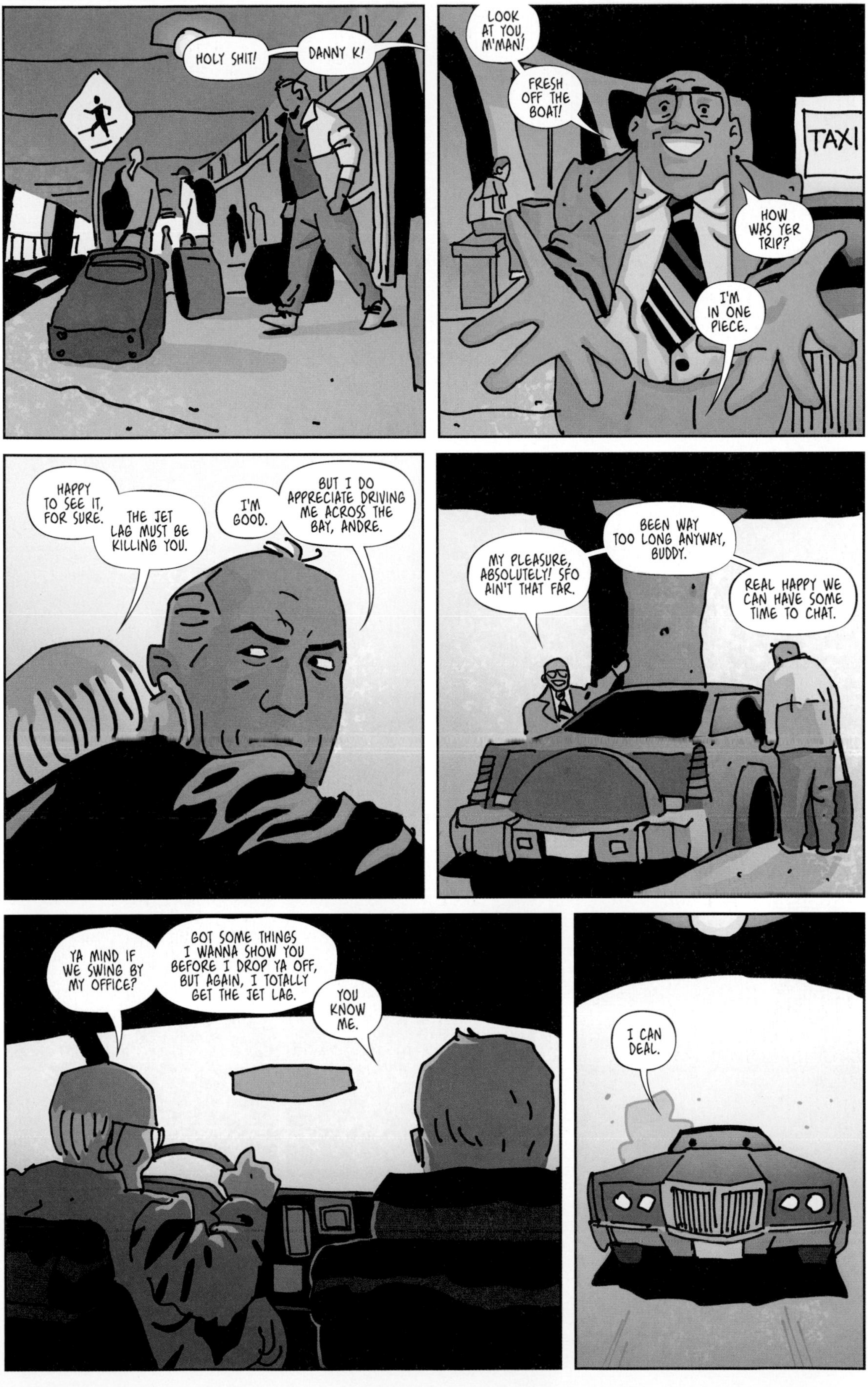
HOLY SHIT!
DANNY K!
LOOK AT YOU, M'MAN!
FRESH OFF THE BOAT!
HOW WAS YER TRIP?
I'M IN ONE PIECE.
HAPPY TO SEE IT, FOR SURE.
THE JET LAG MUST BE KILLING YOU.
I'M GOOD.
BUT I DO APPRECIATE DRIVING ME ACROSS THE BAY, ANDRE.
MY PLEASURE, ABSOLUTELY! SFO AIN'T THAT FAR.
BEEN WAY TOO LONG ANYWAY, BUDDY.
REAL HAPPY WE CAN HAVE SOME TIME TO CHAT.
YA MIND IF WE SWING BY MY OFFICE?
GOT SOME THINGS I WANNA SHOW YOU BEFORE I DROP YA OFF, BUT AGAIN, I TOTALLY GET THE JET LAG.
YOU KNOW ME.
I CAN DEAL.

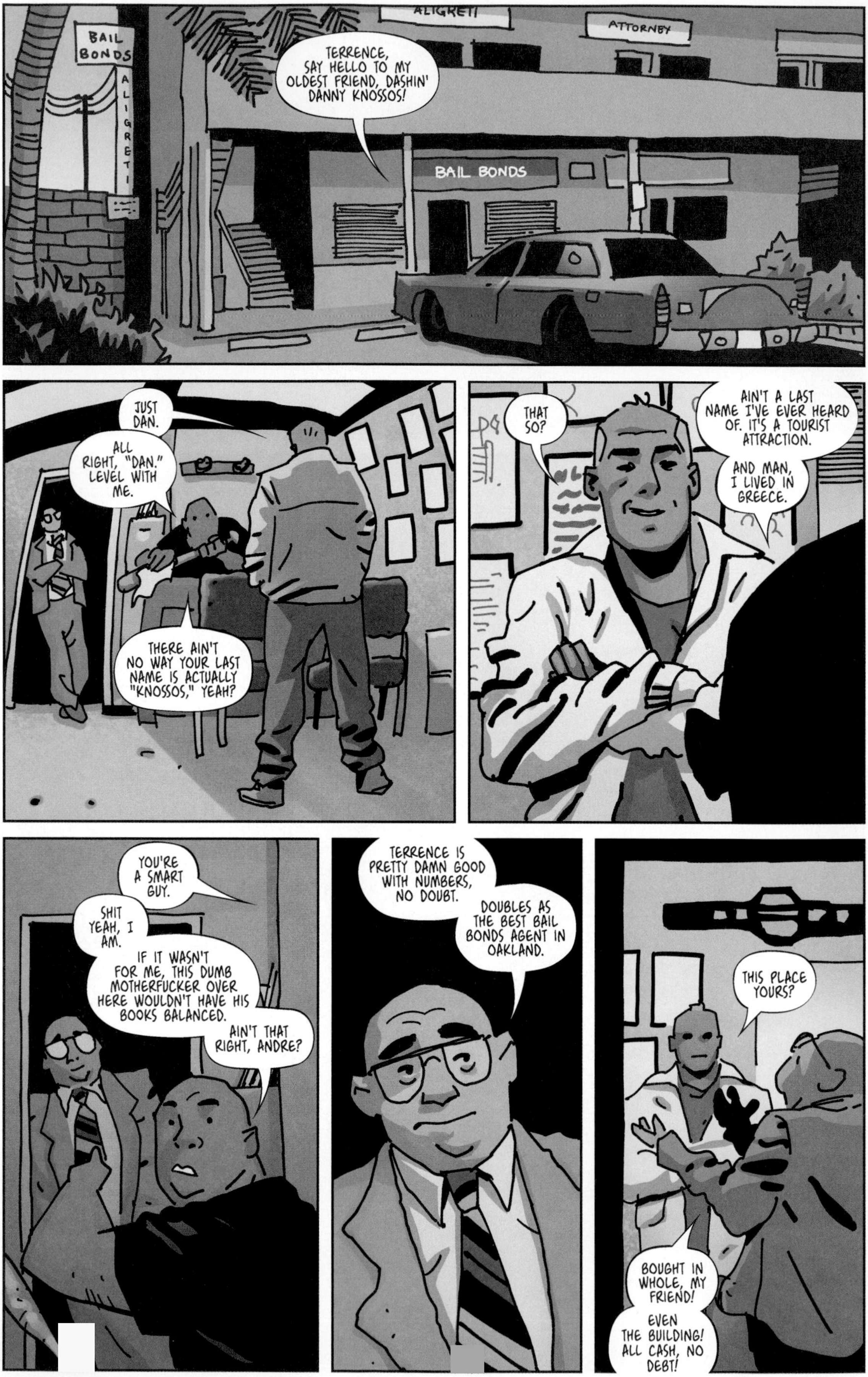
BAIL BONDS
ALIGRETI
ALIGRETI
ATTORNEY
TERRENCE, SAY HELLO TO MY OLDEST FRIEND, DASHIN' DANNY KNOSSOS!
BAIL BONDS
JUST DAN.
ALL RIGHT, "DAN." LEVEL WITH ME.
THERE AIN'T NO WAY YOUR LAST NAME IS ACTUALLY "KNOSSOS," YEAH?
THAT SO?
AIN'T A LAST NAME I'VE EVER HEARD OF. IT'S A TOURIST ATTRACTION.
AND MAN, I LIVED IN GREECE.
YOU'RE A SMART GUY.
SHIT YEAH, I AM.
IF IT WASN'T FOR ME, THIS DUMB MOTHERFUCKER OVER HERE WOULDN'T HAVE HIS BOOKS BALANCED.
AIN'T THAT RIGHT, ANDRE?
TERRENCE IS PRETTY DAMN GOOD WITH NUMBERS, NO DOUBT.
DOUBLES AS THE BEST BAIL BONDS AGENT IN OAKLAND.
THIS PLACE YOURS?
BOUGHT IN WHOLE, MY FRIEND!
EVEN THE BUILDING! ALL CASH, NO DEBT!

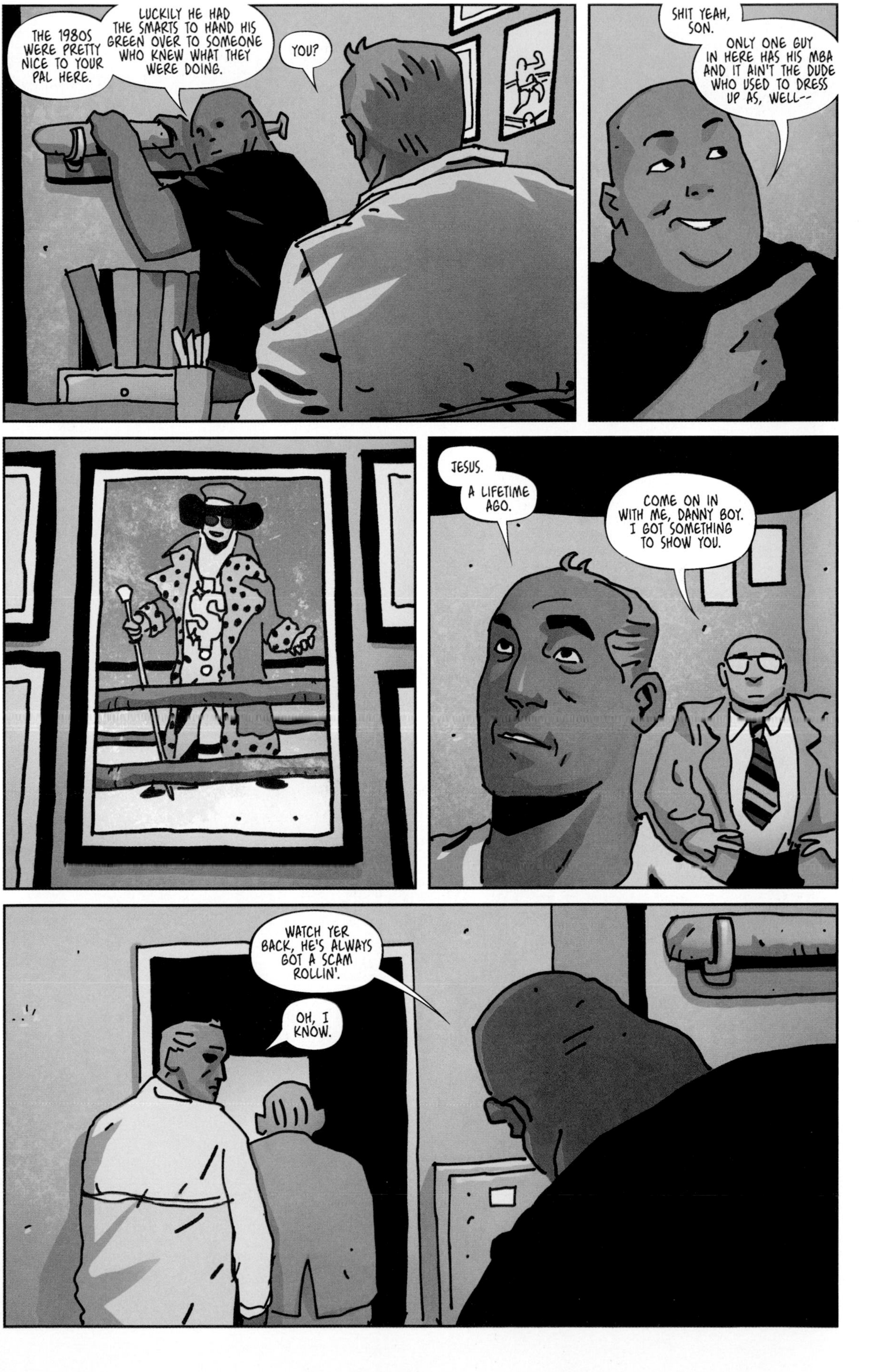
THE 1980s WERE PRETTY NICE TO YOUR PAL HERE.
LUCKILY HE HAD THE SMARTS TO HAND HIS GREEN OVER TO SOMEONE WHO KNEW WHAT THEY WERE DOING.
YOU?
SHIT YEAH, SON.
ONLY ONE GUY IN HERE HAS HIS MBA AND IT AIN'T THE DUDE WHO USED TO DRESS UP AS, WELL--
JESUS.
A LIFETIME AGO.
COME ON IN WITH ME, DANNY BOY. I GOT SOMETHING TO SHOW YOU.
WATCH YER BACK, HE'S ALWAYS GOT A SCAM ROLLIN'.
OH, I KNOW.

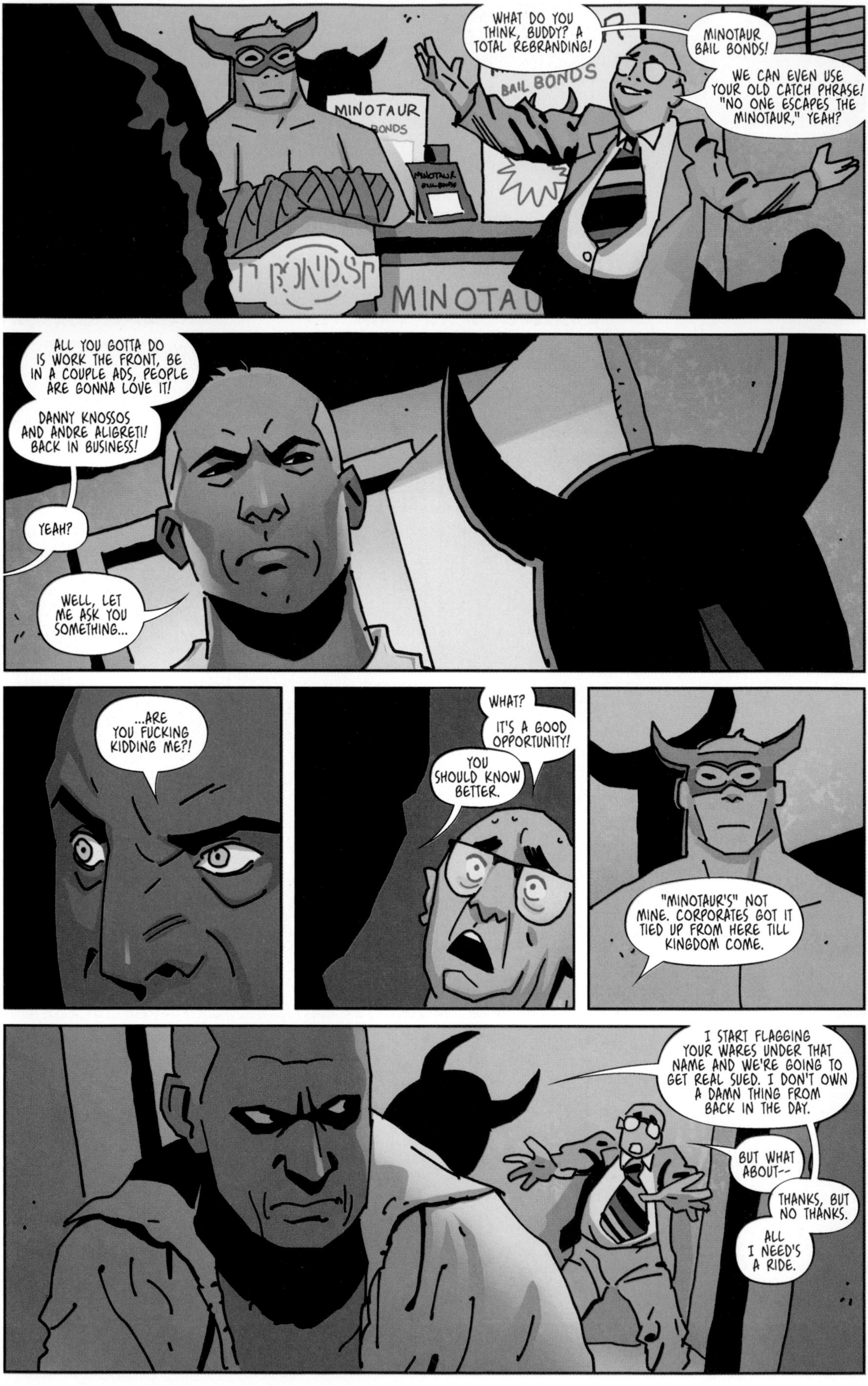
MINOTAUR BONDS
MINOTAUR BAIL BONDS
BAIL BONDS
WHAT DO YOU THINK, BUDDY? A TOTAL REBRANDING!
MINOTAUR BAIL BONDS!
WE CAN EVEN USE YOUR OLD CATCH PHRASE! "NO ONE ESCAPES THE MINOTAUR," YEAH?
MINOTAU
ALL YOU GOTTA DO IS WORK THE FRONT, BE IN A COUPLE ADS, PEOPLE ARE GONNA LOVE IT!
DANNY KNOSSOS AND ANDRE ALIGRETI! BACK IN BUSINESS!
YEAH?
WELL, LET ME ASK YOU SOMETHING...
...ARE YOU FUCKING KIDDING ME?!
WHAT?
IT'S A GOOD OPPORTUNITY!
YOU SHOULD KNOW BETTER.
"MINOTAUR'S" NOT MINE. CORPORATES GOT IT TIED UP FROM HERE TILL KINGDOM COME.
I START FLAGGING YOUR WARES UNDER THAT NAME AND WE'RE GOING TO GET REAL SUED. I DON'T OWN A DAMN THING FROM BACK IN THE DAY.
BUT WHAT ABOUT--
THANKS, BUT NO THANKS.
ALL I NEED'S A RIDE.

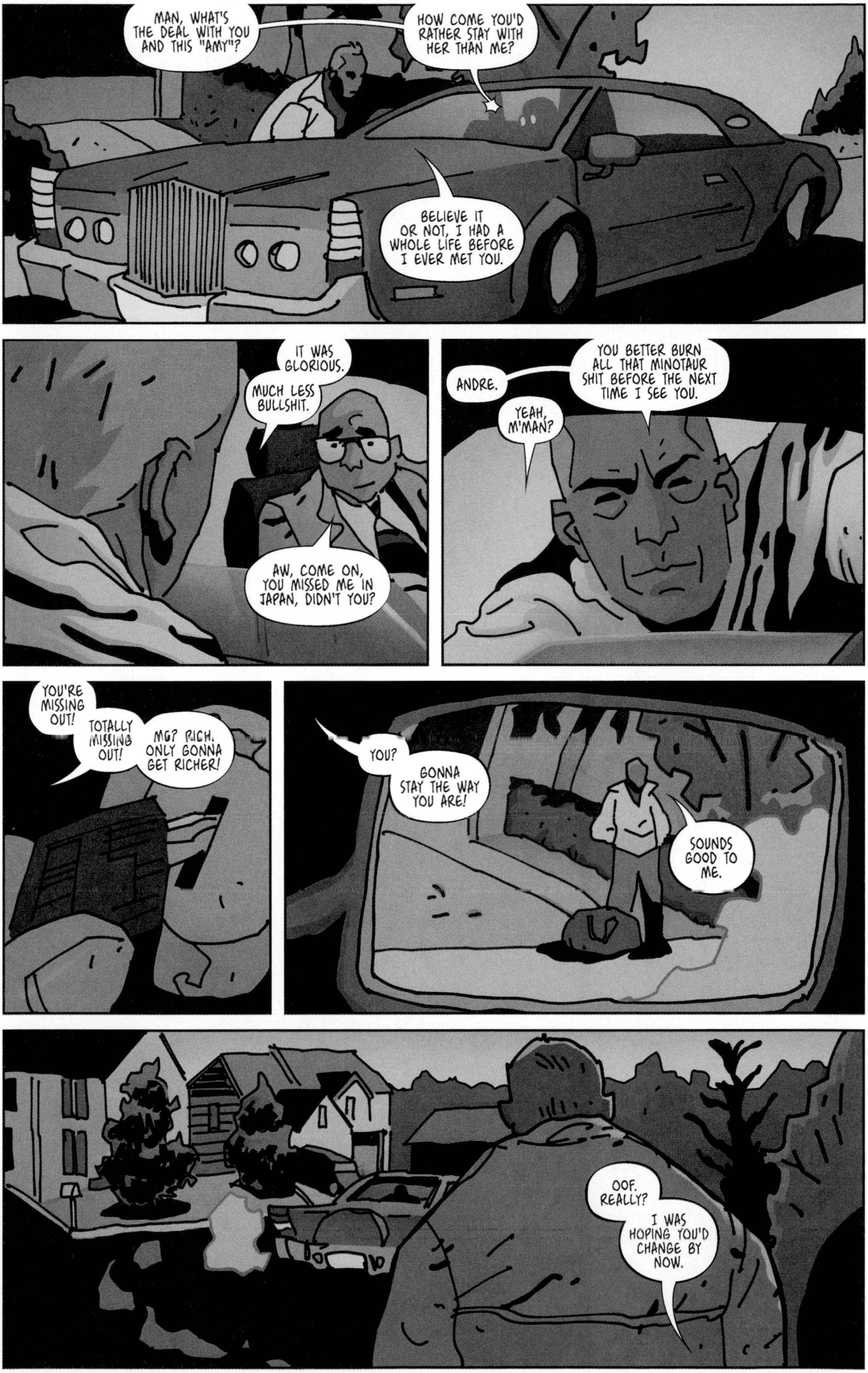
MAN, WHAT'S THE DEAL WITH YOU AND THIS "AMY"?
HOW COME YOU'D RATHER STAY WITH HER THAN ME?
BELIEVE IT OR NOT, I HAD A WHOLE LIFE BEFORE I EVER MET YOU.
IT WAS GLORIOUS.
MUCH LESS BULLSHIT.
AW, COME ON, YOU MISSED ME IN JAPAN, DIDN'T YOU?
ANDRE.
YOU BETTER BURN ALL THAT MINOTAUR SHIT BEFORE THE NEXT TIME I SEE YOU.
YEAH, M'MAN?
YOU'RE MISSING OUT!
TOTALLY MISSING OUT!
ME? RICH. ONLY GONNA GET RICHER!
YOU?
GONNA STAY THE WAY YOU ARE!
SOUNDS GOOD TO ME.
OOF. REALLY?
I WAS HOPING YOU'D CHANGE BY NOW.

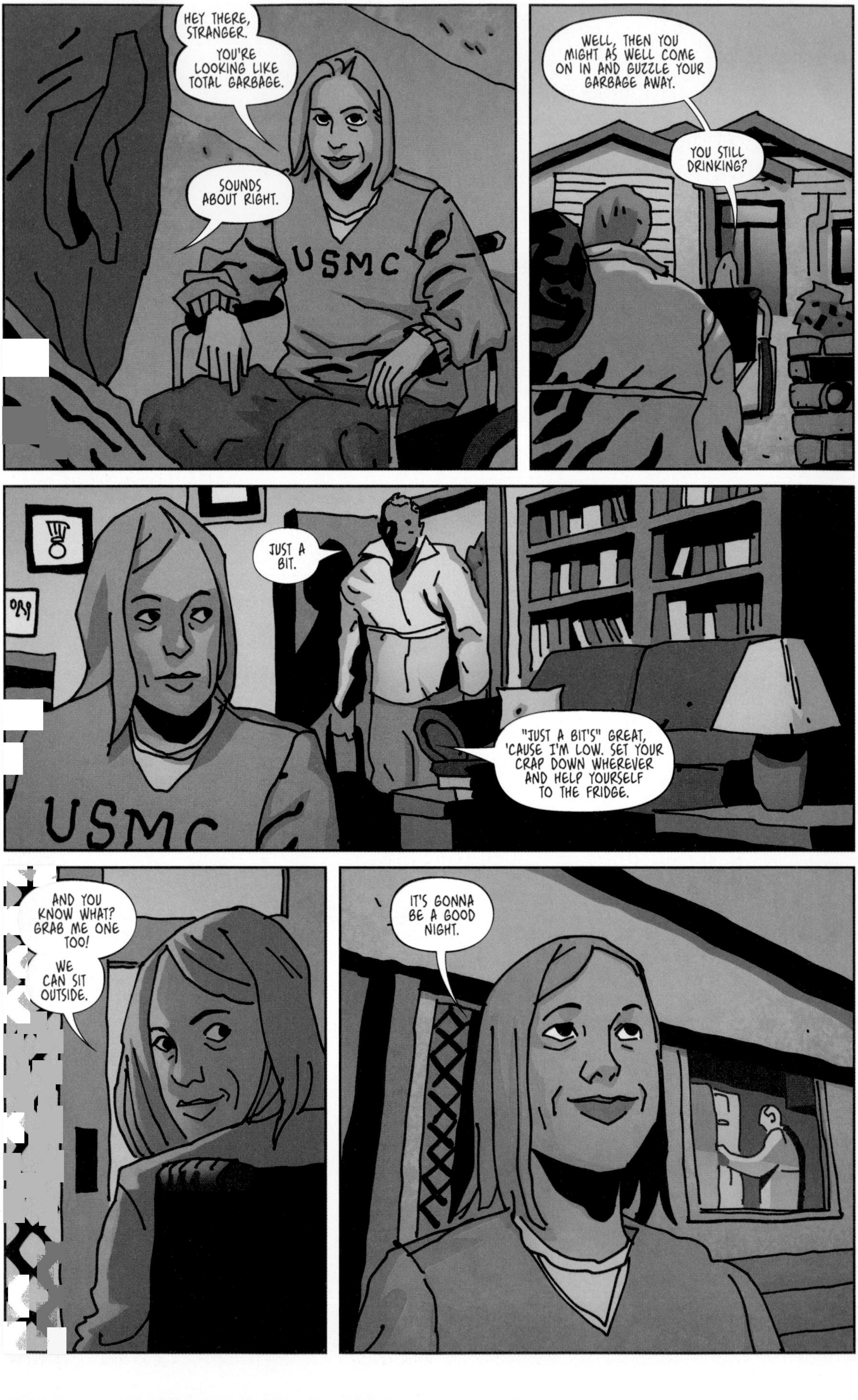
HEY THERE, STRANGER.
YOU'RE LOOKING LIKE TOTAL GARBAGE.
SOUNDS ABOUT RIGHT.
WELL, THEN YOU MIGHT AS WELL COME ON IN AND GUZZLE YOUR GARBAGE AWAY.
YOU STILL DRINKING?
JUST A BIT.
"JUST A BIT'S" GREAT, 'CAUSE I'M LOW. SET YOUR CRAP DOWN WHEREVER AND HELP YOURSELF TO THE FRIDGE.
AND YOU KNOW WHAT? GRAB ME ONE TOO!
WE CAN SIT OUTSIDE.
IT'S GONNA BE A GOOD NIGHT.

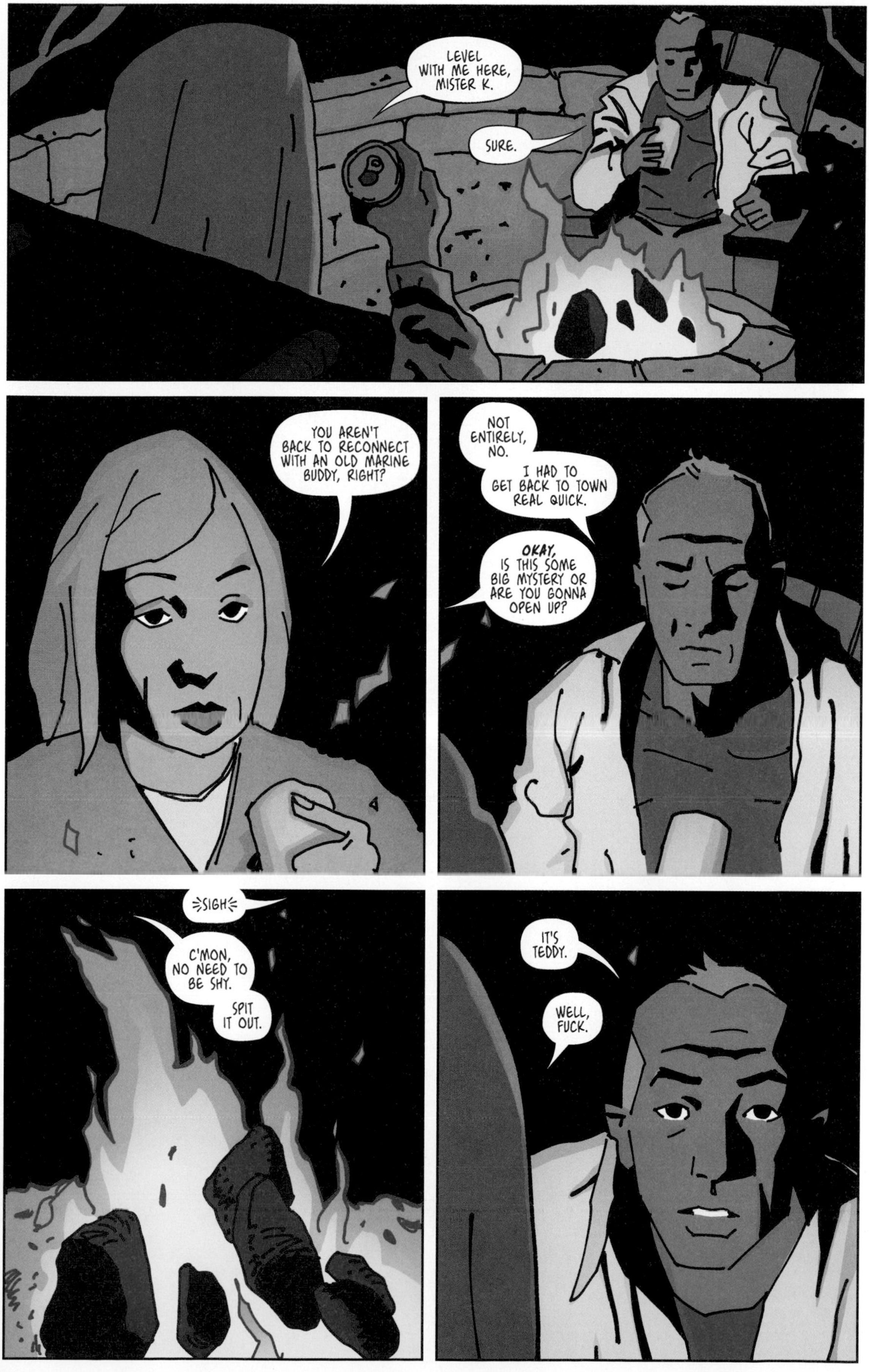
LEVEL WITH ME HERE, MISTER K.
SURE.
YOU AREN'T BACK TO RECONNECT WITH AN OLD MARINE BUDDY, RIGHT?
NOT ENTIRELY, NO.
I HAD TO GET BACK TO TOWN REAL QUICK.
OKAY, IS THIS SOME BIG MYSTERY OR ARE YOU GONNA OPEN UP?
SIGH
C'MON, NO NEED TO BE SHY.
SPIT IT OUT.
IT'S TEDDY.
WELL, FUCK.

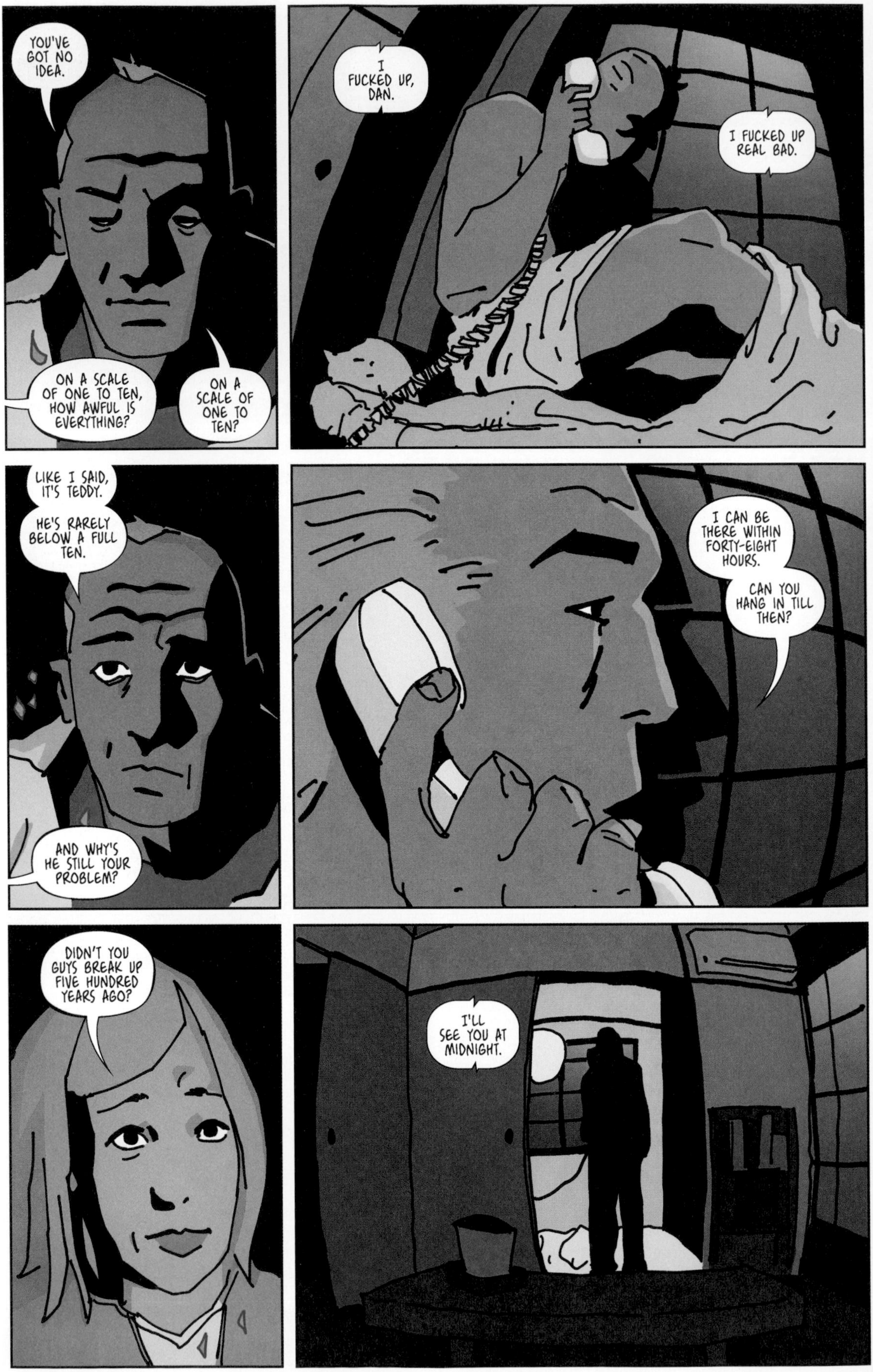
YOU'VE GOT NO IDEA.
I FUCKED UP, DAN.
I FUCKED UP REAL BAD.
ON A SCALE OF ONE TO TEN, HOW AWFUL IS EVERYTHING?
ON A SCALE OF ONE TO TEN?
LIKE I SAID, IT'S TEDDY.
HE'S RARELY BELOW A FULL TEN.
I CAN BE THERE WITHIN FORTY-EIGHT HOURS.
CAN YOU HANG IN TILL THEN?
AND WHY'S HE STILL YOUR PROBLEM?
DIDN'T YOU GUYS BREAK UP FIVE HUNDRED YEARS AGO?
I'LL SEE YOU AT MIDNIGHT.

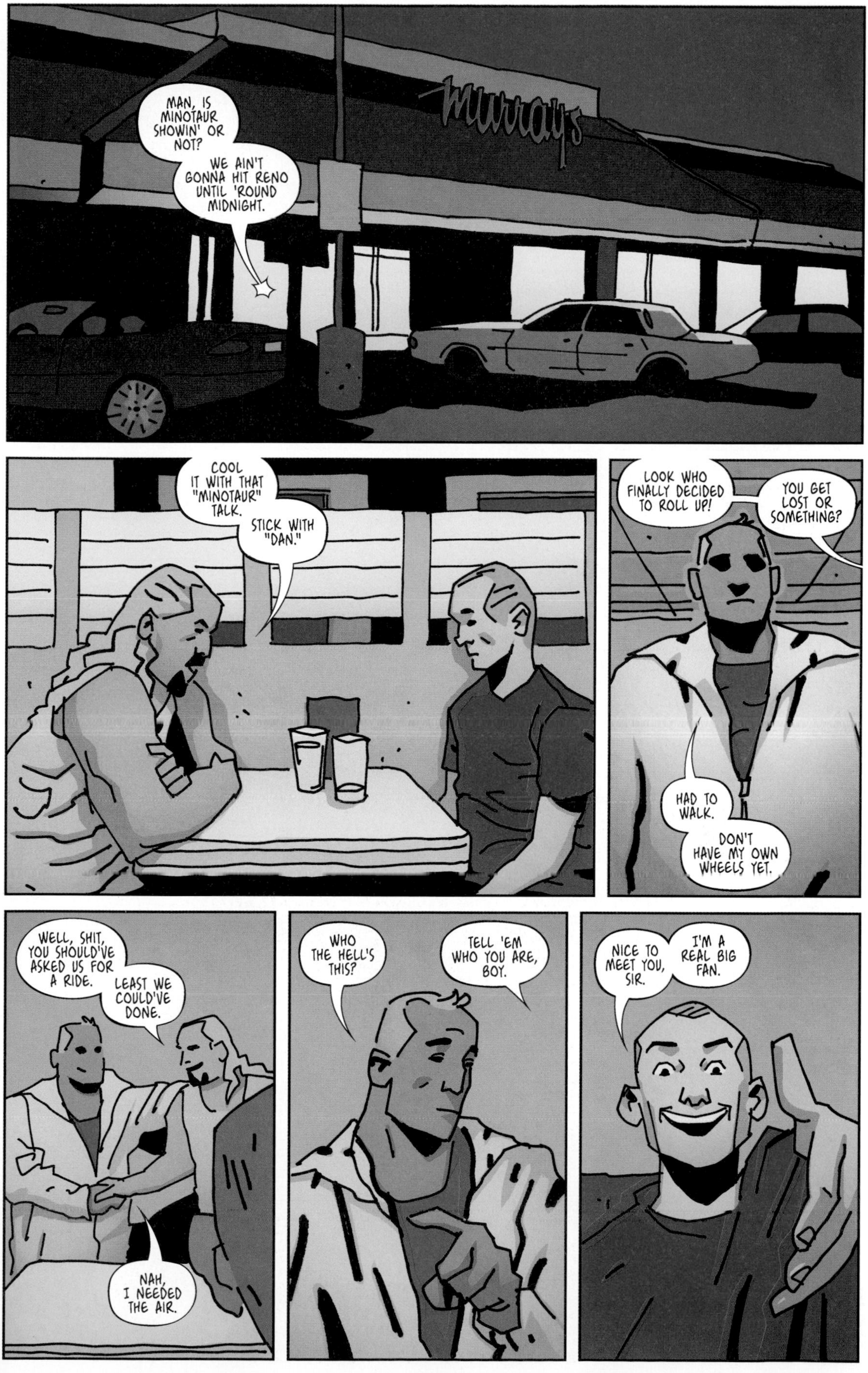
murray's
MAN, IS MINOTAUR SHOWIN' OR NOT?
WE AIN'T GONNA HIT RENO UNTIL 'ROUND MIDNIGHT.
COOL IT WITH THAT "MINOTAUR" TALK.
STICK WITH "DAN."
LOOK WHO FINALLY DECIDED TO ROLL UP!
YOU GET LOST OR SOMETHING?
HAD TO WALK.
DON'T HAVE MY OWN WHEELS YET.
WELL, SHIT, YOU SHOULD'VE ASKED US FOR A RIDE.
LEAST WE COULD'VE DONE.
NAH, I NEEDED THE AIR.
WHO THE HELL'S THIS?
TELL 'EM WHO YOU ARE, BOY.
NICE TO MEET YOU, SIR.
I'M A REAL BIG FAN.

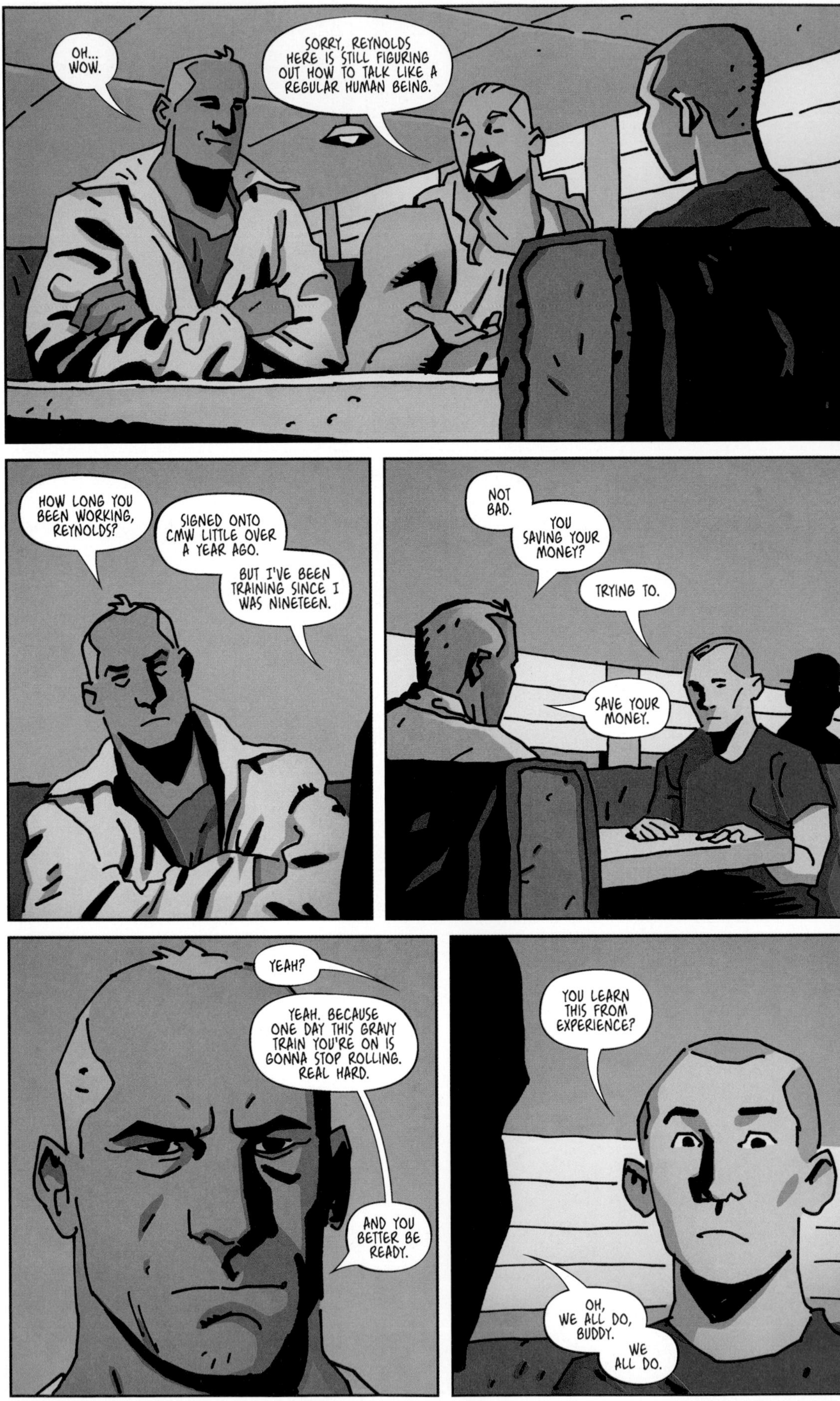
OH... WOW.
SORRY, REYNOLDS HERE IS STILL FIGURING OUT HOW TO TALK LIKE A REGULAR HUMAN BEING.
HOW LONG YOU BEEN WORKING, REYNOLDS?
SIGNED ONTO CMW LITTLE OVER A YEAR AGO.
BUT I'VE BEEN TRAINING SINCE I WAS NINETEEN.
NOT BAD.
YOU SAVING YOUR MONEY?
TRYING TO.
SAVE YOUR MONEY.
YEAH?
YEAH. BECAUSE ONE DAY THIS GRAVY TRAIN YOU'RE ON IS GONNA STOP ROLLING. REAL HARD.
AND YOU BETTER BE READY.
YOU LEARN THIS FROM EXPERIENCE?
OH, WE ALL DO, BUDDY.
WE ALL DO.

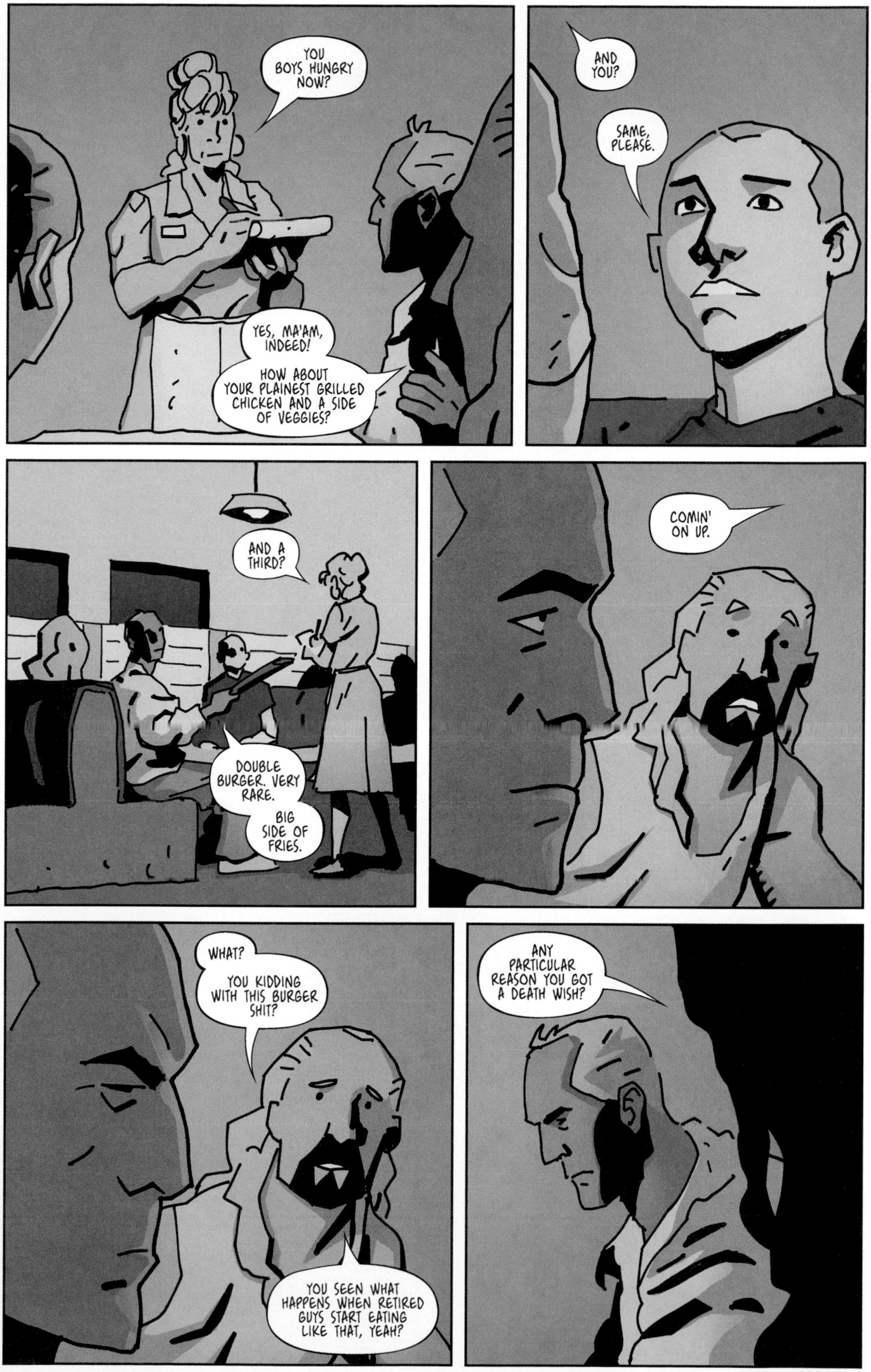
YOU BOYS HUNGRY NOW?
YES, MA'AM, INDEED!
HOW ABOUT YOUR PLAINEST GRILLED CHICKEN AND A SIDE OF VEGGIES?
AND YOU?
SAME, PLEASE.
AND A THIRD?
DOUBLE BURGER. VERY RARE.
BIG SIDE OF FRIES.
COMIN' ON UP.
WHAT?
YOU KIDDING WITH THIS BURGER SHIT?
YOU SEEN WHAT HAPPENS WHEN RETIRED GUYS START EATING LIKE THAT, YEAH?
ANY PARTICULAR REASON YOU GOT A DEATH WISH?

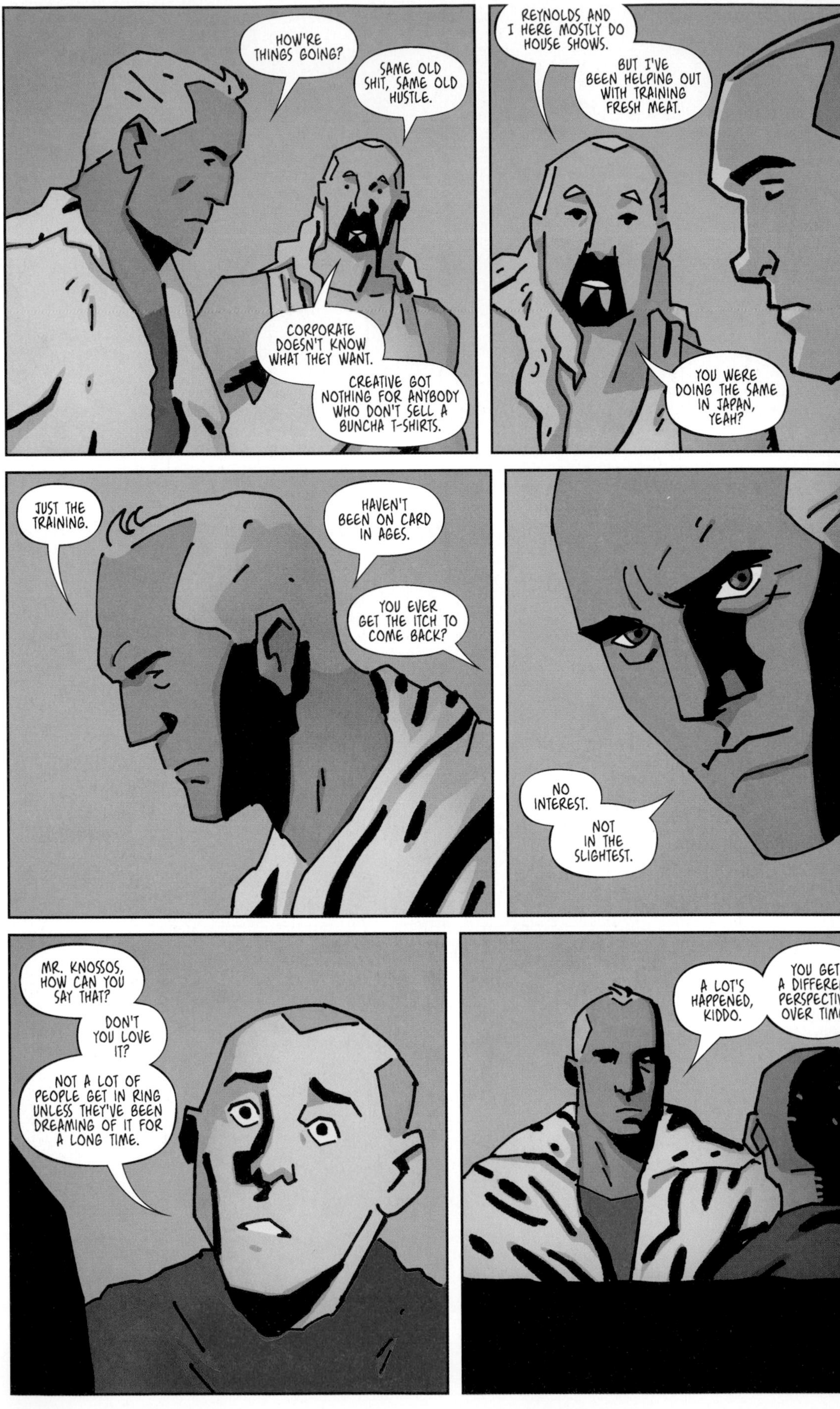
HOW'RE THINGS GOING?
SAME OLD SHIT, SAME OLD HUSTLE.
CORPORATE DOESN'T KNOW WHAT THEY WANT.
CREATIVE GOT NOTHING FOR ANYBODY WHO DON'T SELL A BUNCHA T-SHIRTS.
REYNOLDS AND I HERE MOSTLY DO HOUSE SHOWS.
BUT I'VE BEEN HELPING OUT WITH TRAINING FRESH MEAT.
YOU WERE DOING THE SAME IN JAPAN, YEAH?
JUST THE TRAINING.
HAVEN'T BEEN ON CARD IN AGES.
YOU EVER GET THE ITCH TO COME BACK?
NO INTEREST.
NOT IN THE SLIGHTEST.
MR. KNOSSOS, HOW CAN YOU SAY THAT?
DON'T YOU LOVE IT?
NOT A LOT OF PEOPLE GET IN RING UNLESS THEY'VE BEEN DREAMING OF IT FOR A LONG TIME.
A LOT'S HAPPENED, KIDDO.
YOU GET A DIFFERENT PERSPECTIVE OVER TIME.

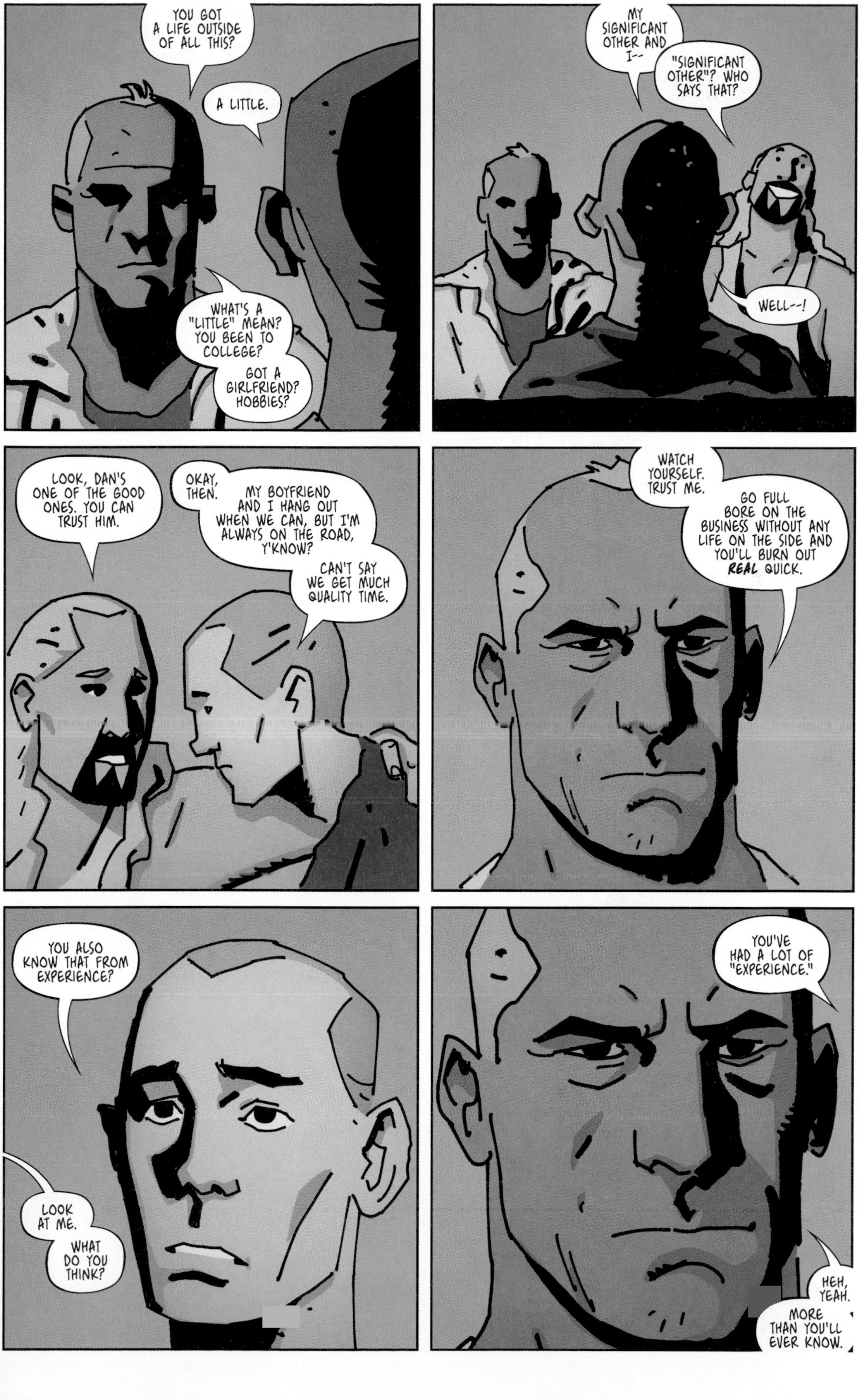
YOU GOT A LIFE OUTSIDE OF ALL THIS?
A LITTLE.
WHAT'S A "LITTLE" MEAN? YOU BEEN TO COLLEGE?
GOT A GIRLFRIEND? HOBBIES?
MY SIGNIFICANT OTHER AND I--
"SIGNIFICANT OTHER"? WHO SAYS THAT?
WELL--!
LOOK, DAN'S ONE OF THE GOOD ONES. YOU CAN TRUST HIM.
OKAY, THEN.
MY BOYFRIEND AND I HANG OUT WHEN WE CAN, BUT I'M ALWAYS ON THE ROAD, Y'KNOW?
CAN'T SAY WE GET MUCH QUALITY TIME.
WATCH YOURSELF. TRUST ME.
GO FULL BORE ON THE BUSINESS WITHOUT ANY LIFE ON THE SIDE AND YOU'LL BURN OUT REAL QUICK.
YOU ALSO KNOW THAT FROM EXPERIENCE?
LOOK AT ME.
WHAT DO YOU THINK?
YOU'VE HAD A LOT OF "EXPERIENCE."
HEH, YEAH.
MORE THAN YOU'LL EVER KNOW.

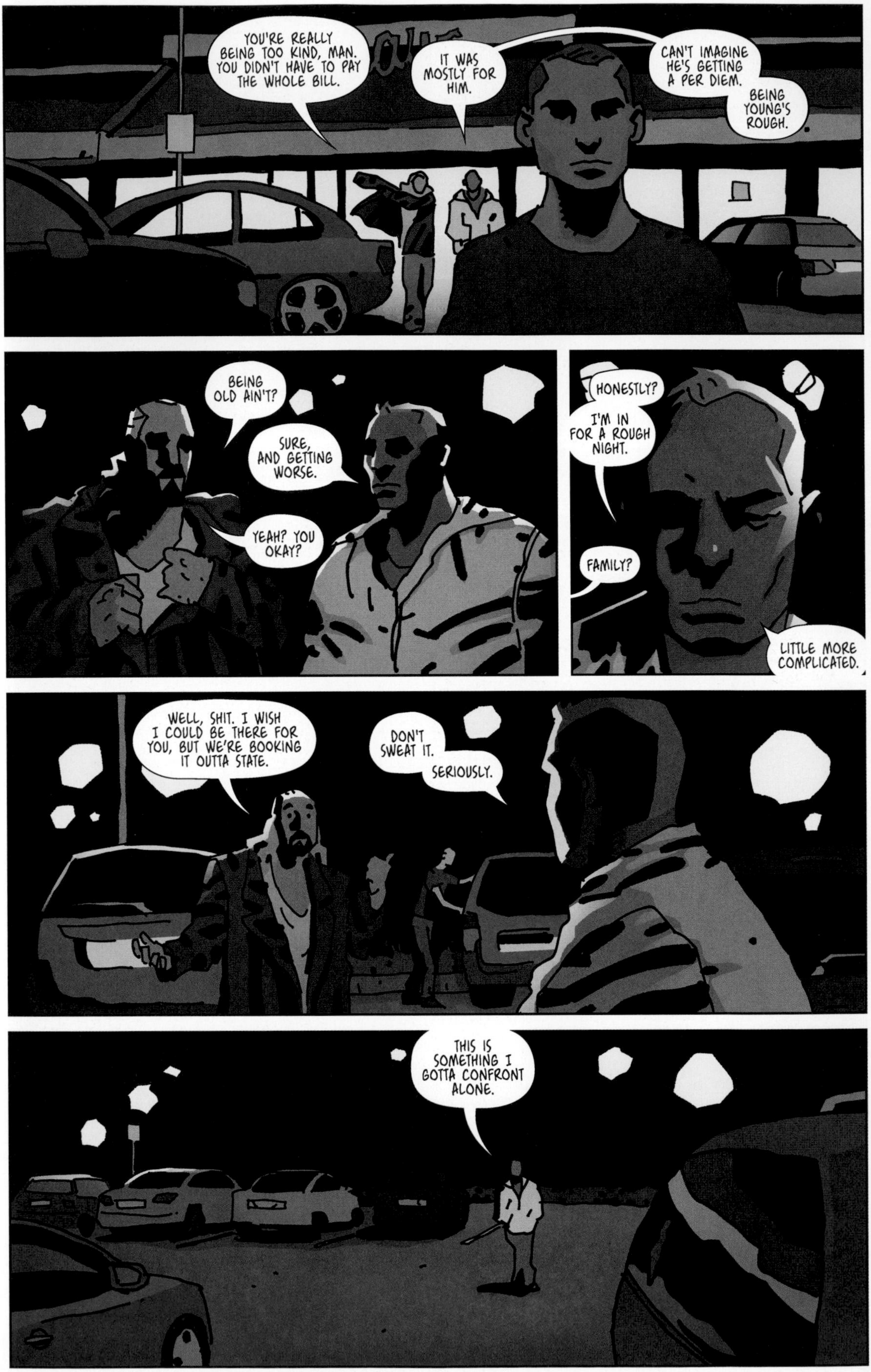
YOU'RE REALLY BEING TOO KIND, MAN. YOU DIDN'T HAVE TO PAY THE WHOLE BILL.
IT WAS MOSTLY FOR HIM.
CAN'T IMAGINE HE'S GETTING A PER DIEM.
BEING YOUNG'S ROUGH.
BEING OLD AIN'T?
SURE, AND GETTING WORSE.
YEAH? YOU OKAY?
HONESTLY?
I'M IN FOR A ROUGH NIGHT.
FAMILY?
LITTLE MORE COMPLICATED.
WELL, SHIT. I WISH I COULD BE THERE FOR YOU, BUT WE'RE BOOKING IT OUTTA STATE.
DON'T SWEAT IT.
SERIOUSLY.
THIS IS SOMETHING I GOTTA CONFRONT ALONE.

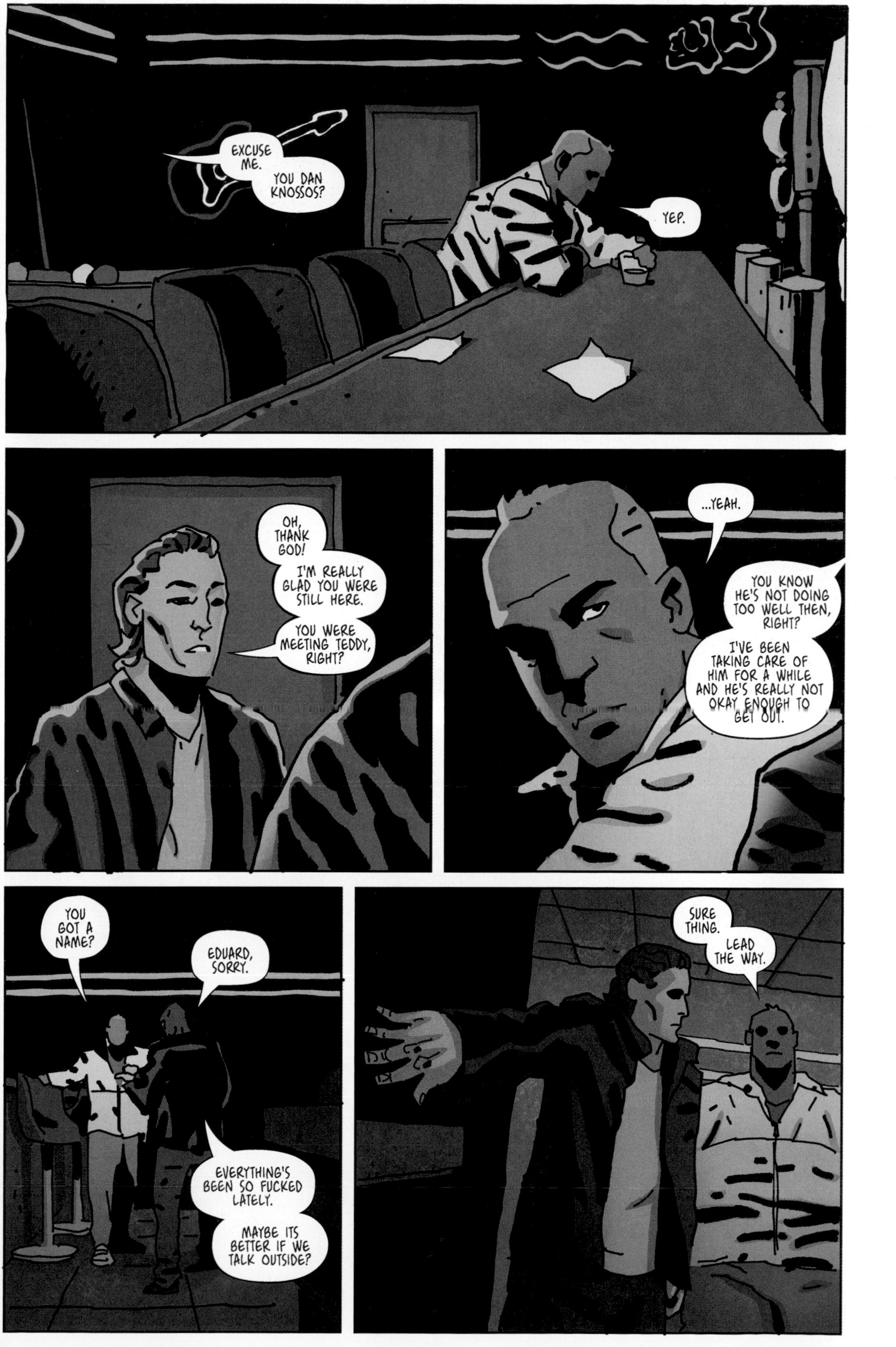
EXCUSE ME. YOU DAN KNOSSOS?
YEP.
OH, THANK GOD!
I'M REALLY GLAD YOU WERE STILL HERE.
YOU WERE MEETING TEDDY, RIGHT?
...YEAH.
YOU KNOW HE'S NOT DOING TOO WELL THEN, RIGHT?
I'VE BEEN TAKING CARE OF HIM FOR A WHILE AND HE'S REALLY NOT OKAY ENOUGH TO GET OUT.
YOU GOT A NAME?
EDUARD, SORRY.
EVERYTHING'S BEEN SO FUCKED LATELY.
MAYBE ITS BETTER IF WE TALK OUTSIDE?
SURE THING.
LEAD THE WAY.

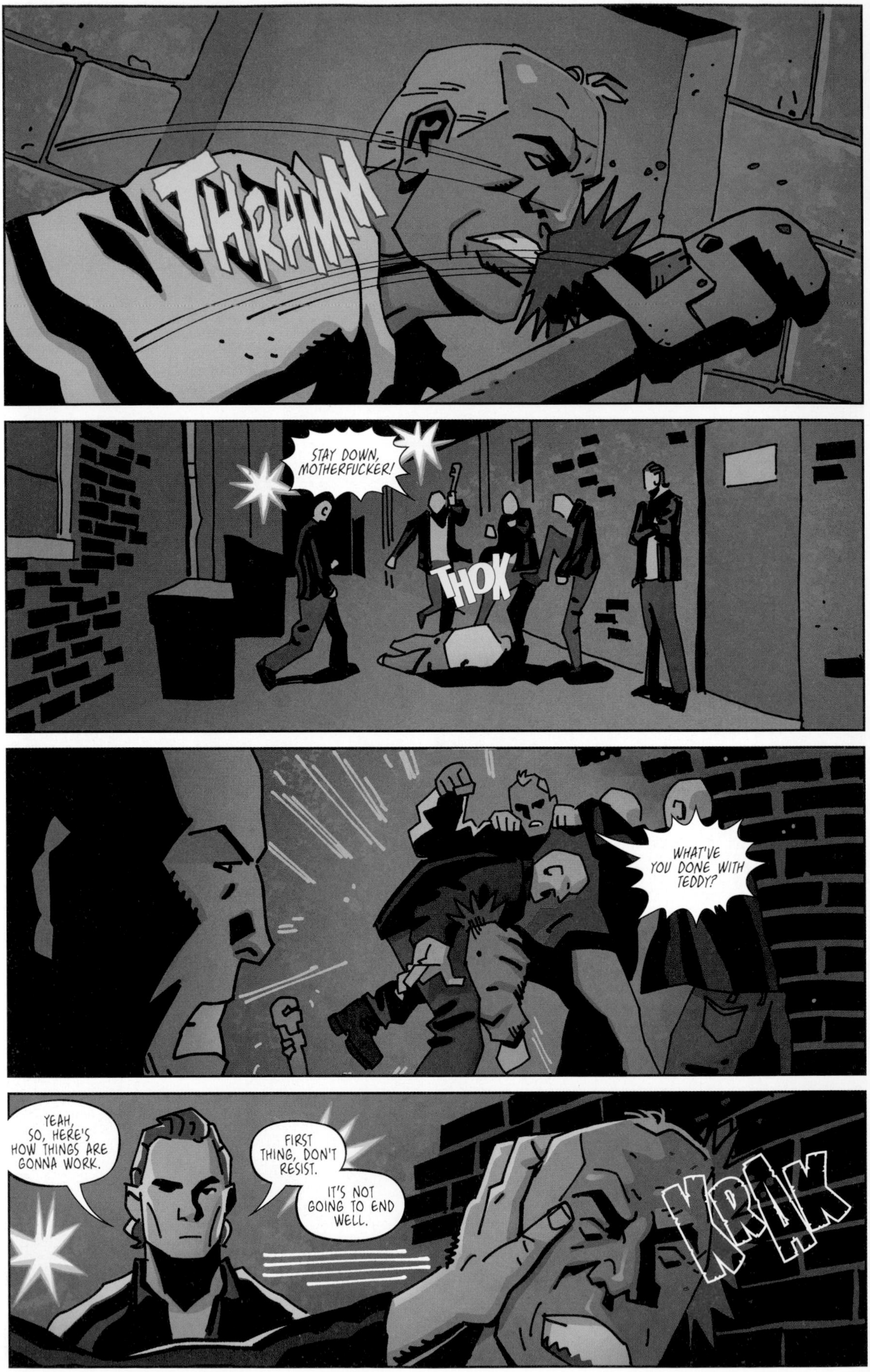
THRAMM
STAY DOWN, MOTHERFUCKER!
THOK
WHAT'VE YOU DONE WITH TEDDY?
YEAH, SO, HERE'S HOW THINGS ARE GONNA WORK.
FIRST THING, DON'T RESIST.
IT'S NOT GOING TO END WELL.
KRAK

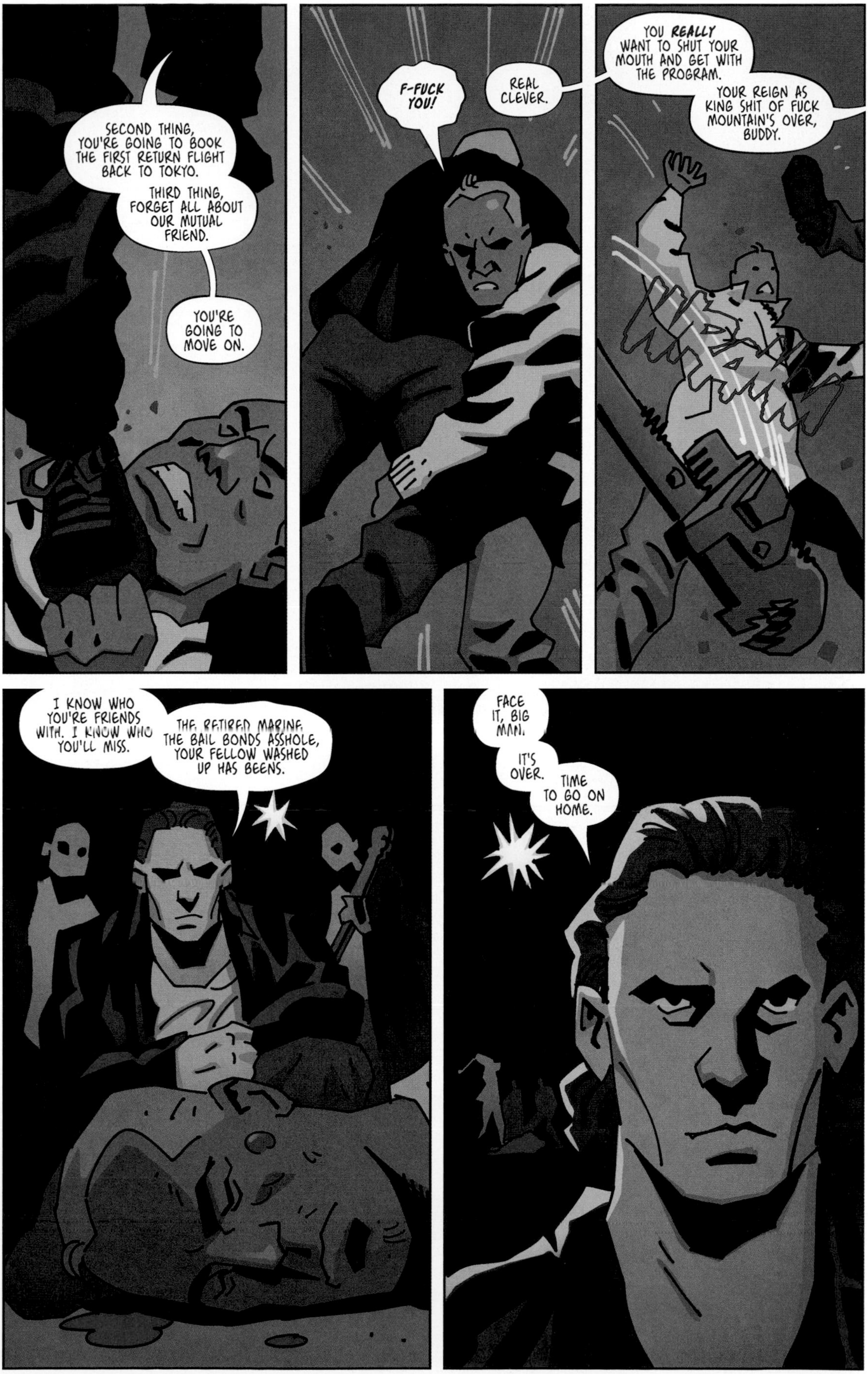

SECOND THING, YOU'RE GOING TO BOOK THE FIRST RETURN FLIGHT BACK TO TOKYO.
THIRD THING, FORGET ALL ABOUT OUR MUTUAL FRIEND.
YOU'RE GOING TO MOVE ON.
F-FUCK YOU!
REAL CLEVER.
YOU REALLY WANT TO SHUT YOUR MOUTH AND GET WITH THE PROGRAM.
YOUR REIGN AS KING SHIT OF FUCK MOUNTAIN'S OVER, BUDDY.
I KNOW WHO YOU'RE FRIENDS WITH. I KNOW WHO YOU'LL MISS.
THE RETIRED MARINE. THE BAIL BONDS ASSHOLE, YOUR FELLOW WASHED UP HAS BEENS.
FACE IT, BIG MAN.
IT'S OVER.
TIME TO GO ON HOME.

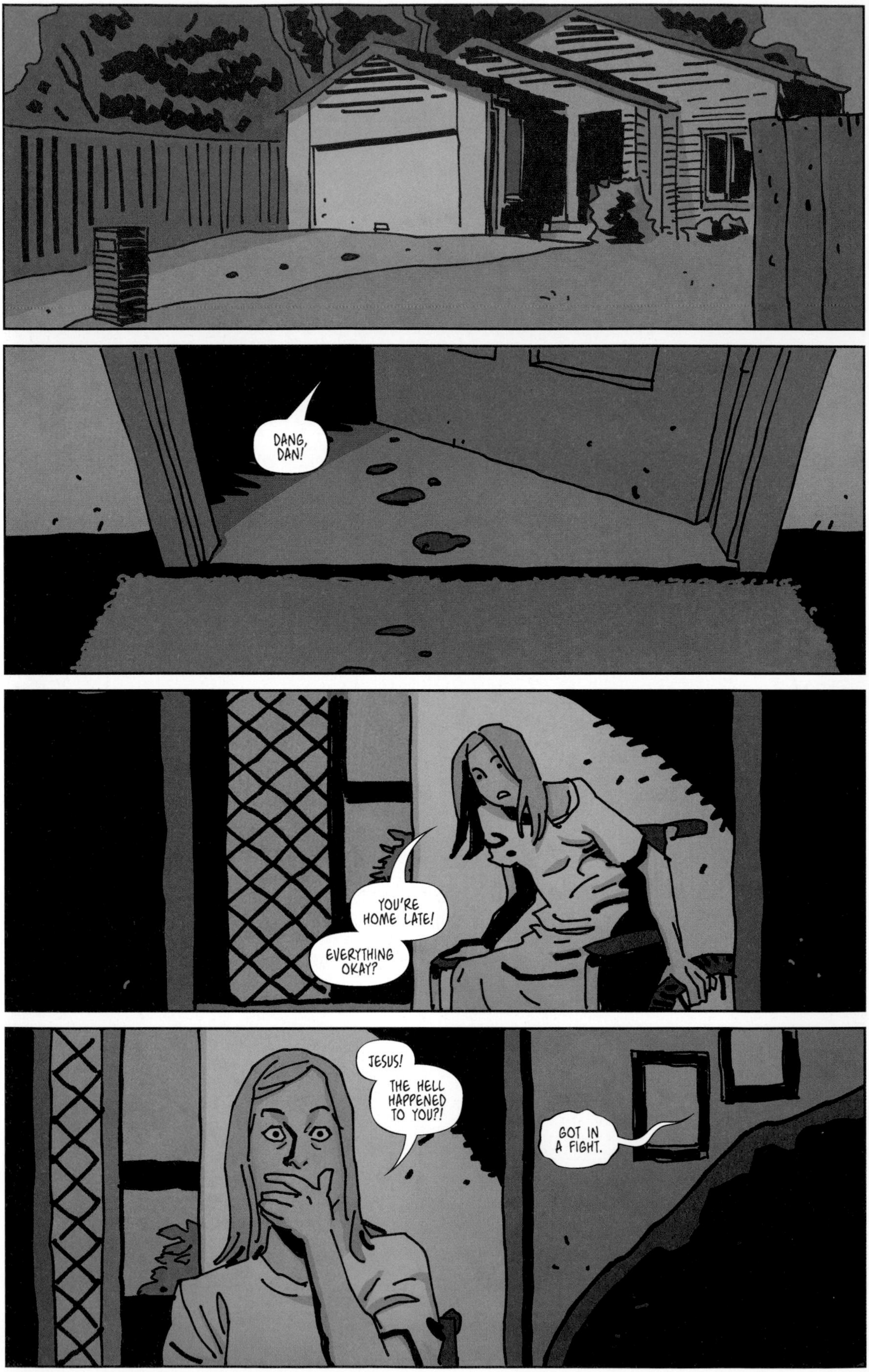
DANG, DAN!
YOU'RE HOME LATE!
EVERYTHING OKAY?
JESUS!
THE HELL HAPPENED TO YOU?!
GOT IN A FIGHT.

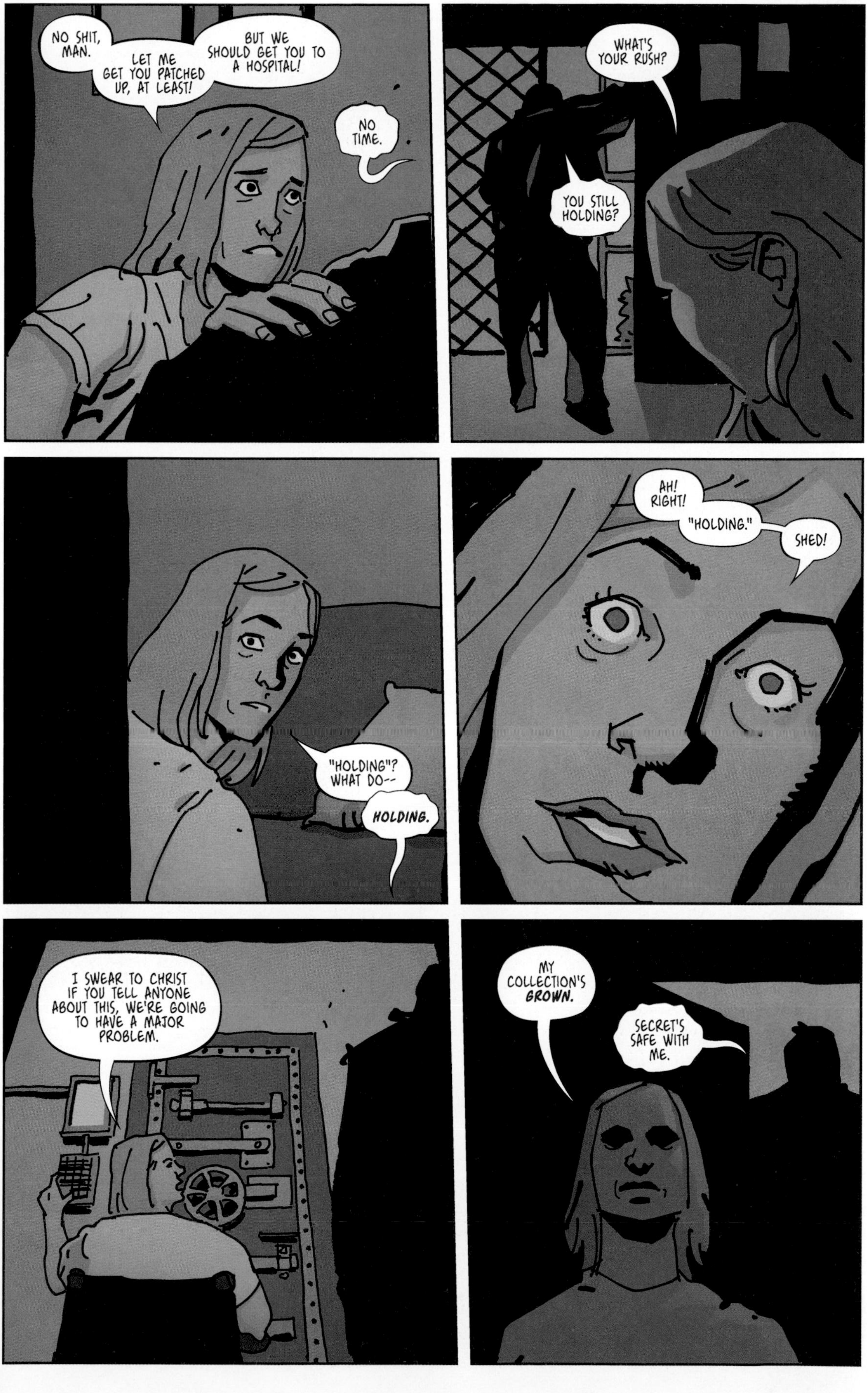
NO SHIT, MAN.
LET ME GET YOU PATCHED UP, AT LEAST!
BUT WE SHOULD GET YOU TO A HOSPITAL!
NO TIME.
WHAT'S YOUR RUSH?
YOU STILL HOLDING?
"HOLDING"? WHAT DO--
HOLDING.
AH! RIGHT!
"HOLDING."
SHED!
I SWEAR TO CHRIST IF YOU TELL ANYONE ABOUT THIS, WE'RE GOING TO HAVE A MAJOR PROBLEM.
MY COLLECTION'S GROWN.
SECRET'S SAFE WITH ME.

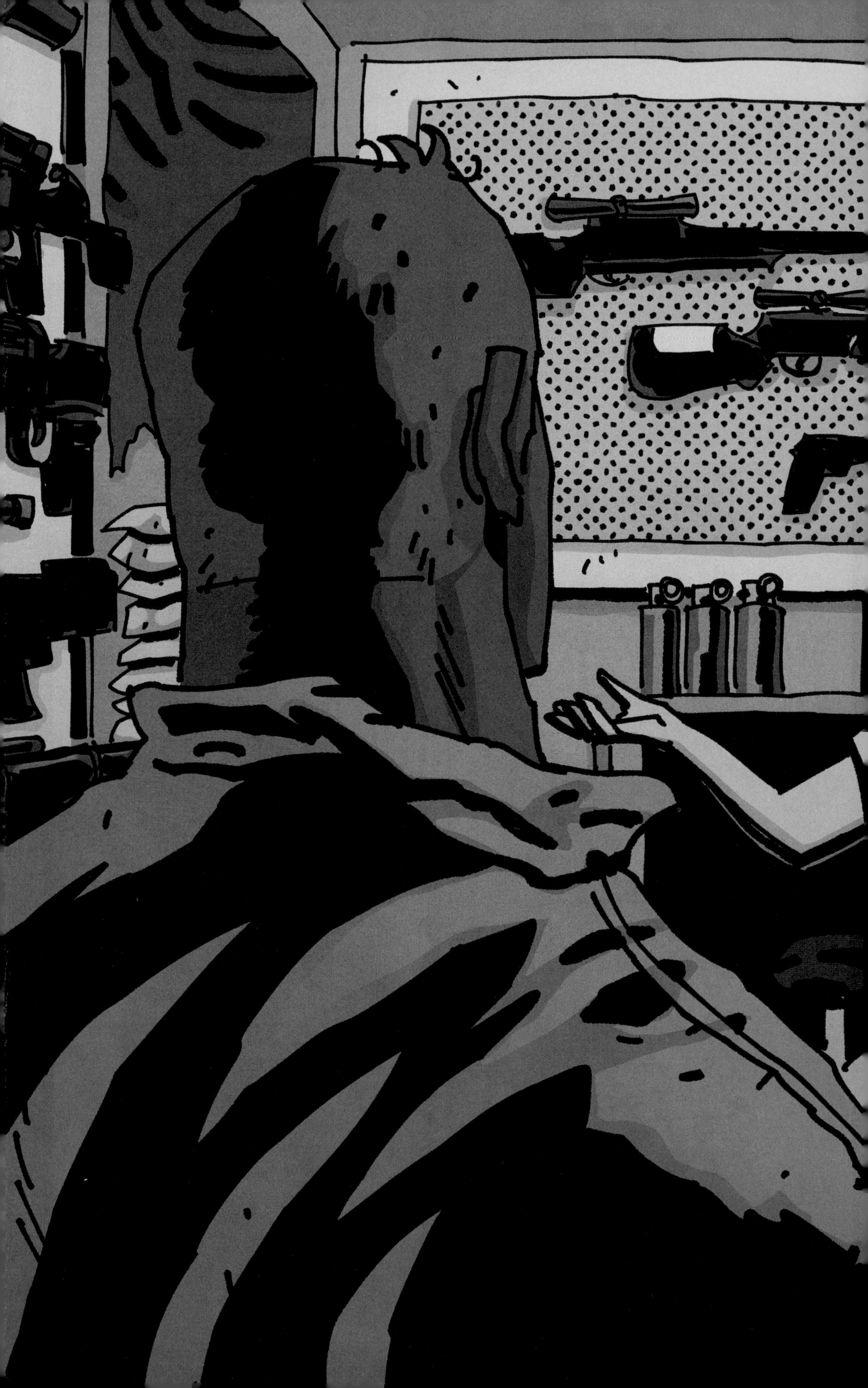

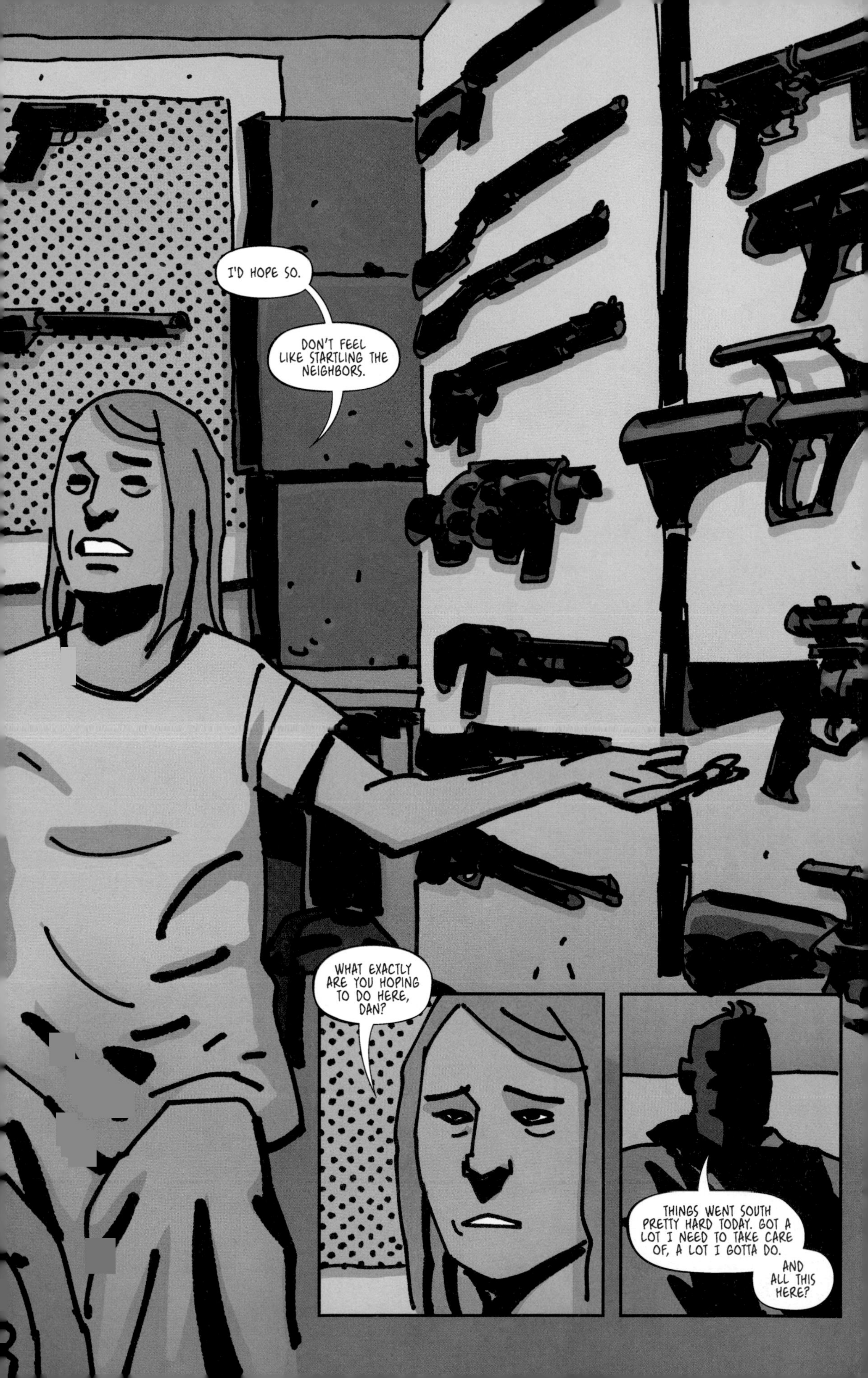
I'D HOPE SO.
DON'T FEEL LIKE STARTLING THE NEIGHBORS.
WHAT EXACTLY ARE YOU HOPING TO DO HERE, DAN?
THINGS WENT SOUTH PRETTY HARD TODAY. GOT A LOT I NEED TO TAKE CARE OF, A LOT I GOTTA DO.
AND ALL THIS HERE?

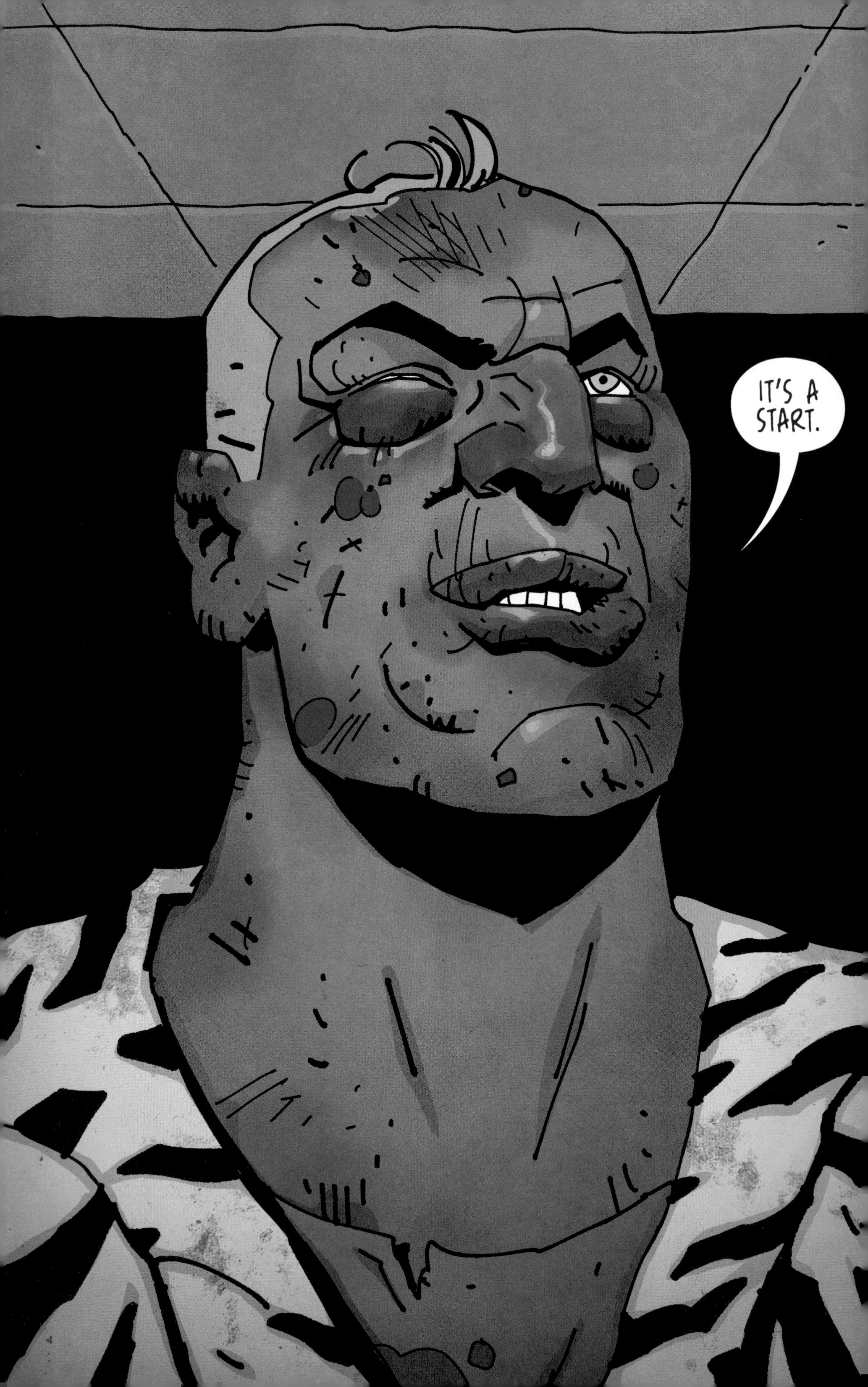
IT'S A START.

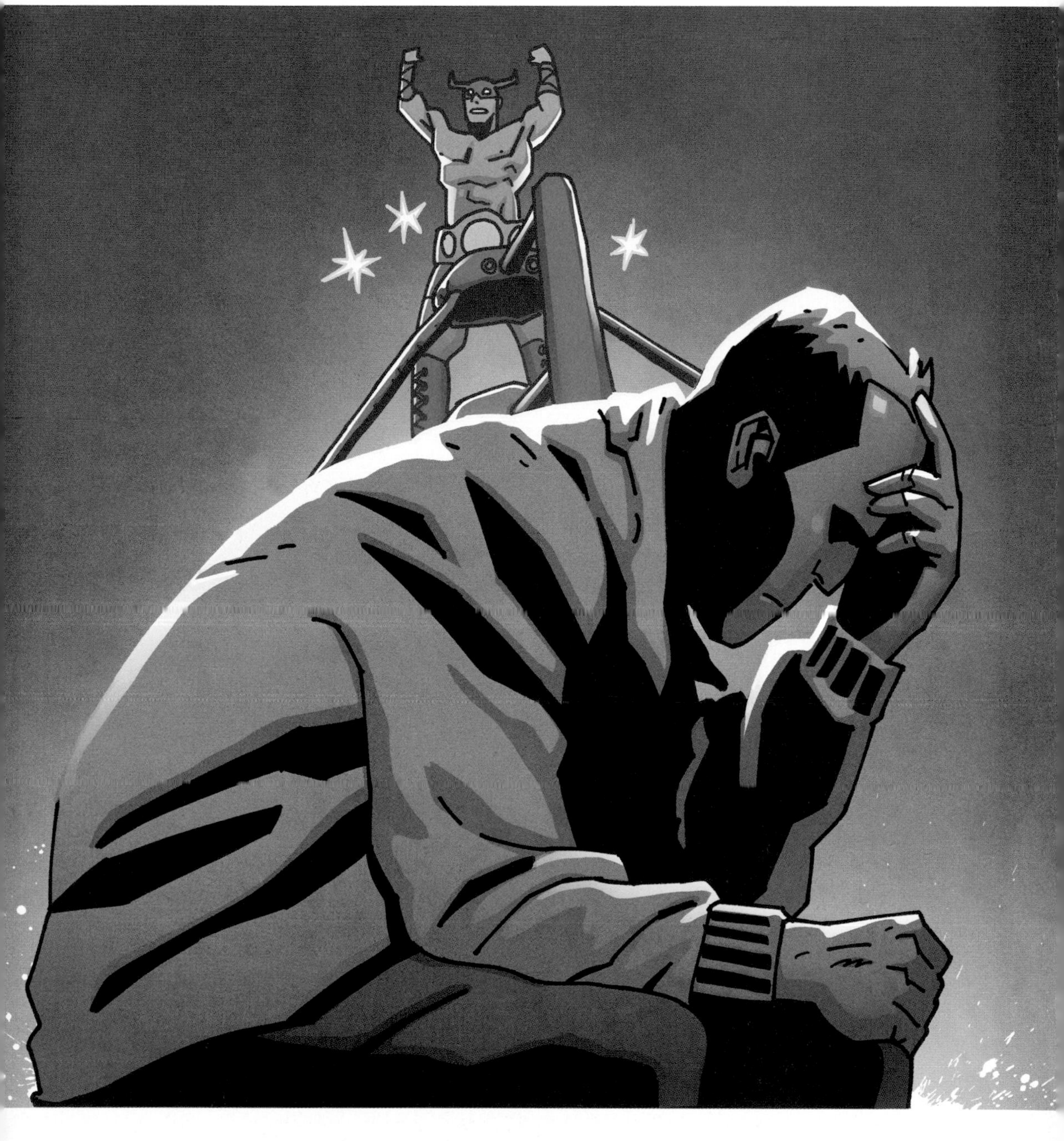

CHAPTER TWO

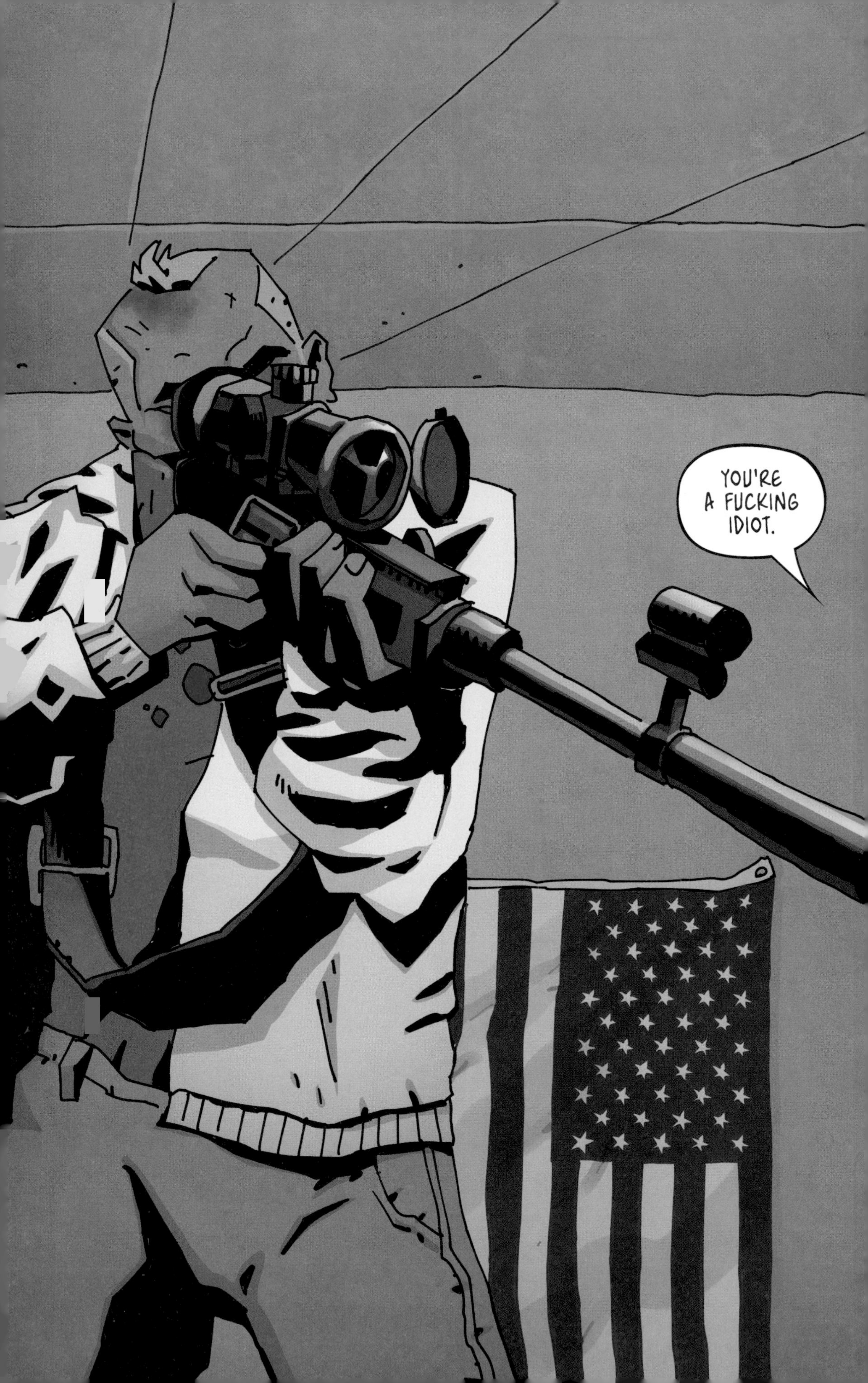
YOU'RE A FUCKING IDIOT.

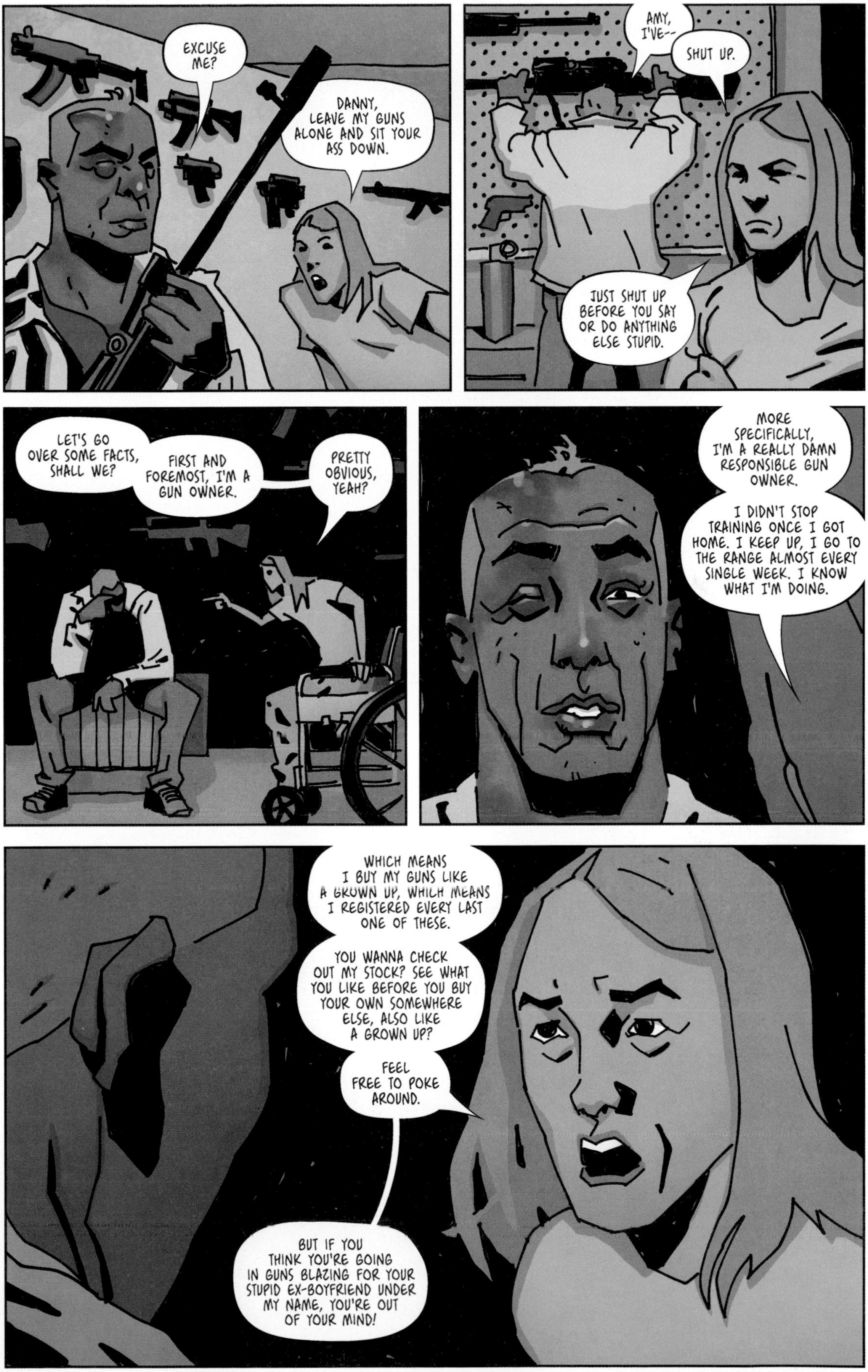
EXCUSE ME?
DANNY, LEAVE MY GUNS ALONE AND SIT YOUR ASS DOWN.
AMY, I'VE--
SHUT UP.
JUST SHUT UP BEFORE YOU SAY OR DO ANYTHING ELSE STUPID.
LET'S GO OVER SOME FACTS, SHALL WE?
FIRST AND FOREMOST, I'M A GUN OWNER.
PRETTY OBVIOUS, YEAH?
MORE SPECIFICALLY, I'M A REALLY DAMN RESPONSIBLE GUN OWNER.
I DIDN'T STOP TRAINING ONCE I GOT HOME. I KEEP UP, I GO TO THE RANGE ALMOST EVERY SINGLE WEEK. I KNOW WHAT I'M DOING.
WHICH MEANS I BUY MY GUNS LIKE A GROWN UP, WHICH MEANS I REGISTERED EVERY LAST ONE OF THESE.
YOU WANNA CHECK OUT MY STOCK? SEE WHAT YOU LIKE BEFORE YOU BUY YOUR OWN SOMEWHERE ELSE, ALSO LIKE A GROWN UP?
FEEL FREE TO POKE AROUND.
BUT IF YOU THINK YOU'RE GOING IN GUNS BLAZING FOR YOUR STUPID EX-BOYFRIEND UNDER MY NAME, YOU'RE OUT OF YOUR MIND!

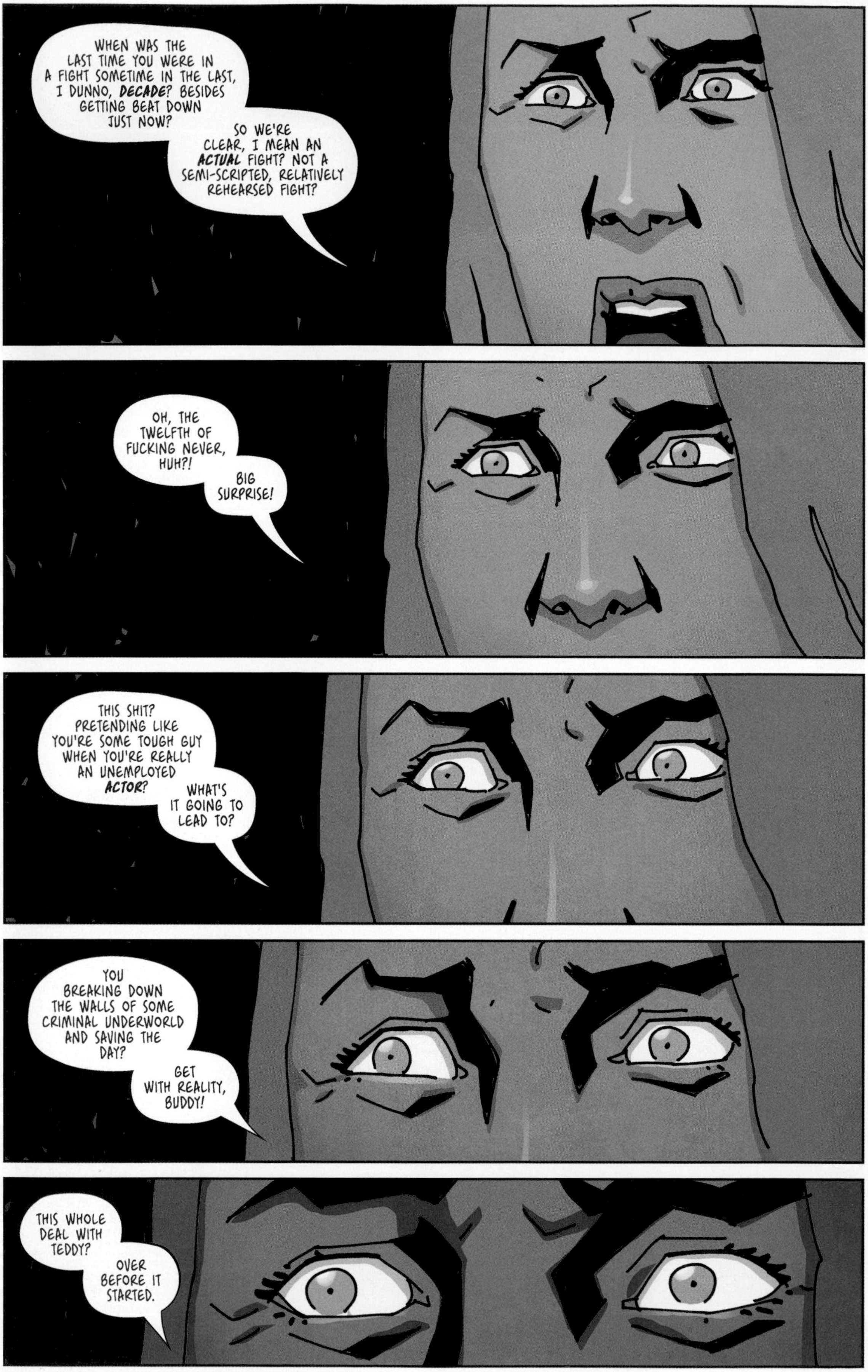
WHEN WAS THE LAST TIME YOU WERE IN A FIGHT SOMETIME IN THE LAST, I DUNNO, DECADE? BESIDES GETTING BEAT DOWN JUST NOW?
SO WE'RE CLEAR, I MEAN AN ACTUAL FIGHT? NOT A SEMI-SCRIPTED, RELATIVELY REHEARSED FIGHT?
OH, THE TWELFTH OF FUCKING NEVER, HUH?!
BIG SURPRISE!
THIS SHIT? PRETENDING LIKE YOU'RE SOME TOUGH GUY WHEN YOU'RE REALLY AN UNEMPLOYED ACTOR?
WHAT'S IT GOING TO LEAD TO?
YOU BREAKING DOWN THE WALLS OF SOME CRIMINAL UNDERWORLD AND SAVING THE DAY?
GET WITH REALITY, BUDDY!
THIS WHOLE DEAL WITH TEDDY?
OVER BEFORE IT STARTED.

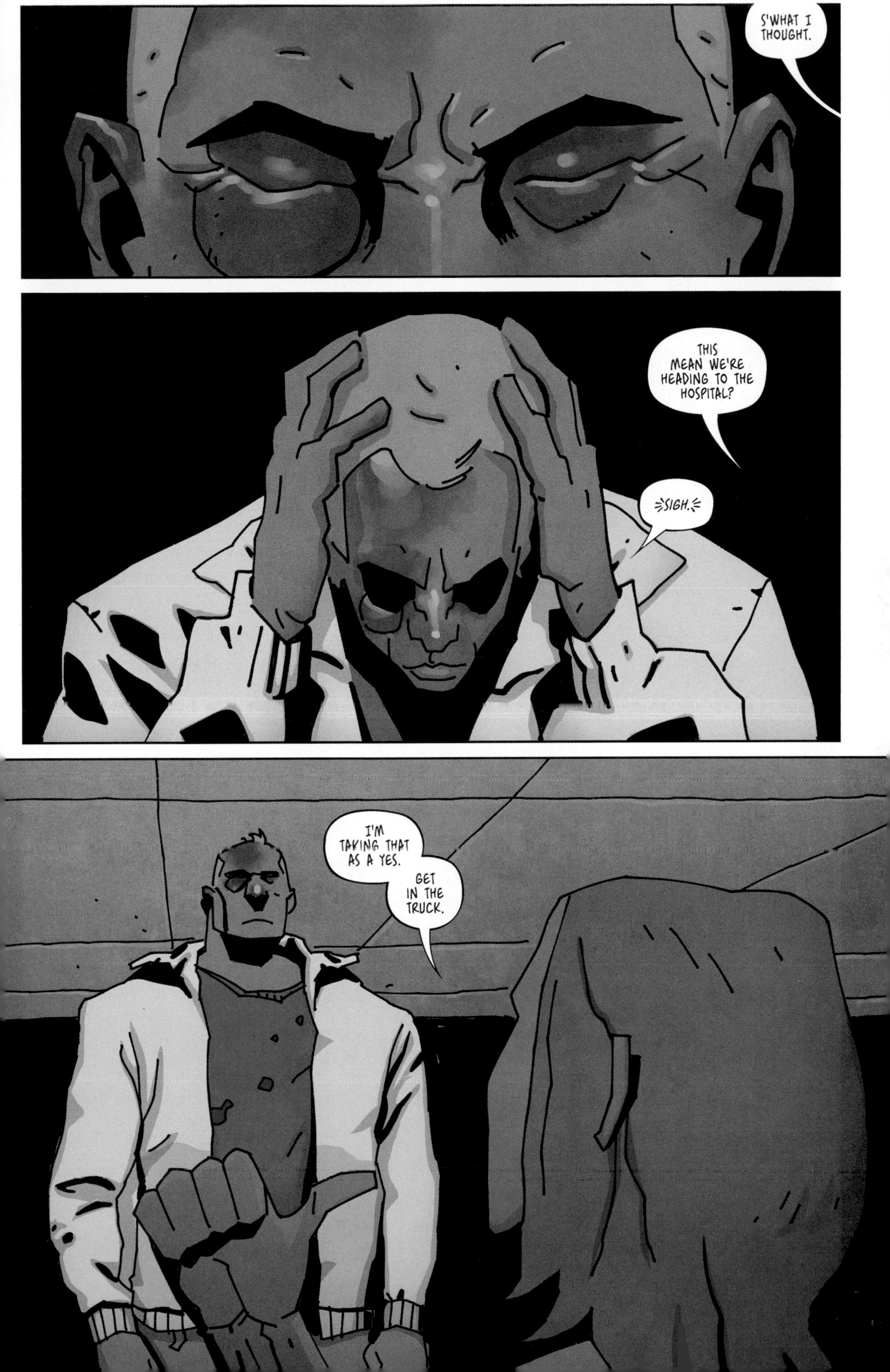
S'WHAT I THOUGHT.
THIS MEAN WE'RE HEADING TO THE HOSPITAL?
SIGH.
I'M TAKING THAT AS A YES.
GET IN THE TRUCK.

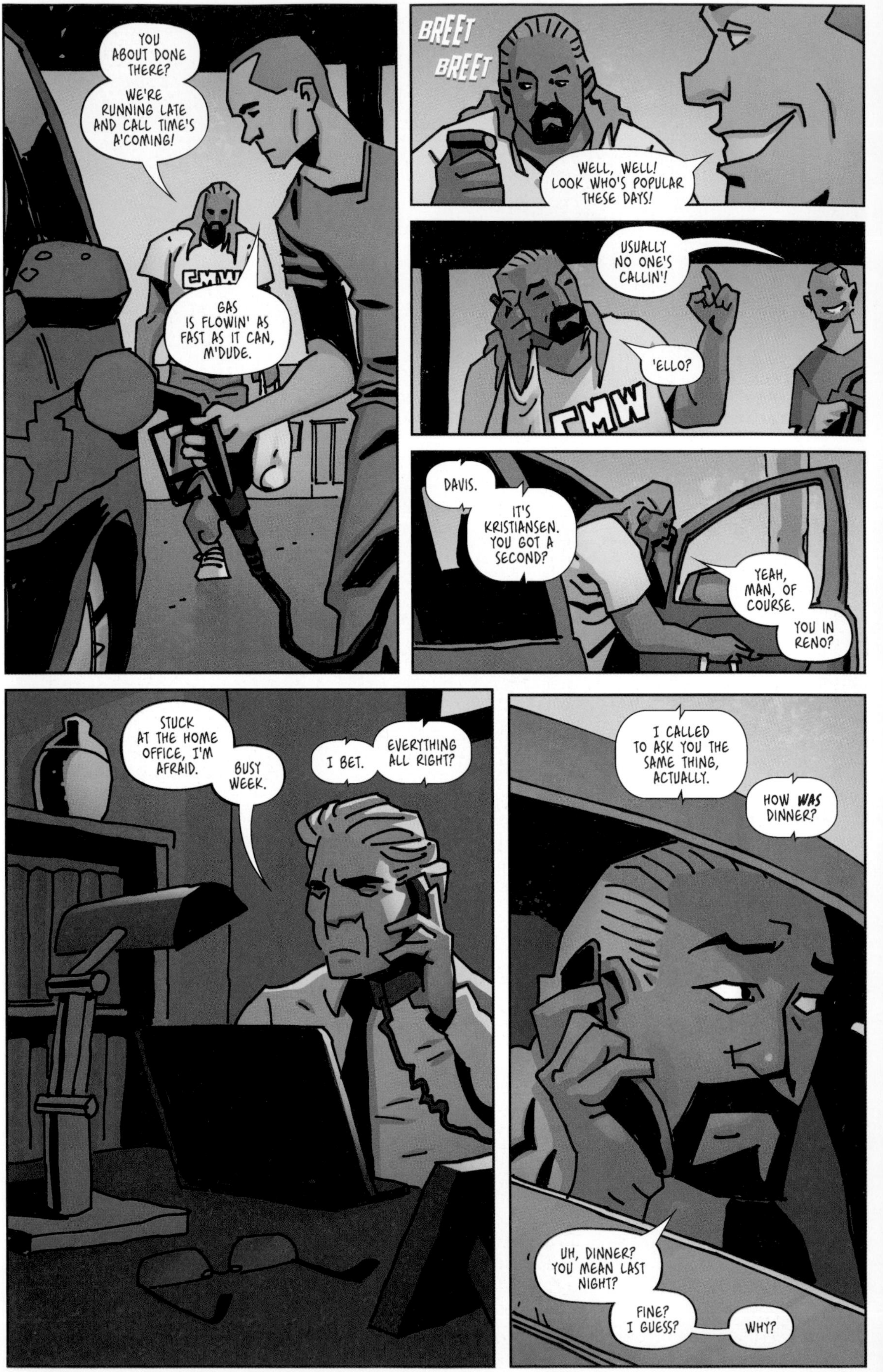
YOU ABOUT DONE THERE?
WE'RE RUNNING LATE AND CALL TIME'S A'COMING!
GAS IS FLOWIN' AS FAST AS IT CAN, M'DUDE.
CMW
BREET BREET
WELL, WELL! LOOK WHO'S POPULAR THESE DAYS!
USUALLY NO ONE'S CALLIN'!
'ELLO?
CMW
DAVIS.
IT'S KRISTIANSEN. YOU GOT A SECOND?
YEAH, MAN, OF COURSE.
YOU IN RENO?
STUCK AT THE HOME OFFICE, I'M AFRAID.
BUSY WEEK.
I BET.
EVERYTHING ALL RIGHT?
I CALLED TO ASK YOU THE SAME THING, ACTUALLY.
HOW WAS DINNER?
UH, DINNER? YOU MEAN LAST NIGHT?
FINE? I GUESS?
WHY?

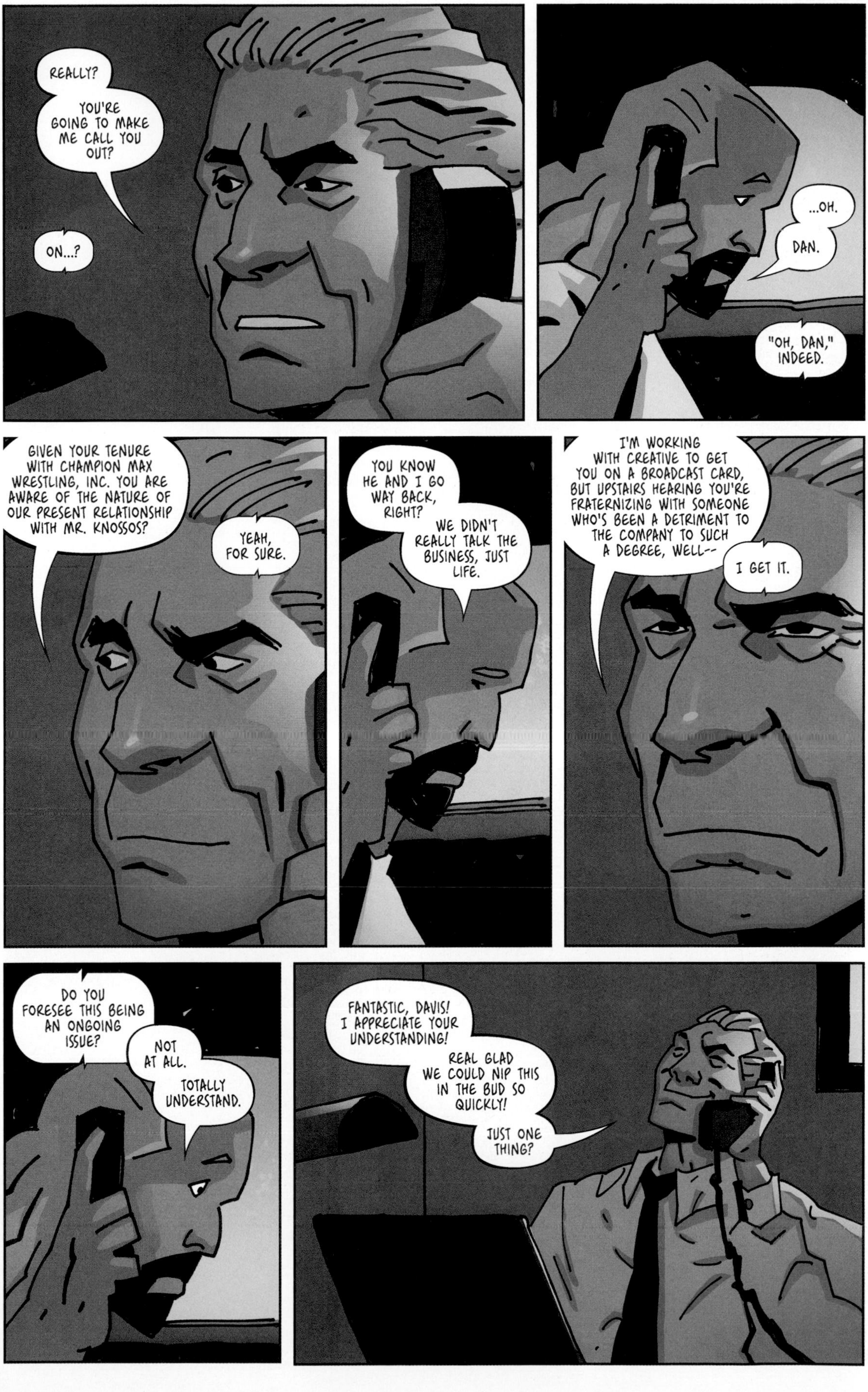
REALLY?
YOU'RE GOING TO MAKE ME CALL YOU OUT?
ON...?
...OH.
DAN.
"OH, DAN," INDEED.
GIVEN YOUR TENURE WITH CHAMPION MAX WRESTLING, INC. YOU ARE AWARE OF THE NATURE OF OUR PRESENT RELATIONSHIP WITH MR. KNOSSOS?
YEAH, FOR SURE.
YOU KNOW HE AND I GO WAY BACK, RIGHT?
WE DIDN'T REALLY TALK THE BUSINESS, JUST LIFE.
I'M WORKING WITH CREATIVE TO GET YOU ON A BROADCAST CARD, BUT UPSTAIRS HEARING YOU'RE FRATERNIZING WITH SOMEONE WHO'S BEEN A DETRIMENT TO THE COMPANY TO SUCH A DEGREE, WELL--
I GET IT.
DO YOU FORESEE THIS BEING AN ONGOING ISSUE?
NOT AT ALL.
TOTALLY UNDERSTAND.
FANTASTIC, DAVIS! I APPRECIATE YOUR UNDERSTANDING!
REAL GLAD WE COULD NIP THIS IN THE BUD SO QUICKLY!
JUST ONE THING?

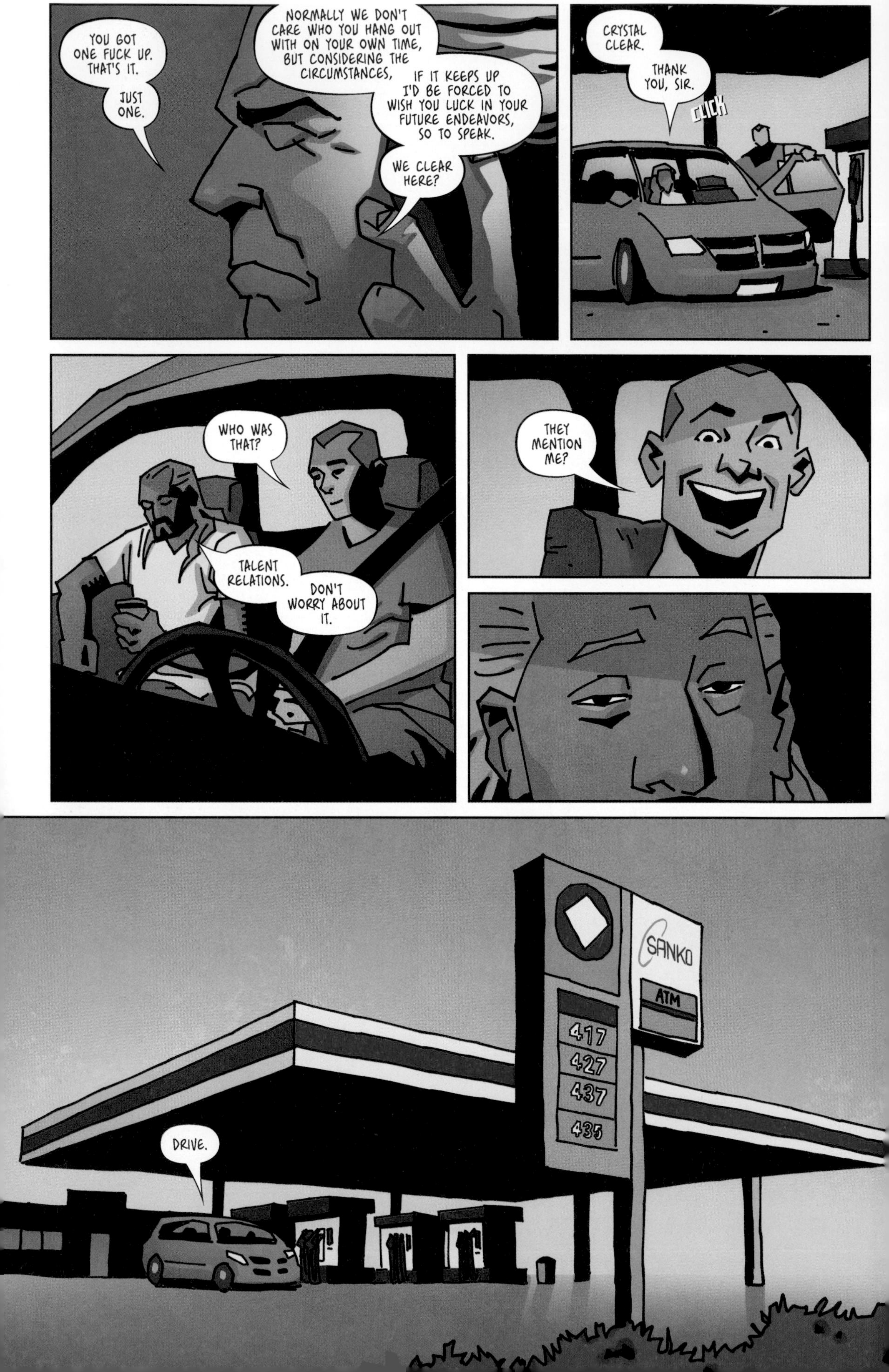
YOU GOT ONE FUCK UP. THAT'S IT.
JUST ONE.
NORMALLY WE DON'T CARE WHO YOU HANG OUT WITH ON YOUR OWN TIME, BUT CONSIDERING THE CIRCUMSTANCES,
IF IT KEEPS UP I'D BE FORCED TO WISH YOU LUCK IN YOUR FUTURE ENDEAVORS, SO TO SPEAK.
WE CLEAR HERE?
CRYSTAL CLEAR.
THANK YOU, SIR.
CLICK
WHO WAS THAT?
TALENT RELATIONS.
DON'T WORRY ABOUT IT.
THEY MENTION ME?
SANKO
ATM
417
427
437
435
DRIVE.

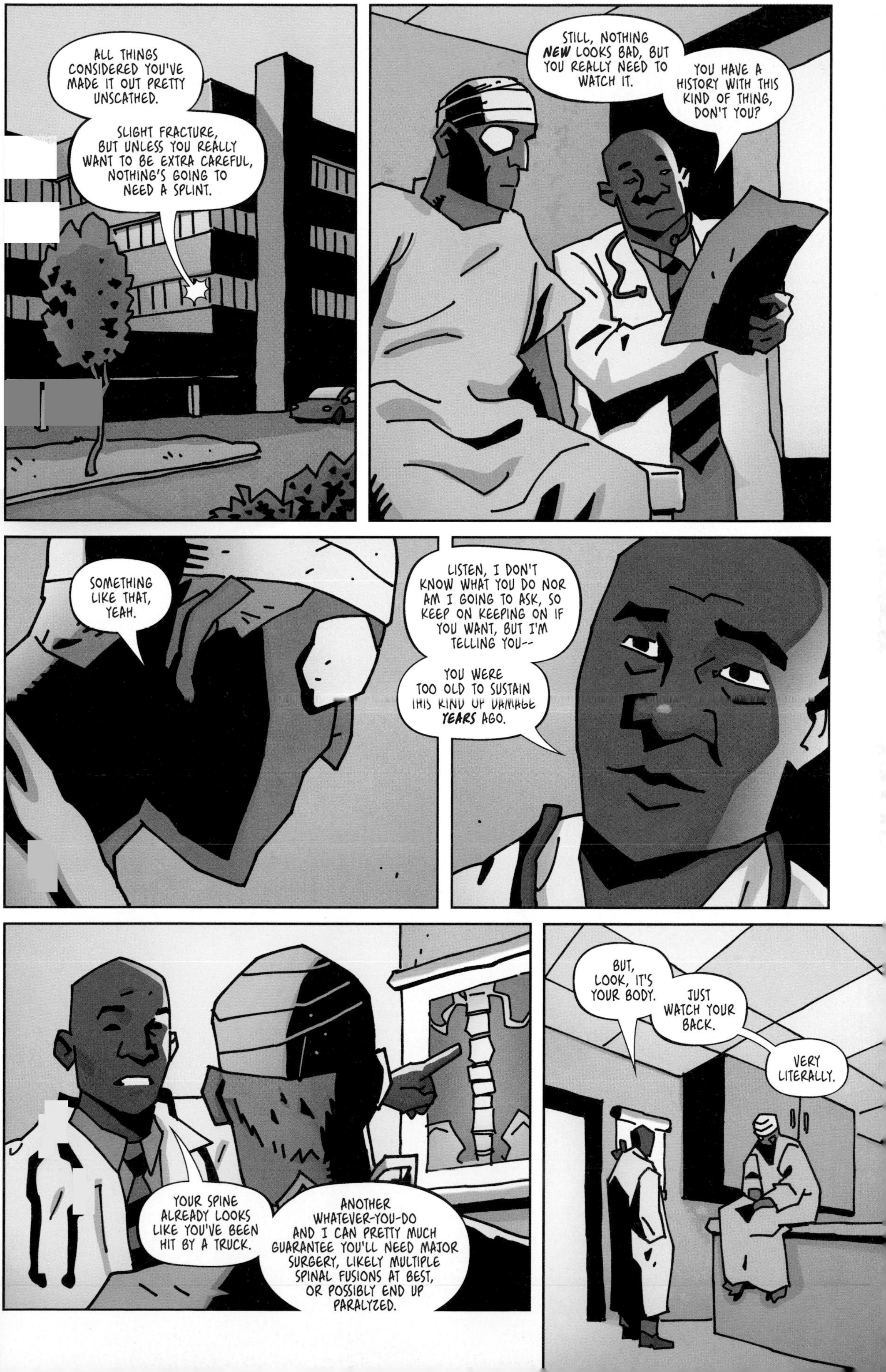
ALL THINGS CONSIDERED YOU'VE MADE IT OUT PRETTY UNSCATHED.
SLIGHT FRACTURE, BUT UNLESS YOU REALLY WANT TO BE EXTRA CAREFUL, NOTHING'S GOING TO NEED A SPLINT.
STILL, NOTHING NEW LOOKS BAD, BUT YOU REALLY NEED TO WATCH IT.
YOU HAVE A HISTORY WITH THIS KIND OF THING, DON'T YOU?
SOMETHING LIKE THAT, YEAH.
LISTEN, I DON'T KNOW WHAT YOU DO NOR AM I GOING TO ASK, SO KEEP ON KEEPING ON IF YOU WANT, BUT I'M TELLING YOU--
YOU WERE TOO OLD TO SUSTAIN THIS KIND OF DAMAGE YEARS AGO.
YOUR SPINE ALREADY LOOKS LIKE YOU'VE BEEN HIT BY A TRUCK.
ANOTHER WHATEVER-YOU-DO AND I CAN PRETTY MUCH GUARANTEE YOU'LL NEED MAJOR SURGERY, LIKELY MULTIPLE SPINAL FUSIONS AT BEST, OR POSSIBLY END UP PARALYZED.
BUT, LOOK, IT'S YOUR BODY.
JUST WATCH YOUR BACK.
VERY LITERALLY.

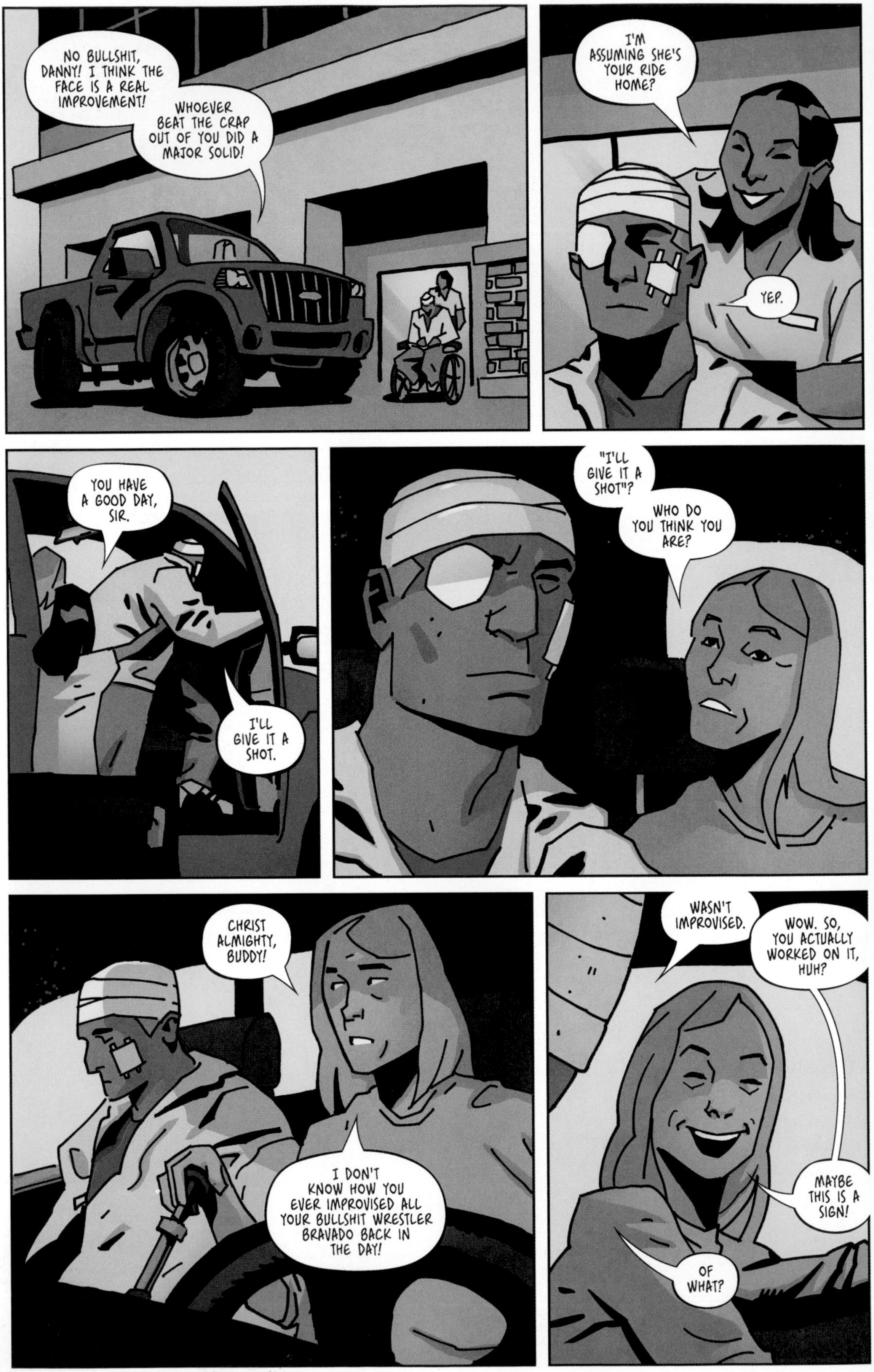
NO BULLSHIT, DANNY! I THINK THE FACE IS A REAL IMPROVEMENT!
WHOEVER BEAT THE CRAP OUT OF YOU DID A MAJOR SOLID!
I'M ASSUMING SHE'S YOUR RIDE HOME?
YEP.
YOU HAVE A GOOD DAY, SIR.
I'LL GIVE IT A SHOT.
"I'LL GIVE IT A SHOT"?
WHO DO YOU THINK YOU ARE?
CHRIST ALMIGHTY, BUDDY!
I DON'T KNOW HOW YOU EVER IMPROVISED ALL YOUR BULLSHIT WRESTLER BRAVADO BACK IN THE DAY!
WASN'T IMPROVISED.
WOW. SO, YOU ACTUALLY WORKED ON IT, HUH?
MAYBE THIS IS A SIGN!
OF WHAT?

MAYBE THIS IS A SIGN YOU SHOULD KEEP YOUR MOUTH SHUT.

PROBABLY.

NO PROBABLY ABOUT IT!

JUST TELL ME THIS REAL QUICK BEFORE YOU SMARTLY CLOSE YOUR YAP...

...WE GOING HOME OR ARE YOU HUNGRY OR WHAT?

I NEED TO STOP BY ANDRE'S.

ANDRE? THE BAIL BONDS JACKASS?

I THOUGHT YOU HATED HIM.

YOU'RE NOT REALLY GOING TO ACCEPT HIS JOB OFFER, ARE YOU?

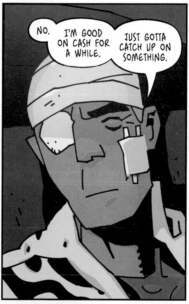

NO.

I'M GOOD ON CASH FOR A WHILE.

JUST GOTTA CATCH UP ON SOMETHING.

...REALLY?

WHAT?

KEEP UP THE VAGUE TOUGH GUY NONSENSE. SEE WHERE IT GETS YOU.

BUT I HOPE YOU GET I'M NOT AN AMBULANCE, NOR AN ENABLER.

I LOVE YOU LIKE A BROTHER, BUT IF YOU KEEP ON NEEDING A HOSPITAL,

I'M NOT LUGGING YOU THERE.

FAIR ENOUGH.

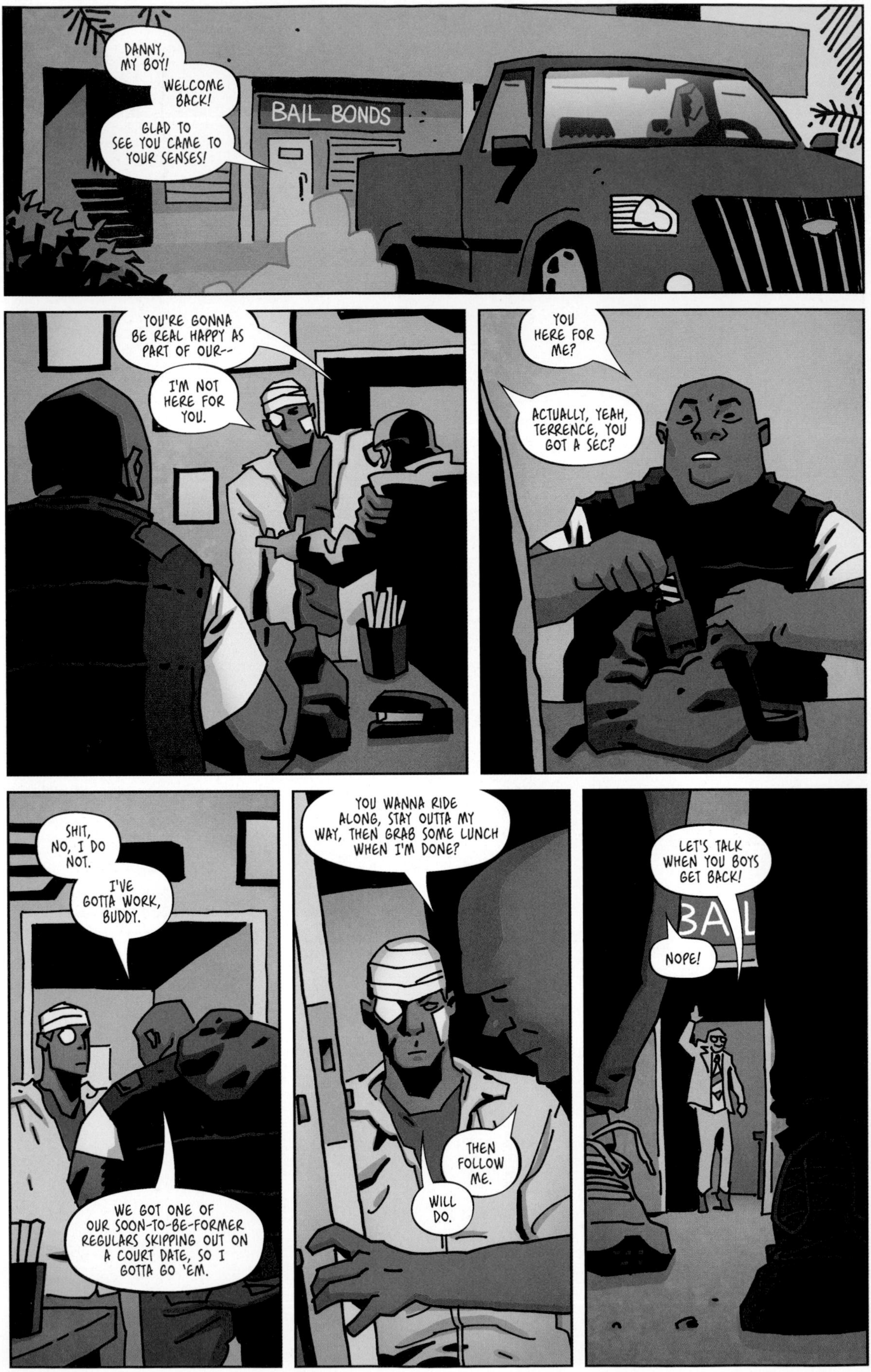
DANNY, MY BOY!
WELCOME BACK!
GLAD TO SEE YOU CAME TO YOUR SENSES!
BAIL BONDS
YOU'RE GONNA BE REAL HAPPY AS PART OF OUR--
I'M NOT HERE FOR YOU.
YOU HERE FOR ME?
ACTUALLY, YEAH, TERRENCE, YOU GOT A SEC?
SHIT, NO, I DO NOT.
I'VE GOTTA WORK, BUDDY.
WE GOT ONE OF OUR SOON-TO-BE-FORMER REGULARS SKIPPING OUT ON A COURT DATE, SO I GOTTA GO 'EM.
YOU WANNA RIDE ALONG, STAY OUTTA MY WAY, THEN GRAB SOME LUNCH WHEN I'M DONE?
WILL DO.
THEN FOLLOW ME.
LET'S TALK WHEN YOU BOYS GET BACK!
NOPE!

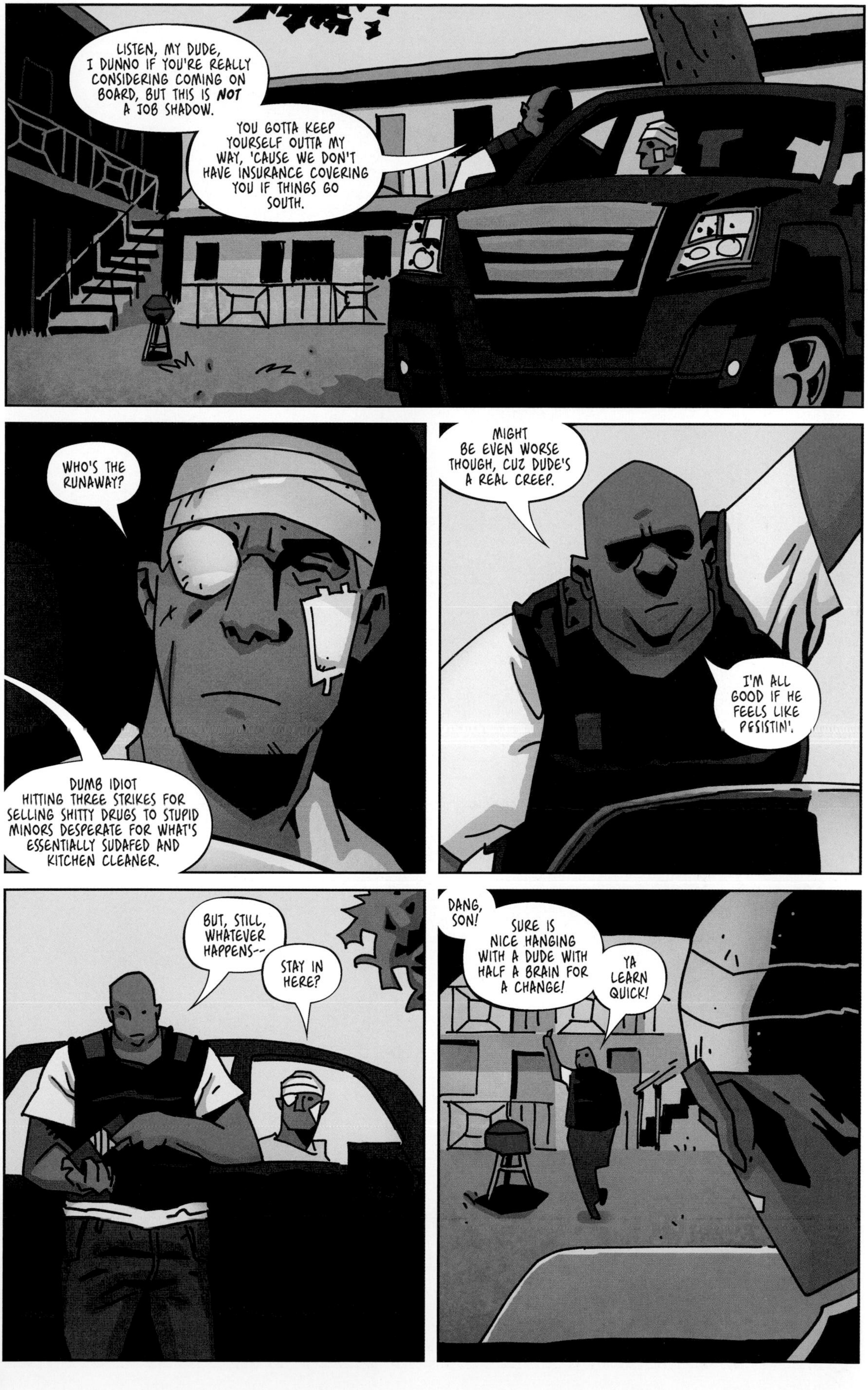
LISTEN, MY DUDE, I DUNNO IF YOU'RE REALLY CONSIDERING COMING ON BOARD, BUT THIS IS **NOT** A JOB SHADOW.
YOU GOTTA KEEP YOURSELF OUTTA MY WAY, 'CAUSE WE DON'T HAVE INSURANCE COVERING YOU IF THINGS GO SOUTH.
WHO'S THE RUNAWAY?
DUMB IDIOT HITTING THREE STRIKES FOR SELLING SHITTY DRUGS TO STUPID MINORS DESPERATE FOR WHAT'S ESSENTIALLY SUDAFED AND KITCHEN CLEANER.
MIGHT BE EVEN WORSE THOUGH, CUZ DUDE'S A REAL CREEP.
I'M ALL GOOD IF HE FEELS LIKE RESISTIN'.
BUT, STILL, WHATEVER HAPPENS--
STAY IN HERE?
DANG, SON!
SURE IS NICE HANGING WITH A DUDE WITH HALF A BRAIN FOR A CHANGE!
YA LEARN QUICK!

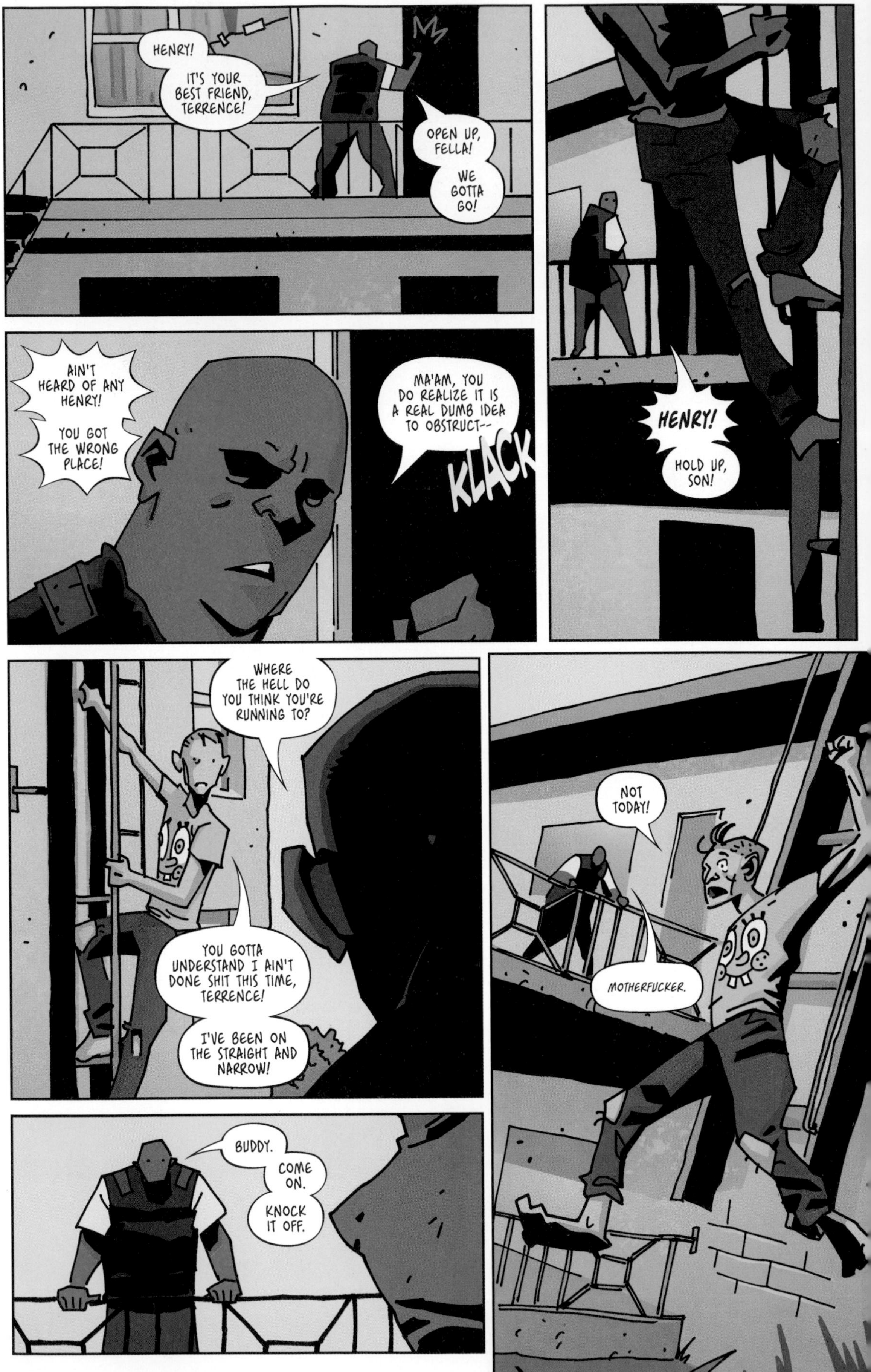
HENRY!
IT'S YOUR BEST FRIEND, TERRENCE!
OPEN UP, FELLA!
WE GOTTA GO!
HENRY!
HOLD UP, SON!
AIN'T HEARD OF ANY HENRY!
YOU GOT THE WRONG PLACE!
MA'AM, YOU DO REALIZE IT IS A REAL DUMB IDEA TO OBSTRUCT--
KLACK
WHERE THE HELL DO YOU THINK YOU'RE RUNNING TO?
YOU GOTTA UNDERSTAND I AIN'T DONE SHIT THIS TIME, TERRENCE!
I'VE BEEN ON THE STRAIGHT AND NARROW!
BUDDY.
COME ON.
KNOCK IT OFF.
NOT TODAY!
MOTHERFUCKER.

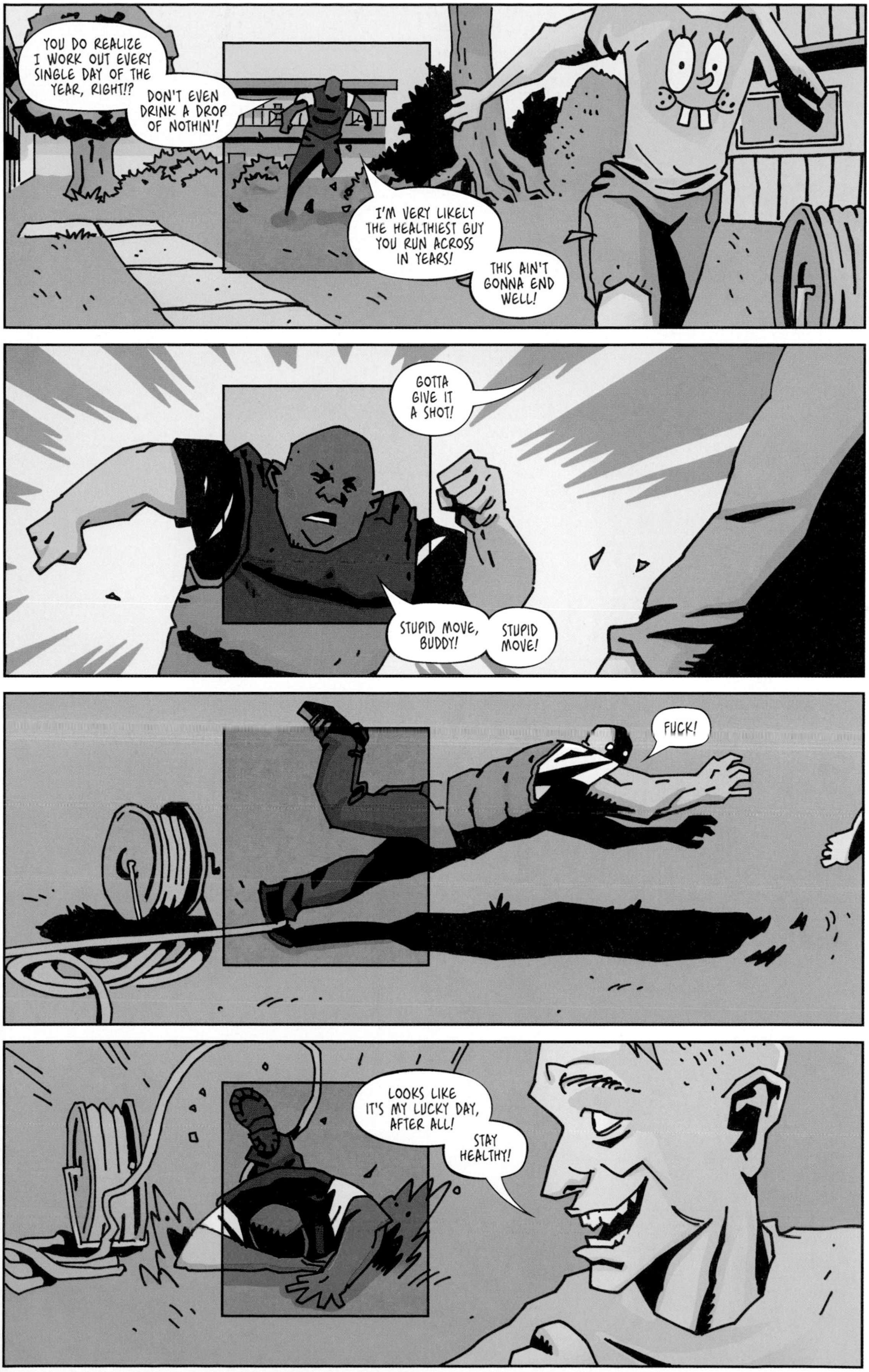
YOU DO REALIZE I WORK OUT EVERY SINGLE DAY OF THE YEAR, RIGHT!?
DON'T EVEN DRINK A DROP OF NOTHIN'!
I'M VERY LIKELY THE HEALTHIEST GUY YOU RUN ACROSS IN YEARS!
THIS AIN'T GONNA END WELL!
GOTTA GIVE IT A SHOT!
STUPID MOVE, BUDDY!
STUPID MOVE!
FUCK!
LOOKS LIKE IT'S MY LUCKY DAY, AFTER ALL!
STAY HEALTHY!

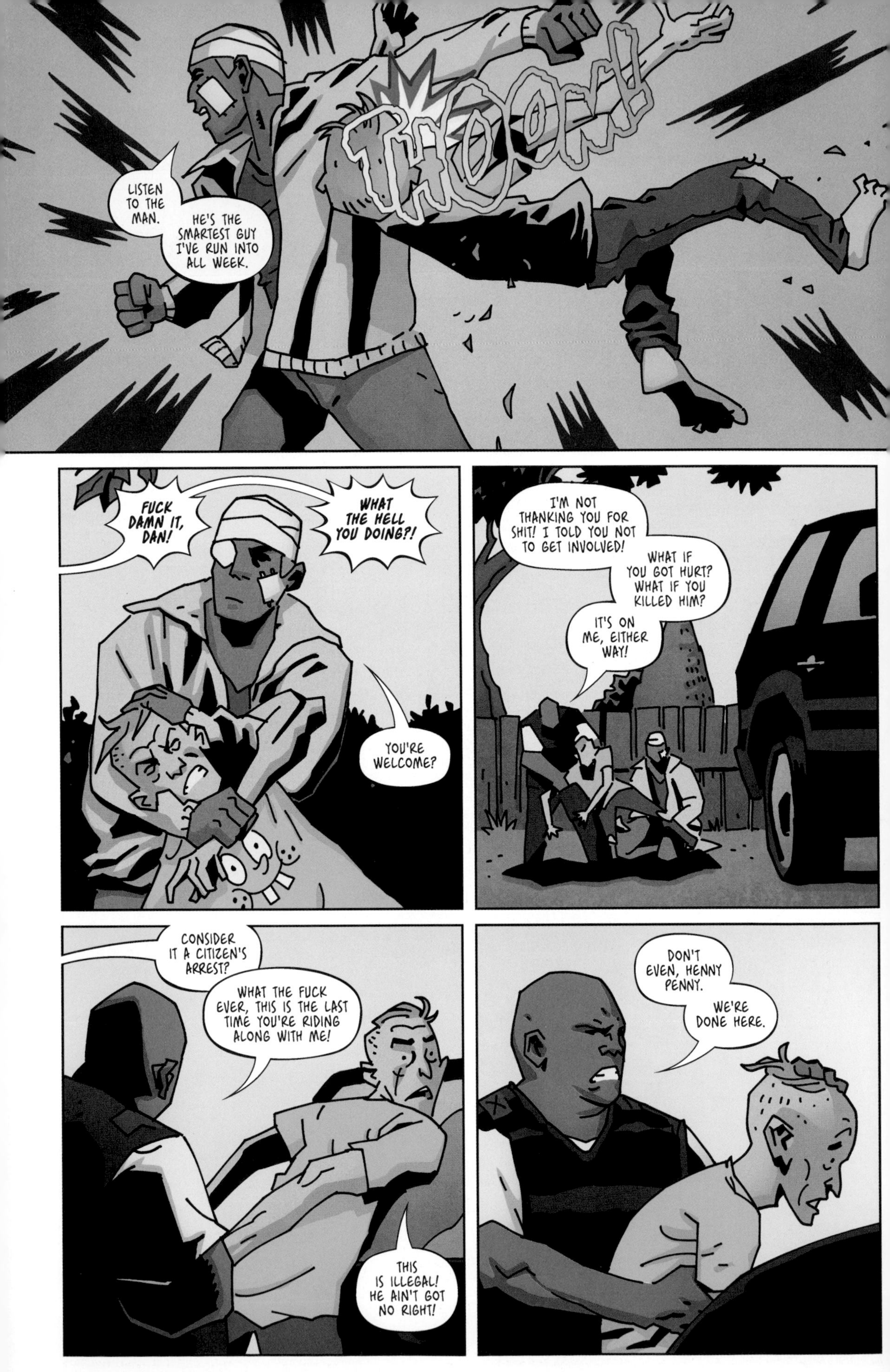
LISTEN TO THE MAN.
HE'S THE SMARTEST GUY I'VE RUN INTO ALL WEEK.
THOOM!
FUCK DAMN IT, DAN!
WHAT THE HELL YOU DOING?!
YOU'RE WELCOME?
I'M NOT THANKING YOU FOR SHIT! I TOLD YOU NOT TO GET INVOLVED!
WHAT IF YOU GOT HURT? WHAT IF YOU KILLED HIM?
IT'S ON ME, EITHER WAY!
CONSIDER IT A CITIZEN'S ARREST?
WHAT THE FUCK EVER, THIS IS THE LAST TIME YOU'RE RIDING ALONG WITH ME!
THIS IS ILLEGAL! HE AIN'T GOT NO RIGHT!
DON'T EVEN, HENNY PENNY.
WE'RE DONE HERE.

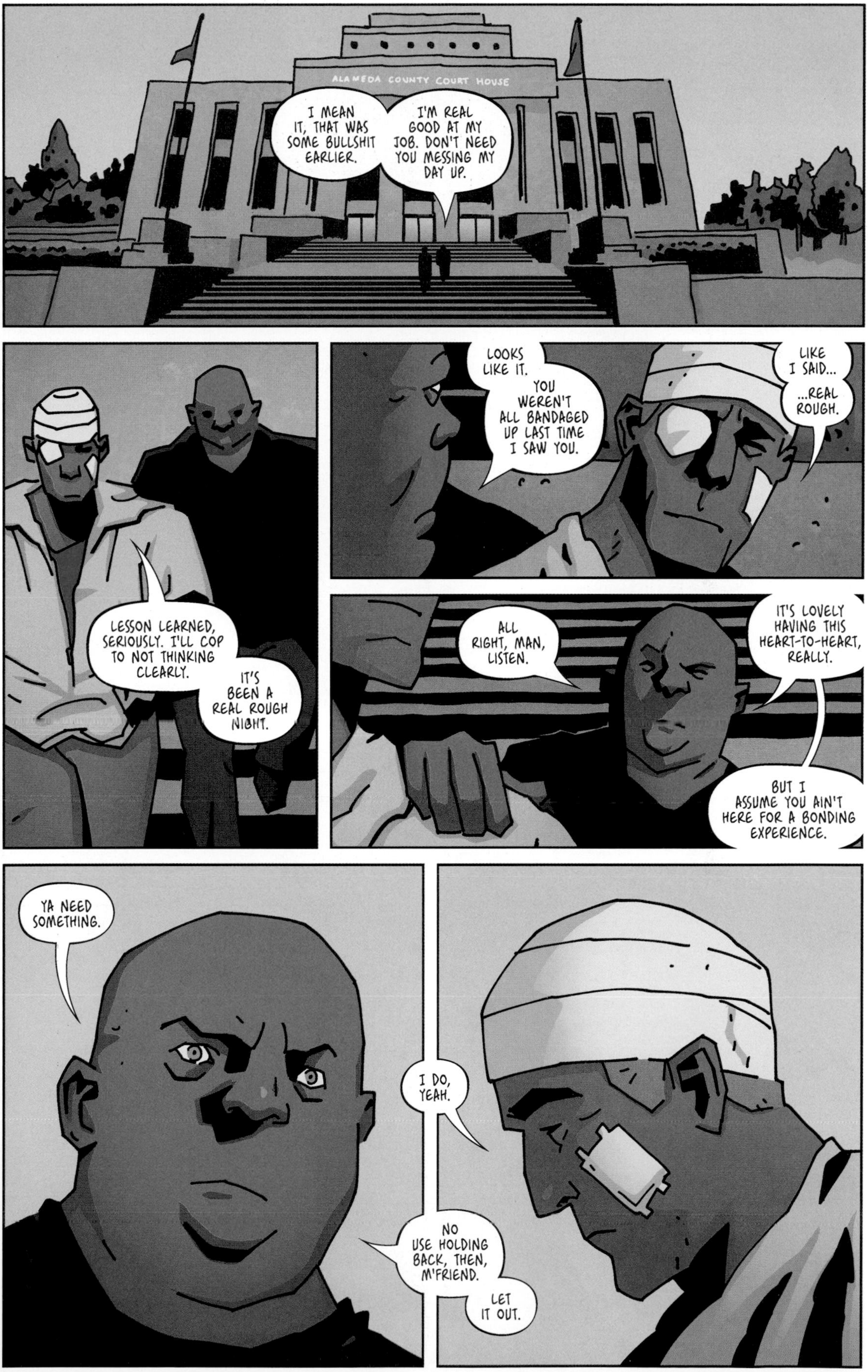
ALAMEDA COUNTY COURT HOUSE
I MEAN IT, THAT WAS SOME BULLSHIT EARLIER.
I'M REAL GOOD AT MY JOB. DON'T NEED YOU MESSING MY DAY UP.
LESSON LEARNED, SERIOUSLY. I'LL COP TO NOT THINKING CLEARLY.
IT'S BEEN A REAL ROUGH NIGHT.
LOOKS LIKE IT.
YOU WEREN'T ALL BANDAGED UP LAST TIME I SAW YOU.
LIKE I SAID...
...REAL ROUGH.
ALL RIGHT, MAN, LISTEN.
IT'S LOVELY HAVING THIS HEART-TO-HEART, REALLY.
BUT I ASSUME YOU AIN'T HERE FOR A BONDING EXPERIENCE.
YA NEED SOMETHING.
I DO, YEAH.
NO USE HOLDING BACK, THEN, M'FRIEND.
LET IT OUT.

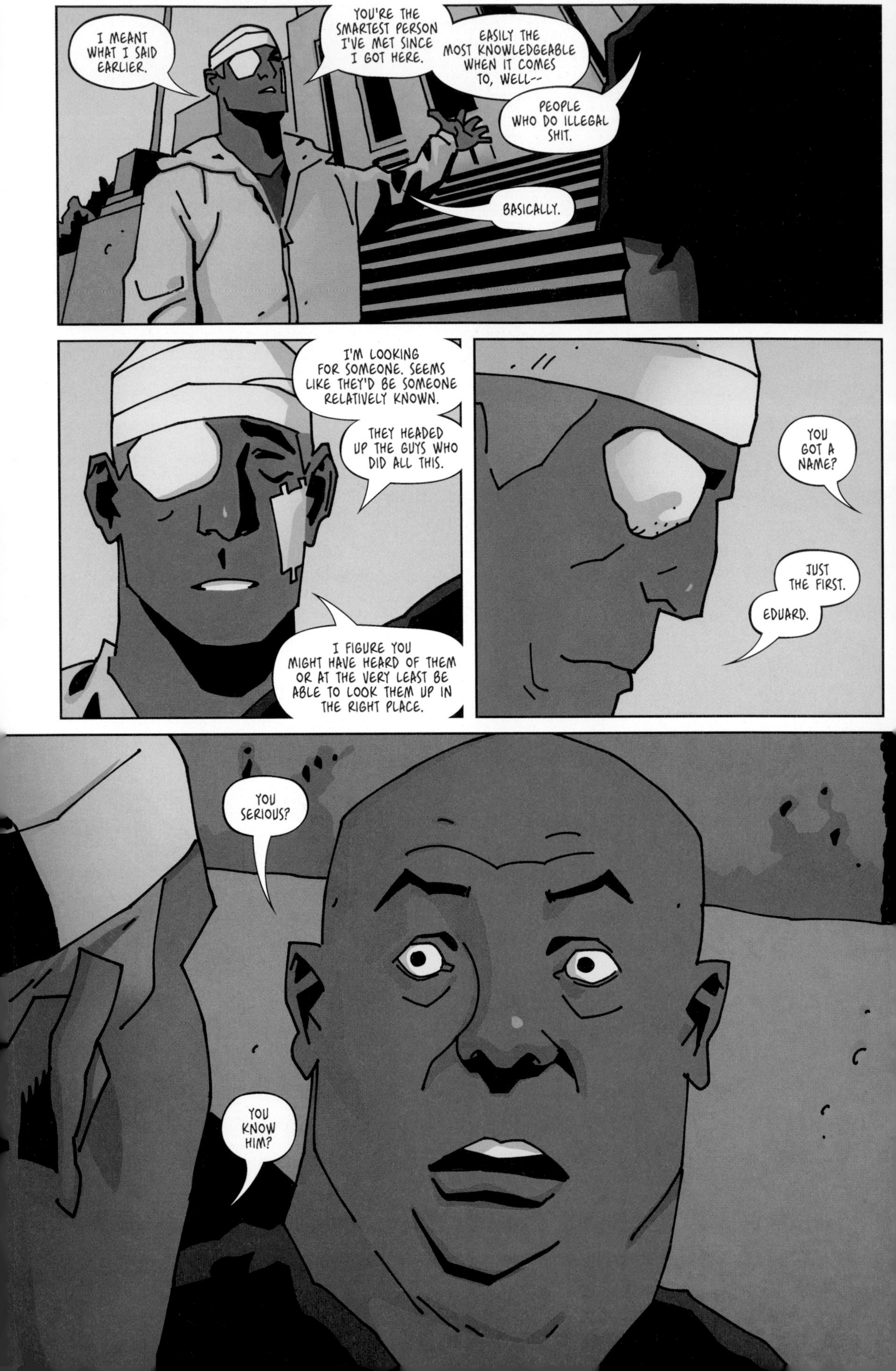
I MEANT WHAT I SAID EARLIER.
YOU'RE THE SMARTEST PERSON I'VE MET SINCE I GOT HERE.
EASILY THE MOST KNOWLEDGEABLE WHEN IT COMES TO, WELL--
PEOPLE WHO DO ILLEGAL SHIT.
BASICALLY.
I'M LOOKING FOR SOMEONE. SEEMS LIKE THEY'D BE SOMEONE RELATIVELY KNOWN.
THEY HEADED UP THE GUYS WHO DID ALL THIS.
I FIGURE YOU MIGHT HAVE HEARD OF THEM OR AT THE VERY LEAST BE ABLE TO LOOK THEM UP IN THE RIGHT PLACE.
YOU GOT A NAME?
JUST THE FIRST.
EDUARD.
YOU SERIOUS?
YOU KNOW HIM?

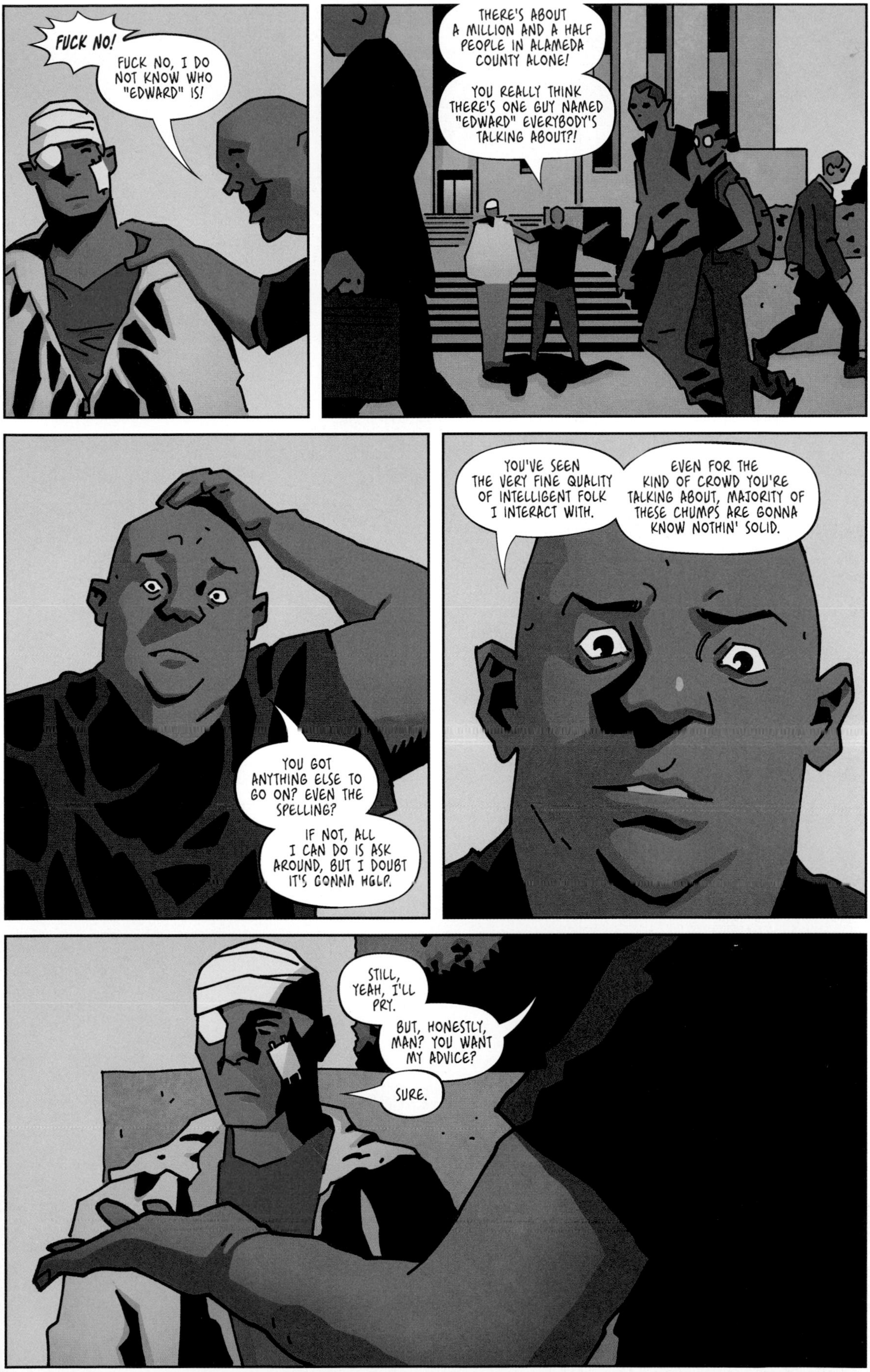
FUCK NO!
FUCK NO, I DO NOT KNOW WHO "EDWARD" IS!
THERE'S ABOUT A MILLION AND A HALF PEOPLE IN ALAMEDA COUNTY ALONE!
YOU REALLY THINK THERE'S ONE GUY NAMED "EDWARD" EVERYBODY'S TALKING ABOUT?!
YOU GOT ANYTHING ELSE TO GO ON? EVEN THE SPELLING?
IF NOT, ALL I CAN DO IS ASK AROUND, BUT I DOUBT IT'S GONNA HELP.
YOU'VE SEEN THE VERY FINE QUALITY OF INTELLIGENT FOLK I INTERACT WITH.
EVEN FOR THE KIND OF CROWD YOU'RE TALKING ABOUT, MAJORITY OF THESE CHUMPS ARE GONNA KNOW NOTHIN' SOLID.
STILL, YEAH, I'LL PRY.
BUT, HONESTLY, MAN? YOU WANT MY ADVICE?
SURE.

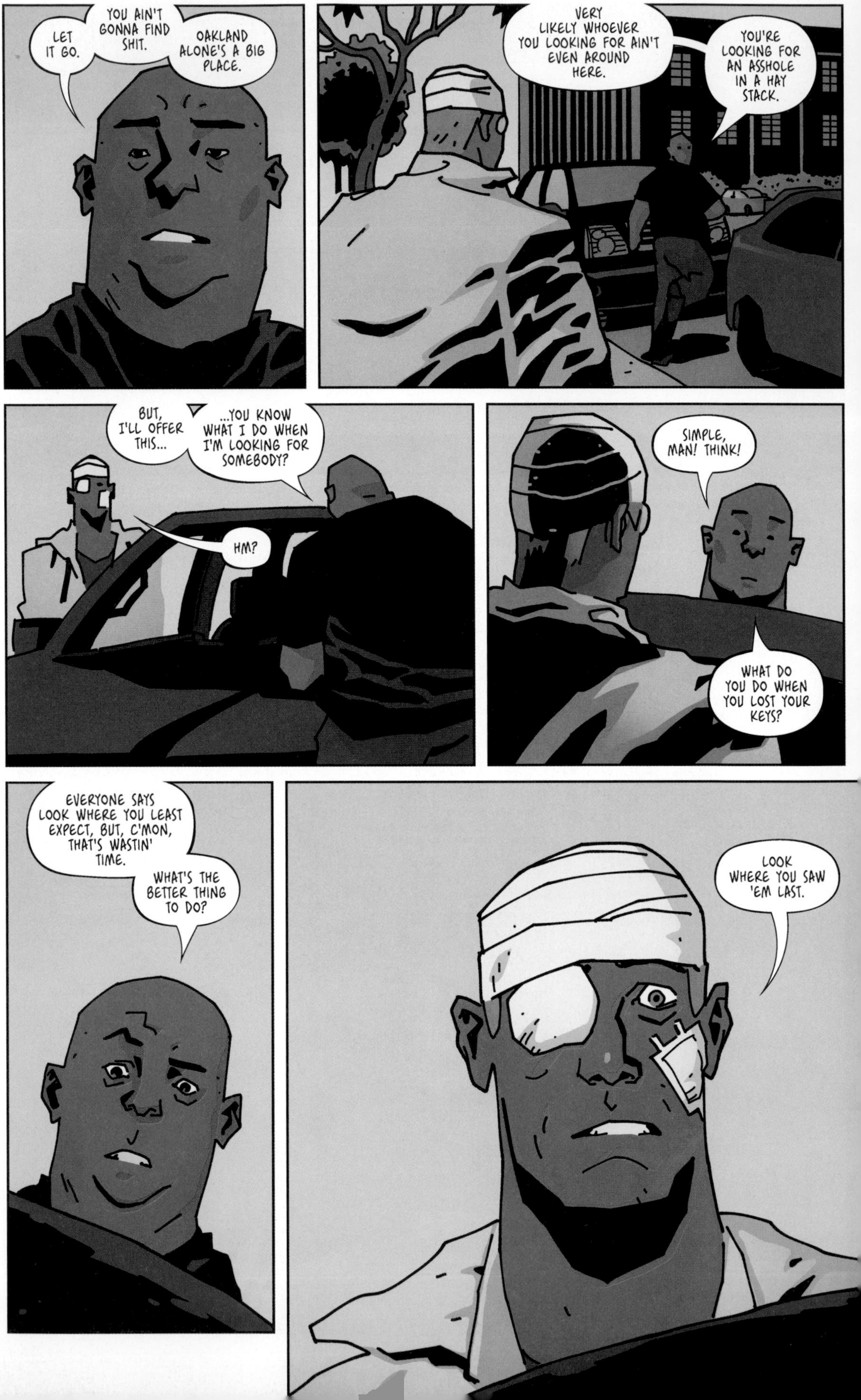
LET IT GO.
YOU AIN'T GONNA FIND SHIT.
OAKLAND ALONE'S A BIG PLACE.
VERY LIKELY WHOEVER YOU LOOKING FOR AIN'T EVEN AROUND HERE.
YOU'RE LOOKING FOR AN ASSHOLE IN A HAY STACK.
BUT, I'LL OFFER THIS...
...YOU KNOW WHAT I DO WHEN I'M LOOKING FOR SOMEBODY?
HM?
SIMPLE, MAN! THINK!
WHAT DO YOU DO WHEN YOU LOST YOUR KEYS?
EVERYONE SAYS LOOK WHERE YOU LEAST EXPECT, BUT, C'MON, THAT'S WASTIN' TIME.
WHAT'S THE BETTER THING TO DO?
LOOK WHERE YOU SAW 'EM LAST.

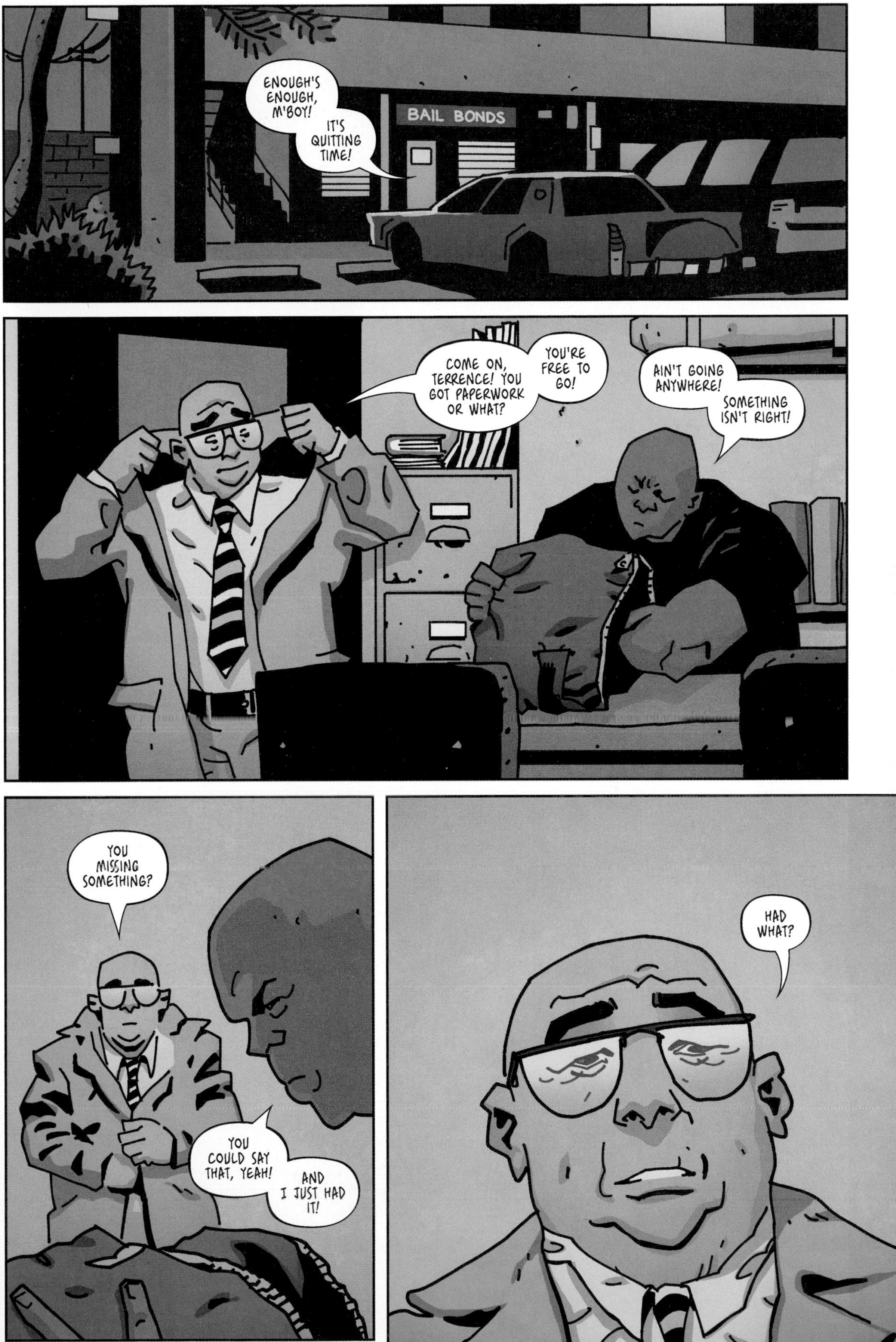

ENOUGH'S ENOUGH, M'BOY!
IT'S QUITTING TIME!
BAIL BONDS
COME ON, TERRENCE! YOU GOT PAPERWORK OR WHAT?
YOU'RE FREE TO GO!
AIN'T GOING ANYWHERE!
SOMETHING ISN'T RIGHT!
YOU MISSING SOMETHING?
YOU COULD SAY THAT, YEAH!
AND I JUST HAD IT!
HAD WHAT?

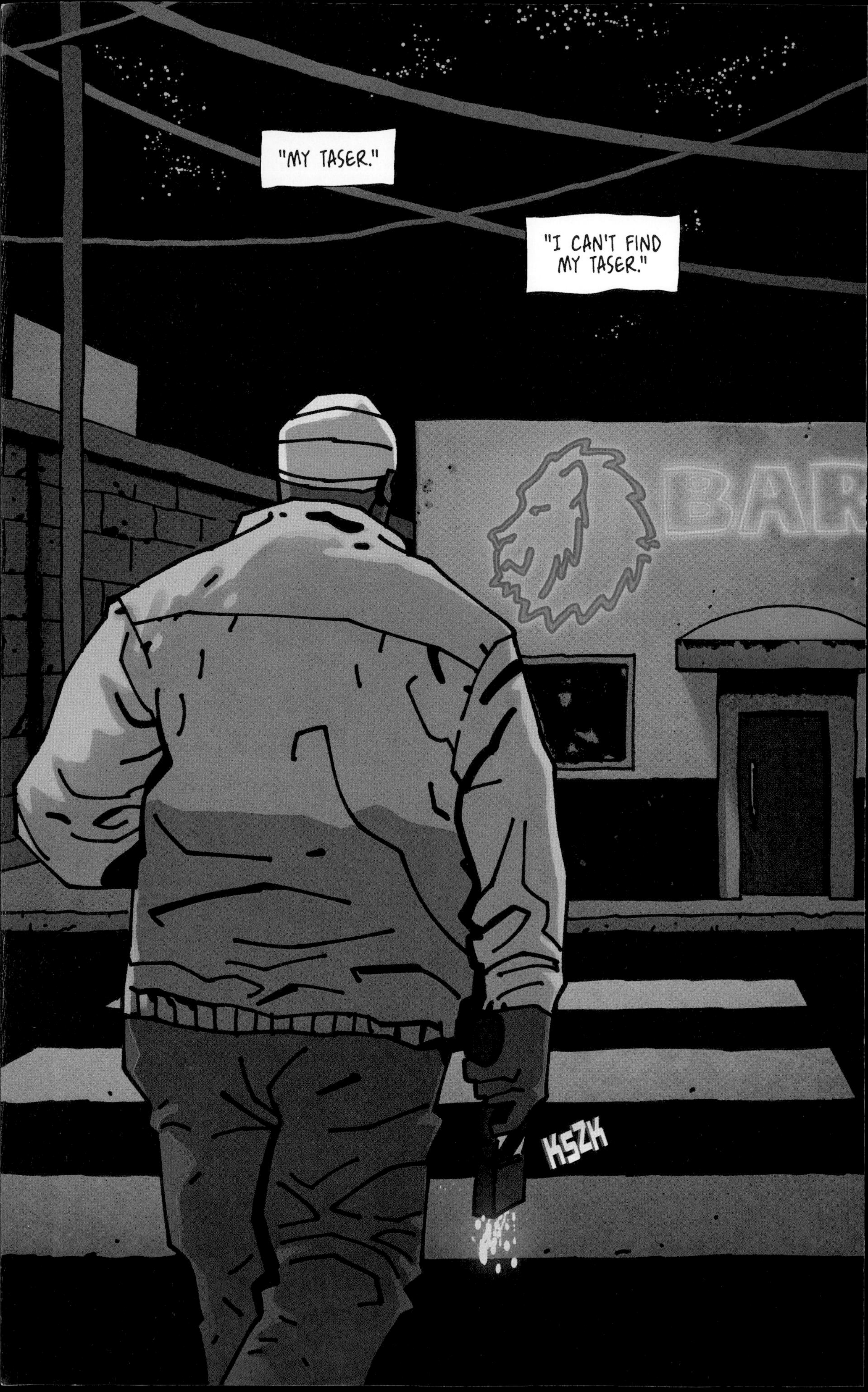
"MY TASER."
"I CAN'T FIND MY TASER."
BAR
KSZK

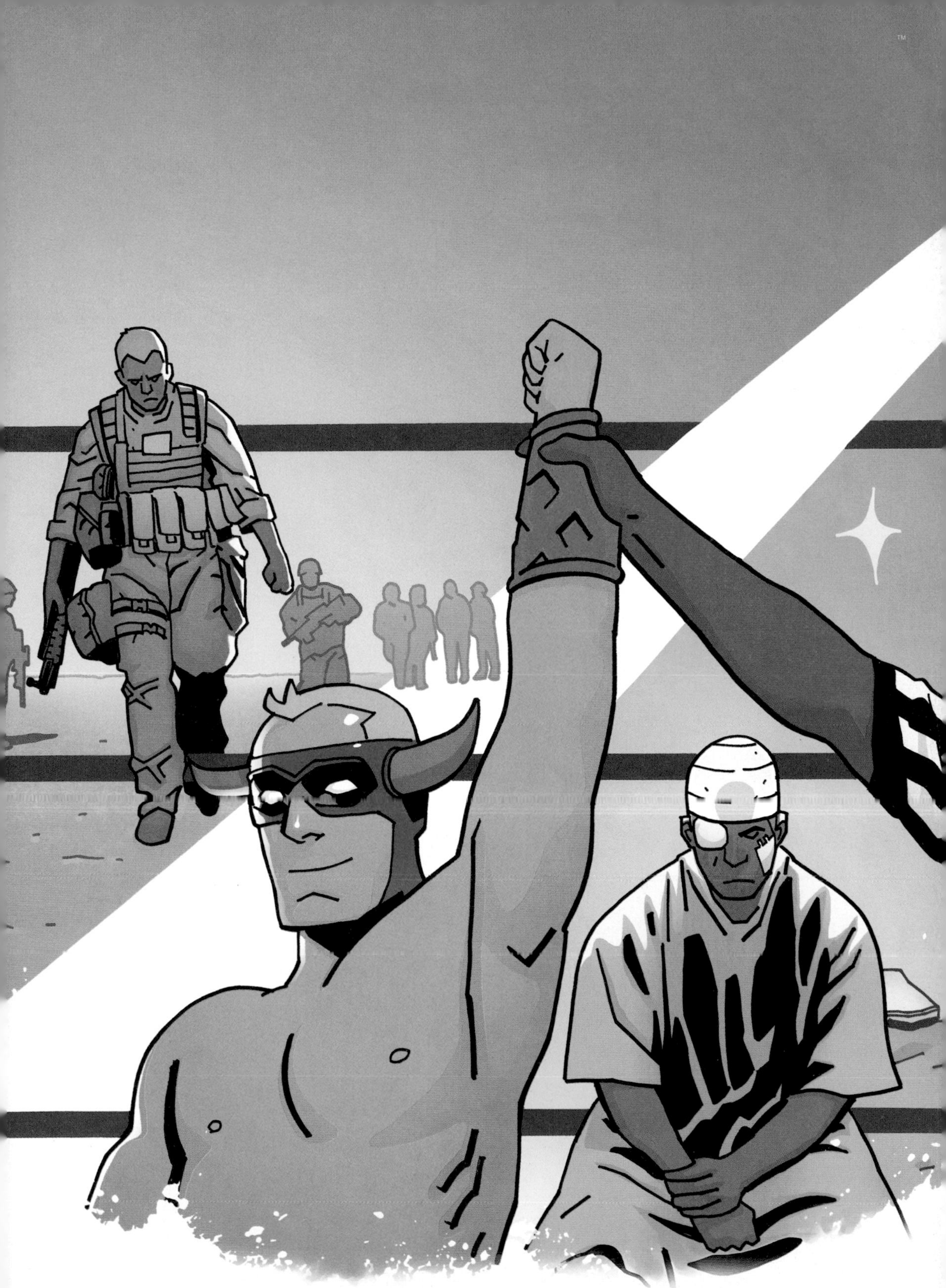

CHAPTER THREE

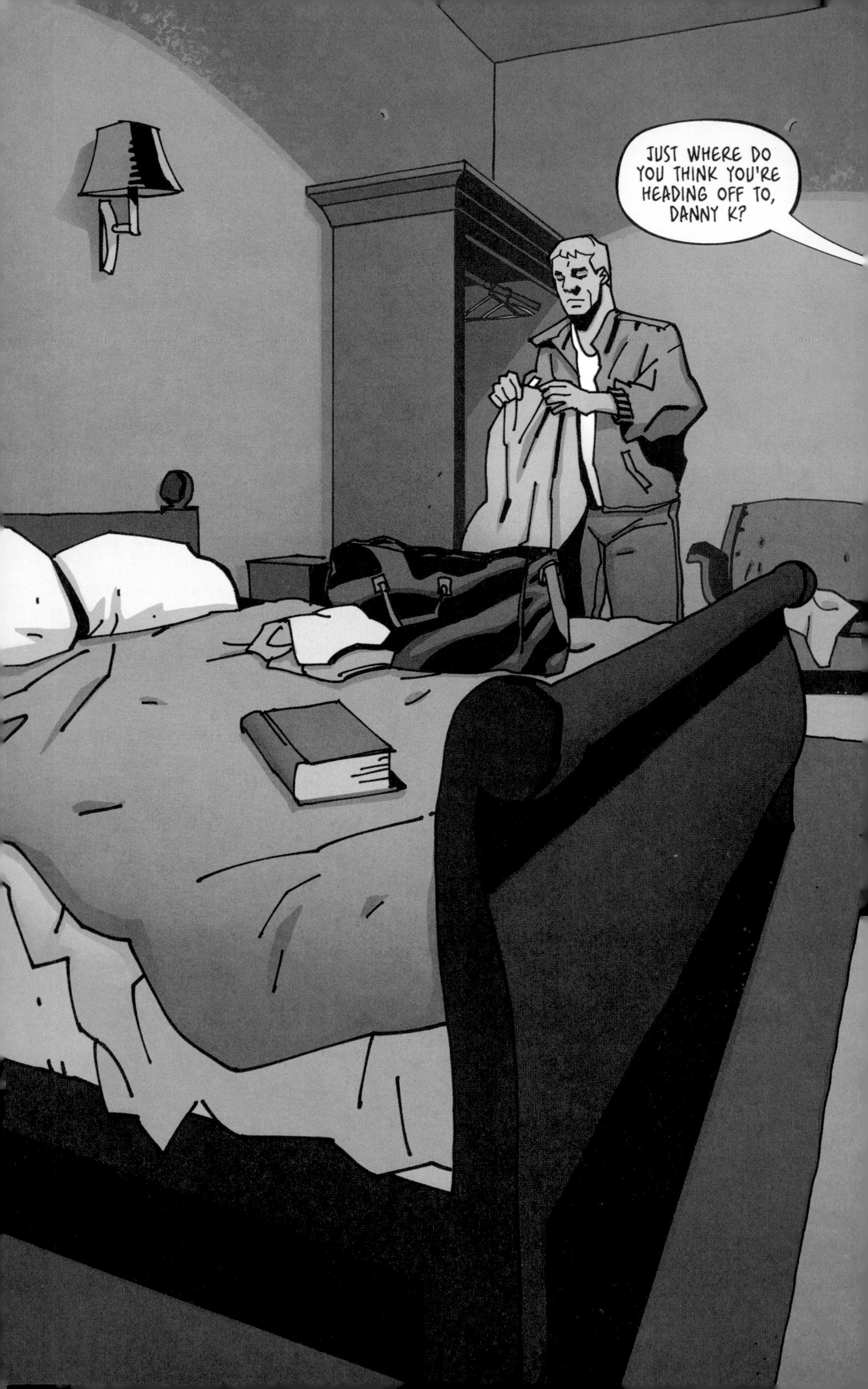
JUST WHERE DO YOU THINK YOU'RE HEADING OFF TO, DANNY K?

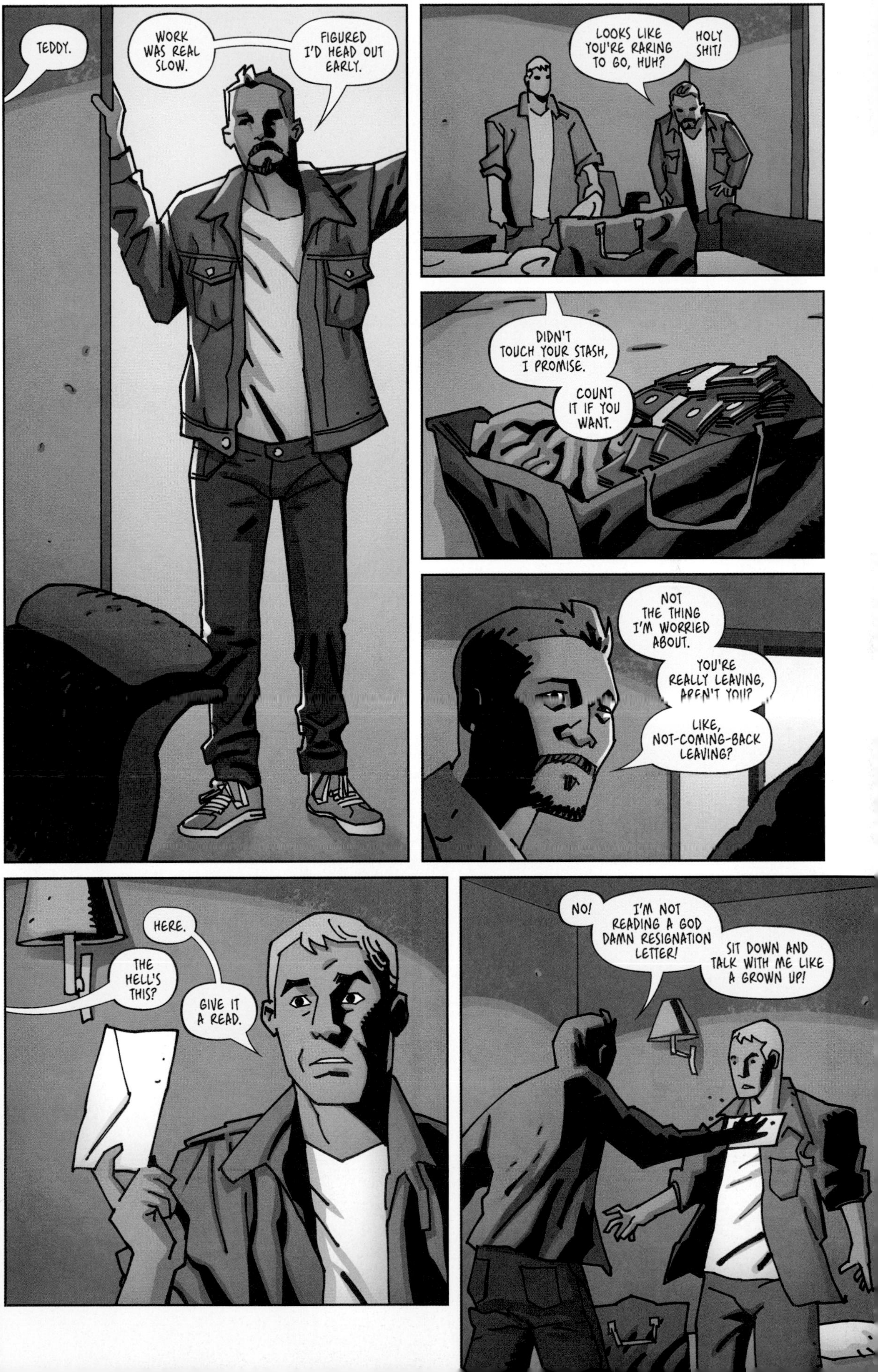
TEDDY.
WORK WAS REAL SLOW.
FIGURED I'D HEAD OUT EARLY.
LOOKS LIKE YOU'RE RARING TO GO, HUH?
HOLY SHIT!
DIDN'T TOUCH YOUR STASH, I PROMISE.
COUNT IT IF YOU WANT.
NOT THE THING I'M WORRIED ABOUT.
YOU'RE REALLY LEAVING, AREN'T YOU?
LIKE, NOT-COMING-BACK LEAVING?
HERE.
THE HELL'S THIS?
GIVE IT A READ.
NO!
I'M NOT READING A GOD DAMN RESIGNATION LETTER!
SIT DOWN AND TALK WITH ME LIKE A GROWN UP!

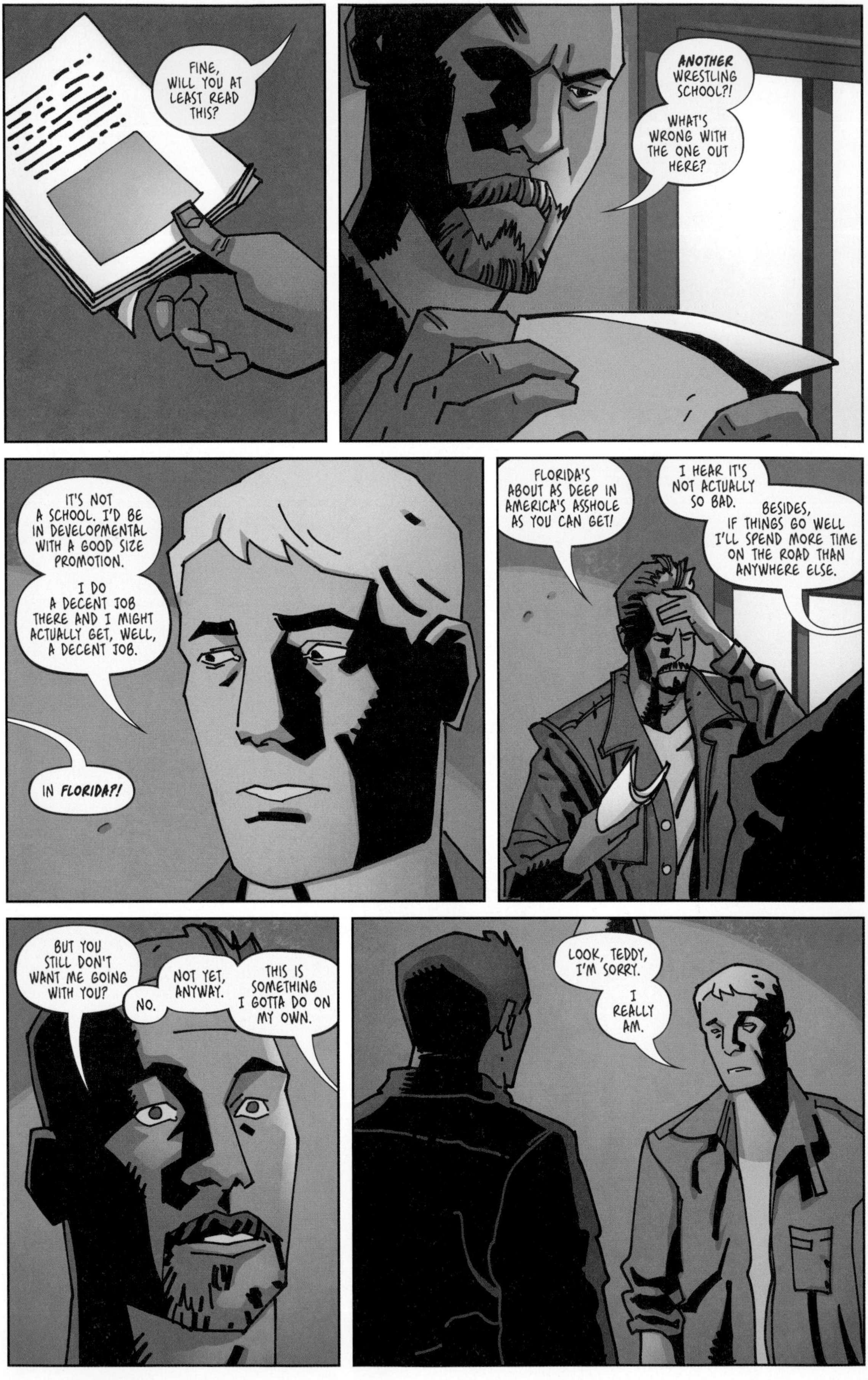
FINE, WILL YOU AT LEAST READ THIS?
ANOTHER WRESTLING SCHOOL?!
WHAT'S WRONG WITH THE ONE OUT HERE?
IT'S NOT A SCHOOL. I'D BE IN DEVELOPMENTAL WITH A GOOD SIZE PROMOTION.
I DO A DECENT JOB THERE AND I MIGHT ACTUALLY GET, WELL, A DECENT JOB.
IN FLORIDA?!
FLORIDA'S ABOUT AS DEEP IN AMERICA'S ASSHOLE AS YOU CAN GET!
I HEAR IT'S NOT ACTUALLY SO BAD.
BESIDES, IF THINGS GO WELL I'LL SPEND MORE TIME ON THE ROAD THAN ANYWHERE ELSE.
BUT YOU STILL DON'T WANT ME GOING WITH YOU?
NO.
NOT YET, ANYWAY.
THIS IS SOMETHING I GOTTA DO ON MY OWN.
LOOK, TEDDY, I'M SORRY.
I REALLY AM.

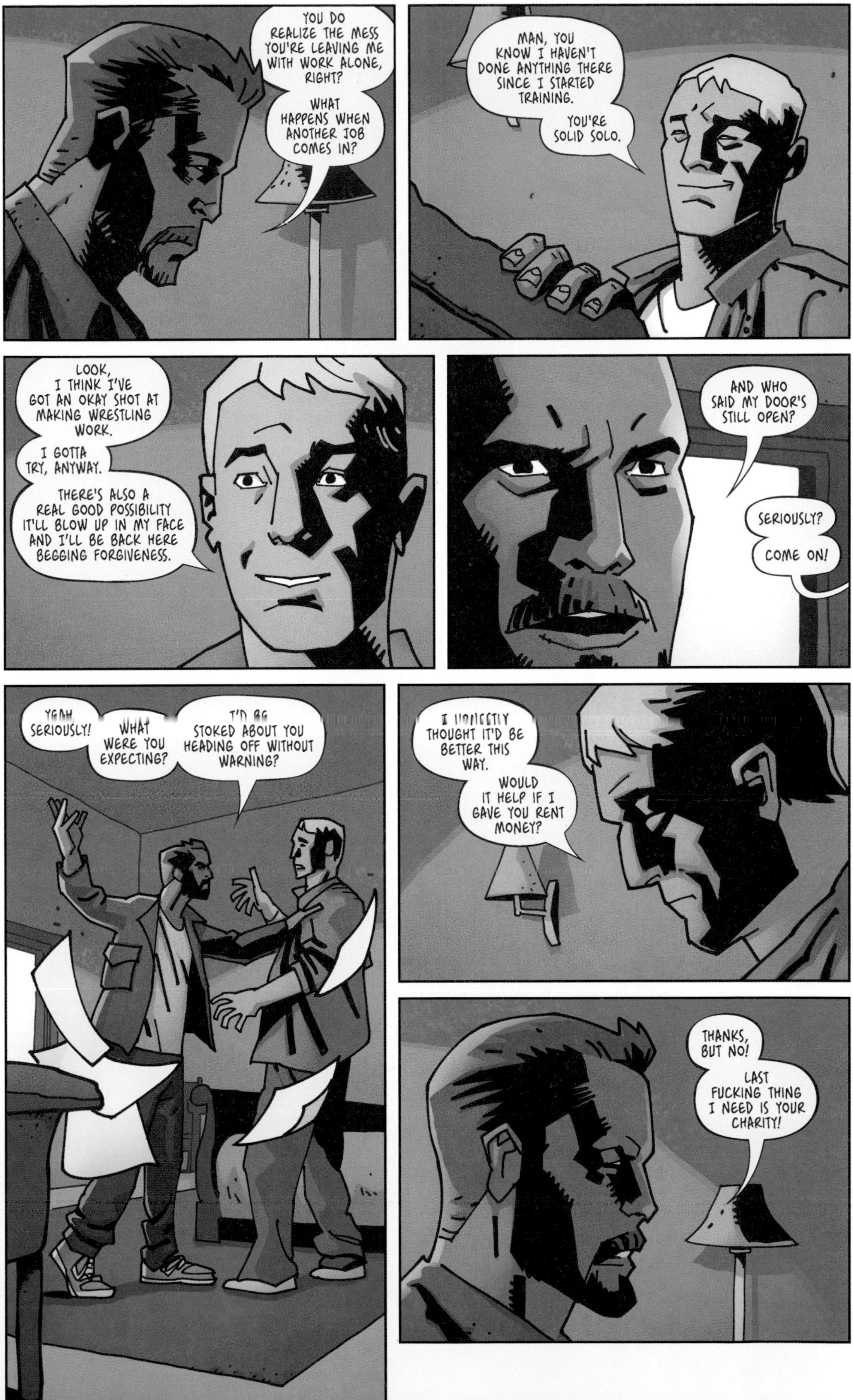
YOU DO REALIZE THE MESS YOU'RE LEAVING ME WITH WORK ALONE, RIGHT?
WHAT HAPPENS WHEN ANOTHER JOB COMES IN?
MAN, YOU KNOW I HAVEN'T DONE ANYTHING THERE SINCE I STARTED TRAINING.
YOU'RE SOLID SOLO.
LOOK, I THINK I'VE GOT AN OKAY SHOT AT MAKING WRESTLING WORK.
I GOTTA TRY, ANYWAY.
THERE'S ALSO A REAL GOOD POSSIBILITY IT'LL BLOW UP IN MY FACE AND I'LL BE BACK HERE BEGGING FORGIVENESS.
AND WHO SAID MY DOOR'S STILL OPEN?
SERIOUSLY?
COME ON!
YEAH, SERIOUSLY!
WHAT WERE YOU EXPECTING?
I'D BE STOKED ABOUT YOU HEADING OFF WITHOUT WARNING?
I HONESTLY THOUGHT IT'D BE BETTER THIS WAY.
WOULD IT HELP IF I GAVE YOU RENT MONEY?
THANKS, BUT NO!
LAST FUCKING THING I NEED IS YOUR CHARITY!

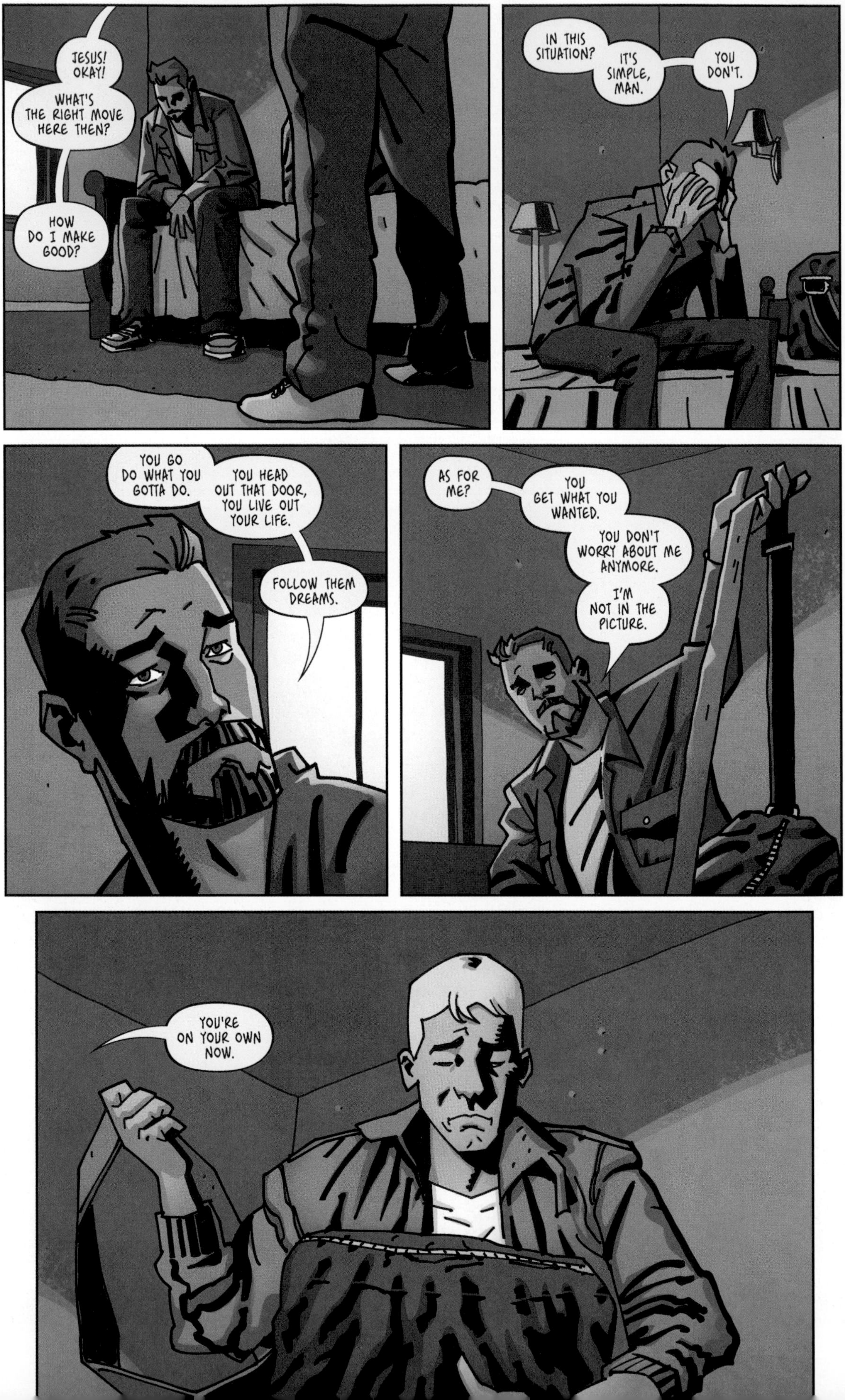
JESUS! OKAY!
WHAT'S THE RIGHT MOVE HERE THEN?
HOW DO I MAKE GOOD?
IN THIS SITUATION?
IT'S SIMPLE, MAN.
YOU DON'T.
YOU GO DO WHAT YOU GOTTA DO.
YOU HEAD OUT THAT DOOR, YOU LIVE OUT YOUR LIFE.
FOLLOW THEM DREAMS.
AS FOR ME?
YOU GET WHAT YOU WANTED.
YOU DON'T WORRY ABOUT ME ANYMORE.
I'M NOT IN THE PICTURE.
YOU'RE ON YOUR OWN NOW.

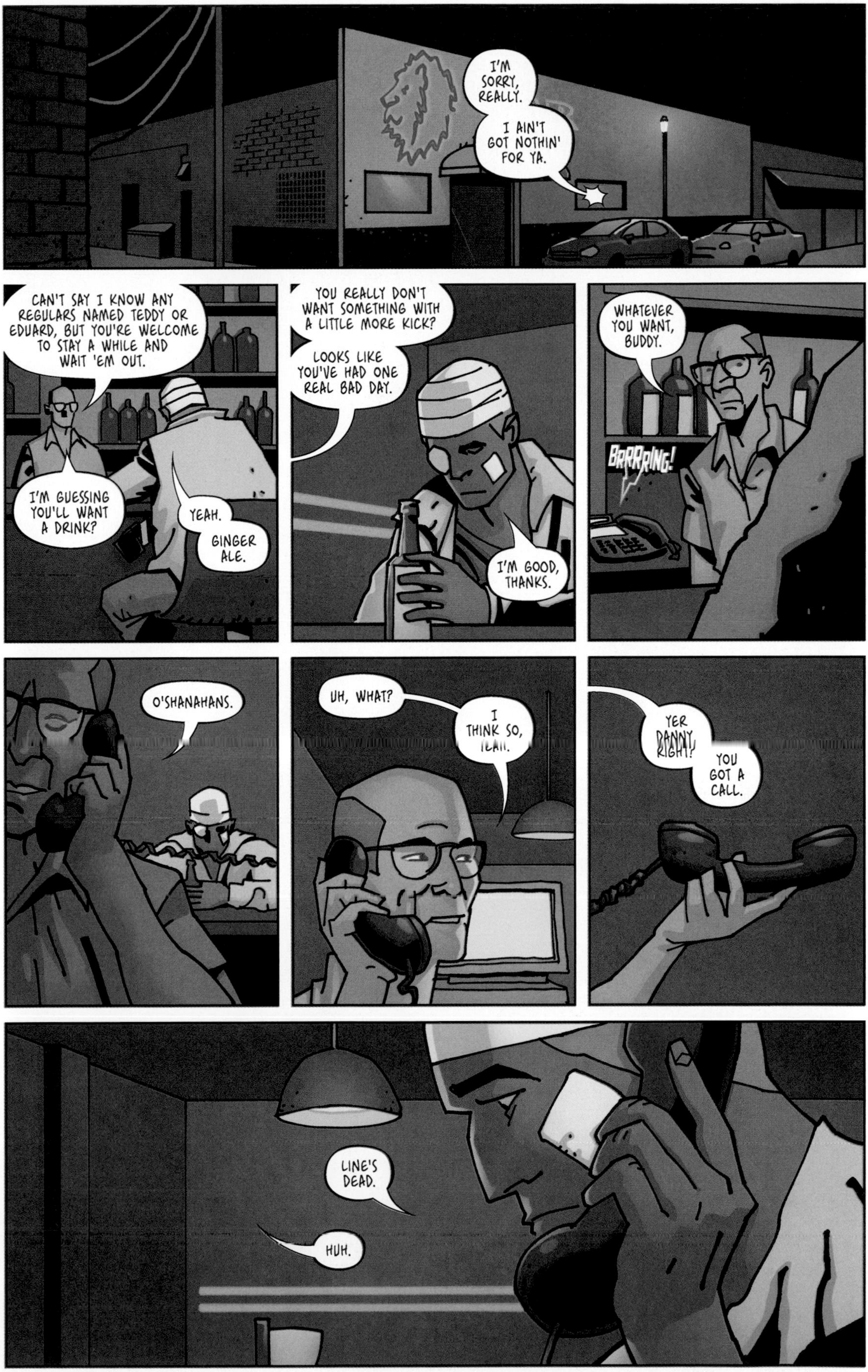
I'M SORRY, REALLY.
I AIN'T GOT NOTHIN' FOR YA.
CAN'T SAY I KNOW ANY REGULARS NAMED TEDDY OR EDUARD, BUT YOU'RE WELCOME TO STAY A WHILE AND WAIT 'EM OUT.
I'M GUESSING YOU'LL WANT A DRINK?
YEAH.
GINGER ALE.
YOU REALLY DON'T WANT SOMETHING WITH A LITTLE MORE KICK?
LOOKS LIKE YOU'VE HAD ONE REAL BAD DAY.
I'M GOOD, THANKS.
WHATEVER YOU WANT, BUDDY.
BRRRRING!
O'SHANAHANS.
UH, WHAT?
I THINK SO,
YER DANNY, RIGHT?
YOU GOT A CALL.
LINE'S DEAD.
HUH.

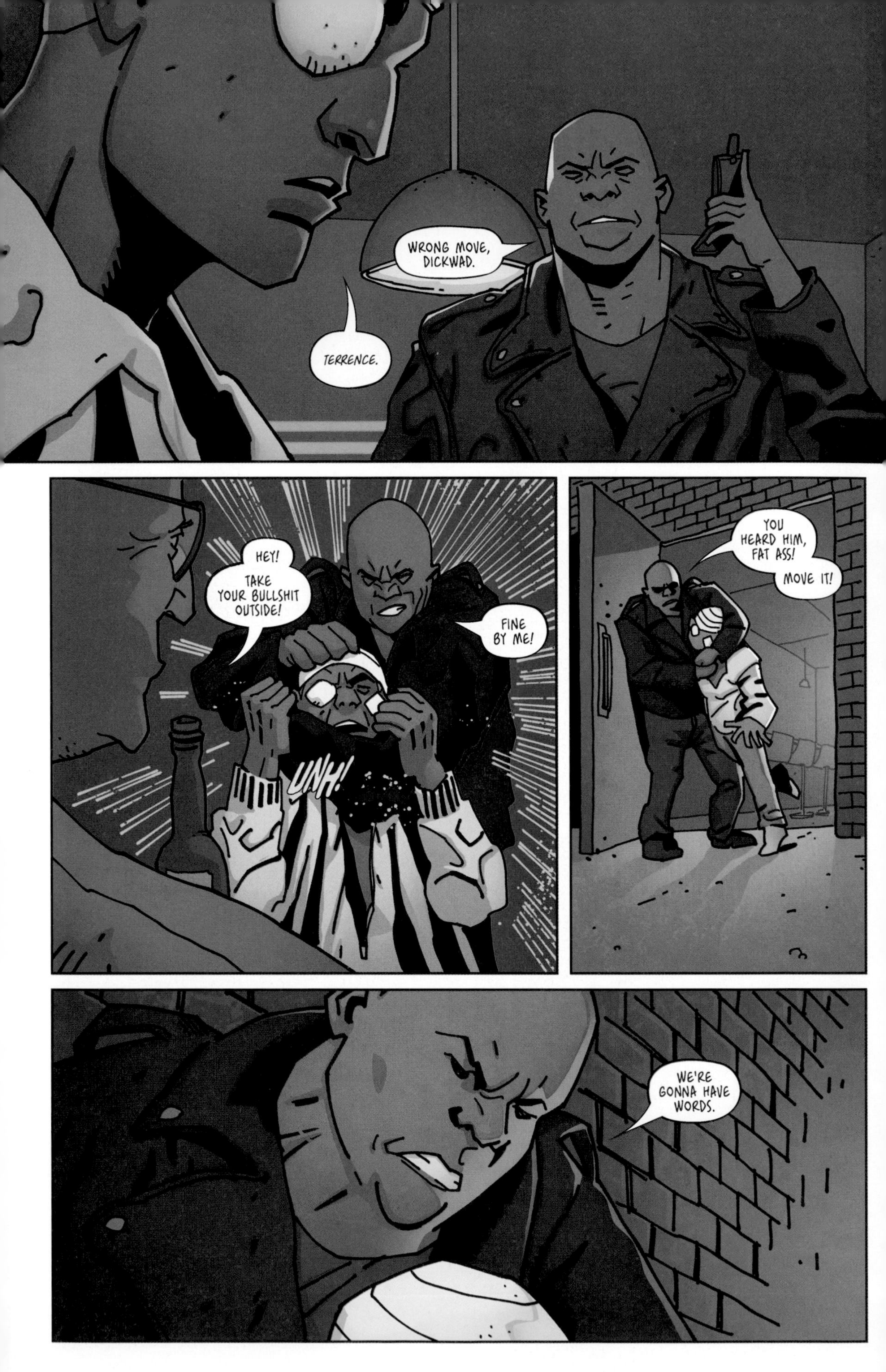
WRONG MOVE, DICKWAD.
TERRENCE.
HEY! TAKE YOUR BULLSHIT OUTSIDE!
FINE BY ME!
UNH!
YOU HEARD HIM, FAT ASS!
MOVE IT!
WE'RE GONNA HAVE WORDS.

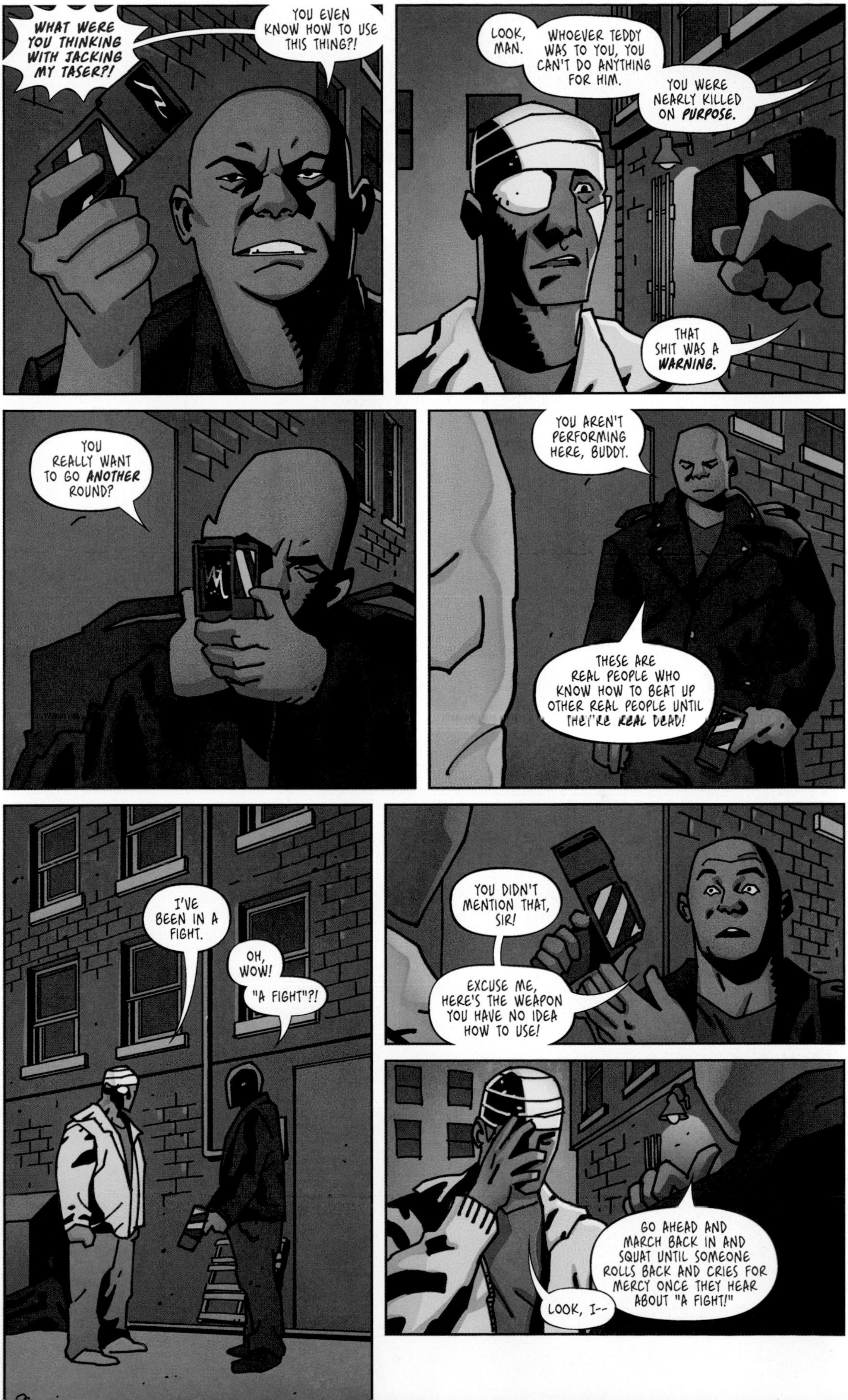
WHAT WERE YOU THINKING WITH JACKING MY TASER?!
YOU EVEN KNOW HOW TO USE THIS THING?!
LOOK, MAN.
WHOEVER TEDDY WAS TO YOU, YOU CAN'T DO ANYTHING FOR HIM.
YOU WERE NEARLY KILLED ON PURPOSE.
THAT SHIT WAS A WARNING.
YOU REALLY WANT TO GO ANOTHER ROUND?
YOU AREN'T PERFORMING HERE, BUDDY.
THESE ARE REAL PEOPLE WHO KNOW HOW TO BEAT UP OTHER REAL PEOPLE UNTIL THEY'RE REAL DEAD!
I'VE BEEN IN A FIGHT.
OH, WOW!
"A FIGHT"?!
YOU DIDN'T MENTION THAT, SIR!
EXCUSE ME, HERE'S THE WEAPON YOU HAVE NO IDEA HOW TO USE!
GO AHEAD AND MARCH BACK IN AND SQUAT UNTIL SOMEONE ROLLS BACK AND CRIES FOR MERCY ONCE THEY HEAR ABOUT "A FIGHT!"
LOOK, I--

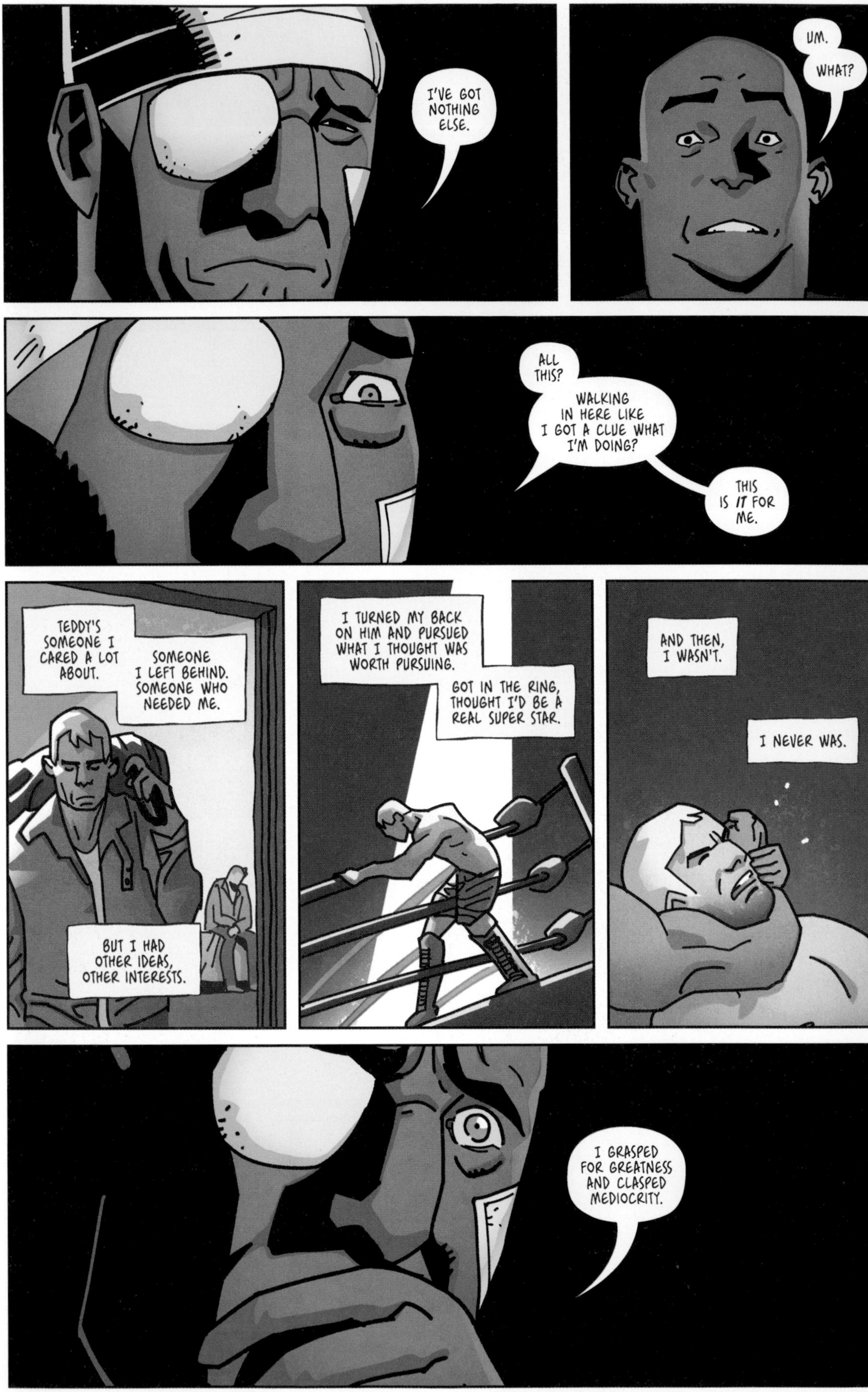
I'VE GOT NOTHING ELSE.
UM.
WHAT?
ALL THIS?
WALKING IN HERE LIKE I GOT A CLUE WHAT I'M DOING?
THIS IS *IT* FOR ME.
TEDDY'S SOMEONE I CARED A LOT ABOUT.
SOMEONE I LEFT BEHIND. SOMEONE WHO NEEDED ME.
BUT I HAD OTHER IDEAS, OTHER INTERESTS.
I TURNED MY BACK ON HIM AND PURSUED WHAT I THOUGHT WAS WORTH PURSUING.
GOT IN THE RING, THOUGHT I'D BE A REAL SUPER STAR.
AND THEN, I WASN'T.
I NEVER WAS.
I GRASPED FOR GREATNESS AND CLASPED MEDIOCRITY.

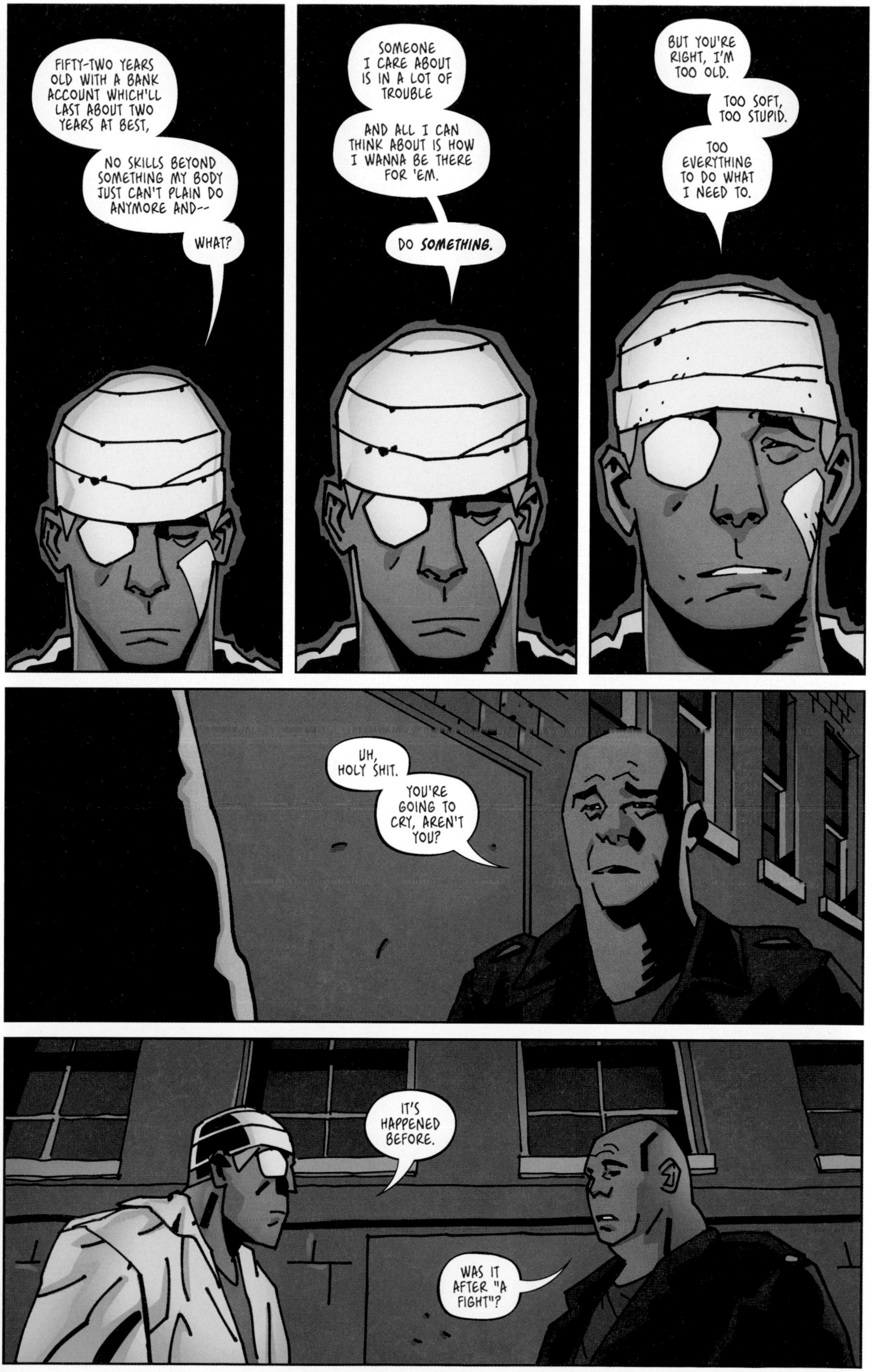
FIFTY-TWO YEARS OLD WITH A BANK ACCOUNT WHICH'LL LAST ABOUT TWO YEARS AT BEST,
NO SKILLS BEYOND SOMETHING MY BODY JUST CAN'T PLAIN DO ANYMORE AND--
WHAT?
SOMEONE I CARE ABOUT IS IN A LOT OF TROUBLE
AND ALL I CAN THINK ABOUT IS HOW I WANNA BE THERE FOR 'EM.
DO SOMETHING.
BUT YOU'RE RIGHT, I'M TOO OLD.
TOO SOFT, TOO STUPID.
TOO EVERYTHING TO DO WHAT I NEED TO.
UH, HOLY SHIT.
YOU'RE GOING TO CRY, AREN'T YOU?
IT'S HAPPENED BEFORE.
WAS IT AFTER "A FIGHT"?

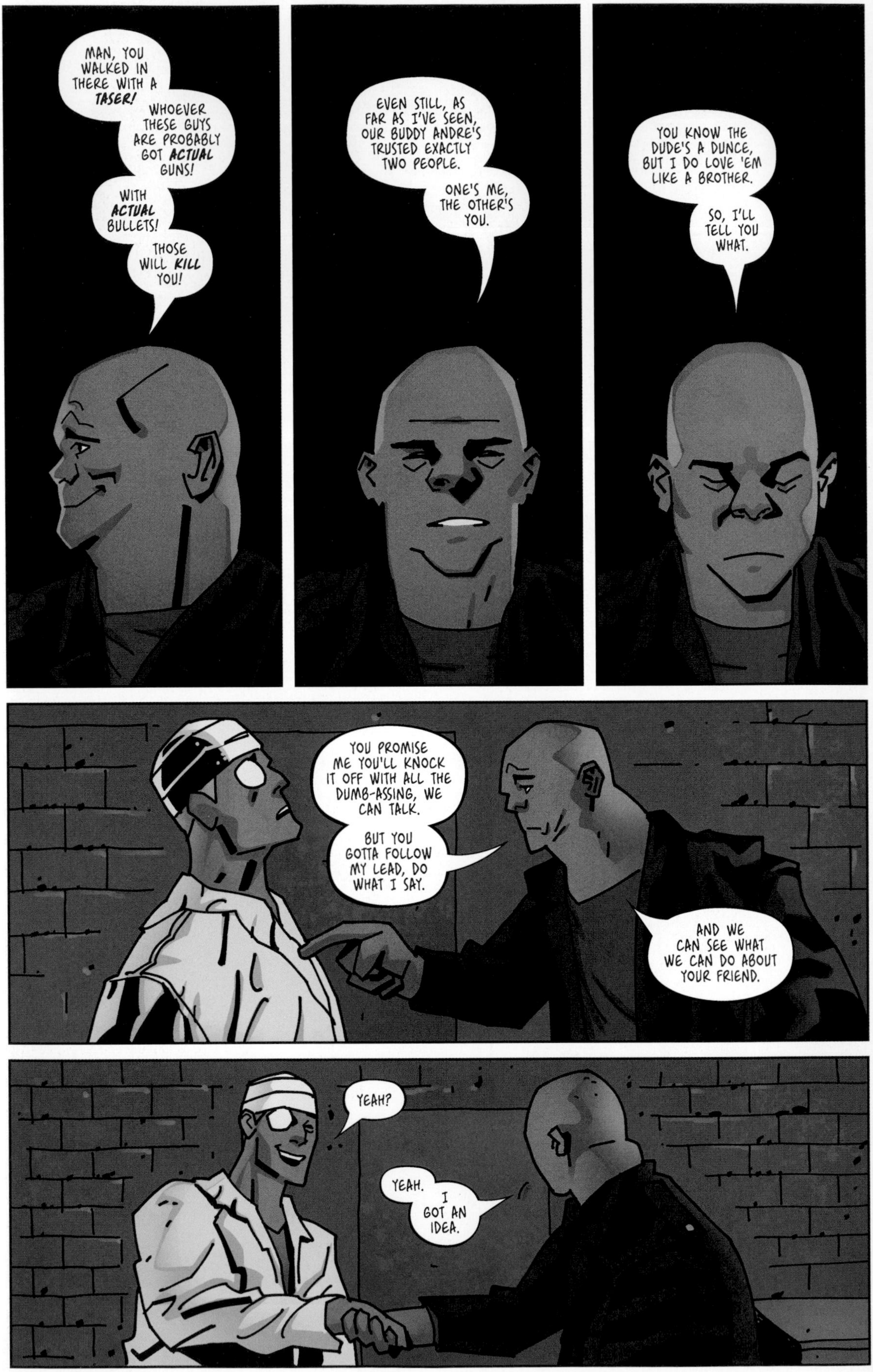
MAN, YOU WALKED IN THERE WITH A *TASER!*
WHOEVER THESE GUYS ARE PROBABLY GOT *ACTUAL* GUNS!
WITH *ACTUAL* BULLETS!
THOSE WILL *KILL* YOU!
EVEN STILL, AS FAR AS I'VE SEEN, OUR BUDDY ANDRE'S TRUSTED EXACTLY TWO PEOPLE.
ONE'S ME, THE OTHER'S YOU.
YOU KNOW THE DUDE'S A DUNCE, BUT I DO LOVE 'EM LIKE A BROTHER.
SO, I'LL TELL YOU WHAT.
YOU PROMISE ME YOU'LL KNOCK IT OFF WITH ALL THE DUMB-ASSING, WE CAN TALK.
BUT YOU GOTTA FOLLOW MY LEAD, DO WHAT I SAY.
AND WE CAN SEE WHAT WE CAN DO ABOUT YOUR FRIEND.
YEAH?
YEAH.
I GOT AN IDEA.

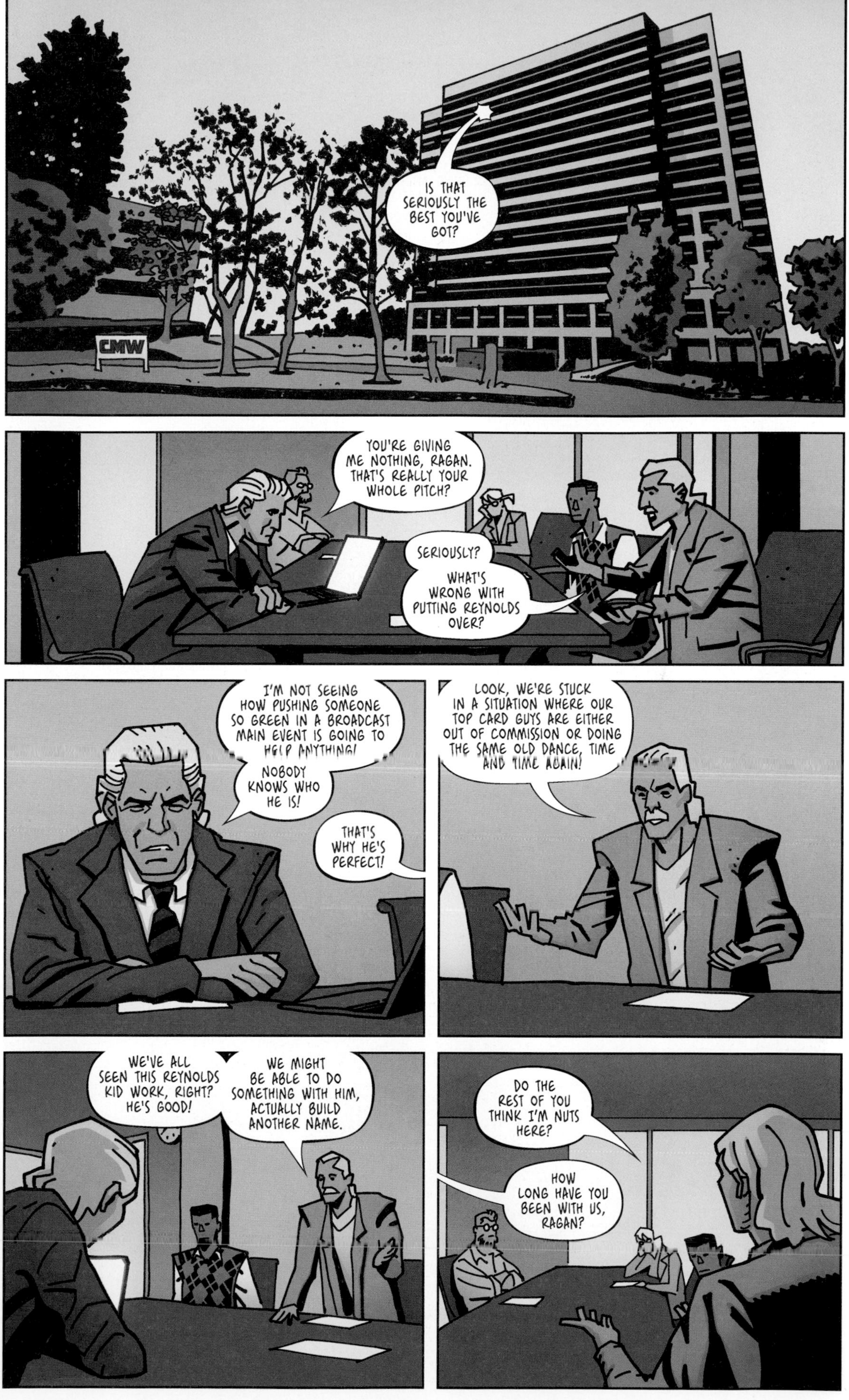
IS THAT SERIOUSLY THE BEST YOU'VE GOT?
CMW
YOU'RE GIVING ME NOTHING, RAGAN. THAT'S REALLY YOUR WHOLE PITCH?
SERIOUSLY?
WHAT'S WRONG WITH PUTTING REYNOLDS OVER?
I'M NOT SEEING HOW PUSHING SOMEONE SO GREEN IN A BROADCAST MAIN EVENT IS GOING TO HELP ANYTHING!
NOBODY KNOWS WHO HE IS!
THAT'S WHY HE'S PERFECT!
LOOK, WE'RE STUCK IN A SITUATION WHERE OUR TOP CARD GUYS ARE EITHER OUT OF COMMISSION OR DOING THE SAME OLD DANCE, TIME AND TIME AGAIN!
WE'VE ALL SEEN THIS REYNOLDS KID WORK, RIGHT? HE'S GOOD!
WE MIGHT BE ABLE TO DO SOMETHING WITH HIM, ACTUALLY BUILD ANOTHER NAME.
DO THE REST OF YOU THINK I'M NUTS HERE?
HOW LONG HAVE YOU BEEN WITH US, RAGAN?

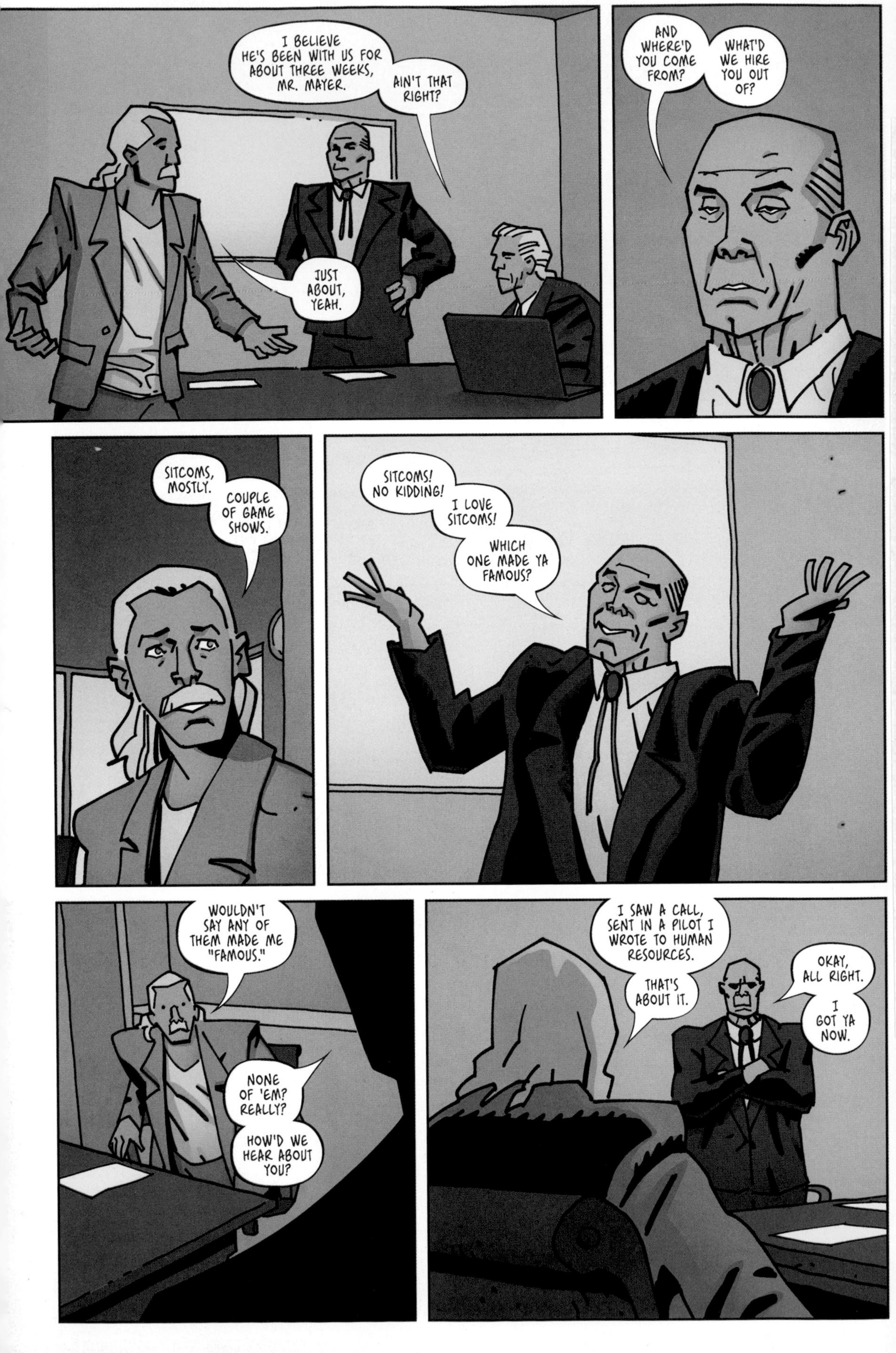
I BELIEVE HE'S BEEN WITH US FOR ABOUT THREE WEEKS, MR. MAYER.
AIN'T THAT RIGHT?
JUST ABOUT, YEAH.
AND WHERE'D YOU COME FROM?
WHAT'D WE HIRE YOU OUT OF?
SITCOMS, MOSTLY.
COUPLE OF GAME SHOWS.
SITCOMS! NO KIDDING!
I LOVE SITCOMS!
WHICH ONE MADE YA FAMOUS?
WOULDN'T SAY ANY OF THEM MADE ME "FAMOUS."
NONE OF 'EM? REALLY?
HOW'D WE HEAR ABOUT YOU?
I SAW A CALL, SENT IN A PILOT I WROTE TO HUMAN RESOURCES.
THAT'S ABOUT IT.
OKAY, ALL RIGHT.
I GOT YA NOW.

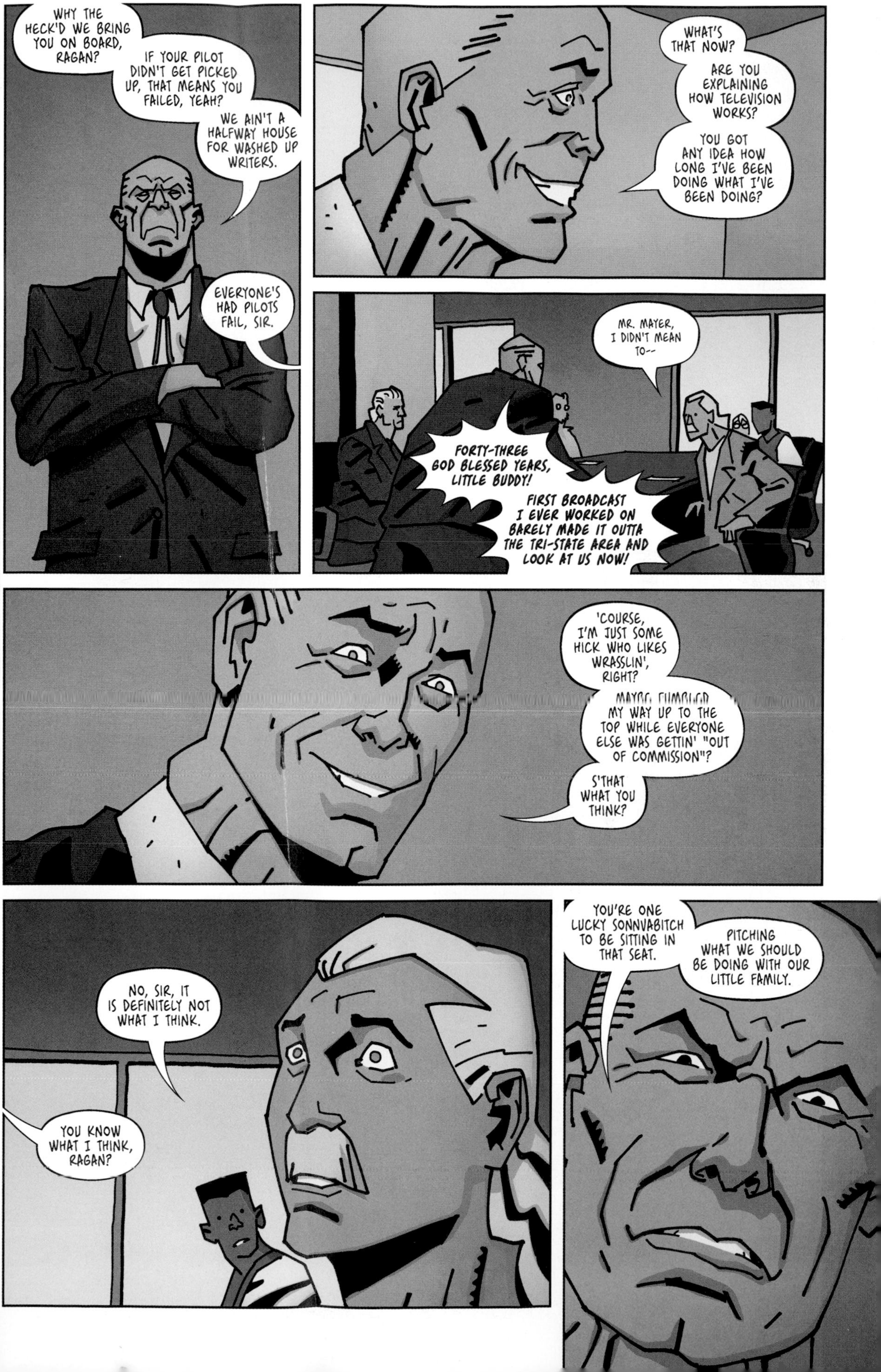
WHY THE HECK'D WE BRING YOU ON BOARD, RAGAN?
IF YOUR PILOT DIDN'T GET PICKED UP, THAT MEANS YOU FAILED, YEAH?
WE AIN'T A HALFWAY HOUSE FOR WASHED UP WRITERS.
EVERYONE'S HAD PILOTS FAIL, SIR.
WHAT'S THAT NOW?
ARE YOU EXPLAINING HOW TELEVISION WORKS?
YOU GOT ANY IDEA HOW LONG I'VE BEEN DOING WHAT I'VE BEEN DOING?
MR. MAYER, I DIDN'T MEAN TO--
FORTY-THREE GOD BLESSED YEARS, LITTLE BUDDY!
FIRST BROADCAST I EVER WORKED ON BARELY MADE IT OUTTA THE TRI-STATE AREA AND LOOK AT US NOW!
'COURSE, I'M JUST SOME HICK WHO LIKES WRASSLIN', RIGHT?
MY WAY UP TO THE TOP WHILE EVERYONE ELSE WAS GETTIN' "OUT OF COMMISSION"?
S'THAT WHAT YOU THINK?
NO, SIR, IT IS DEFINITELY NOT WHAT I THINK.
YOU KNOW WHAT I THINK, RAGAN?
YOU'RE ONE LUCKY SONNVABITCH TO BE SITTING IN THAT SEAT.
PITCHING WHAT WE SHOULD BE DOING WITH OUR LITTLE FAMILY.

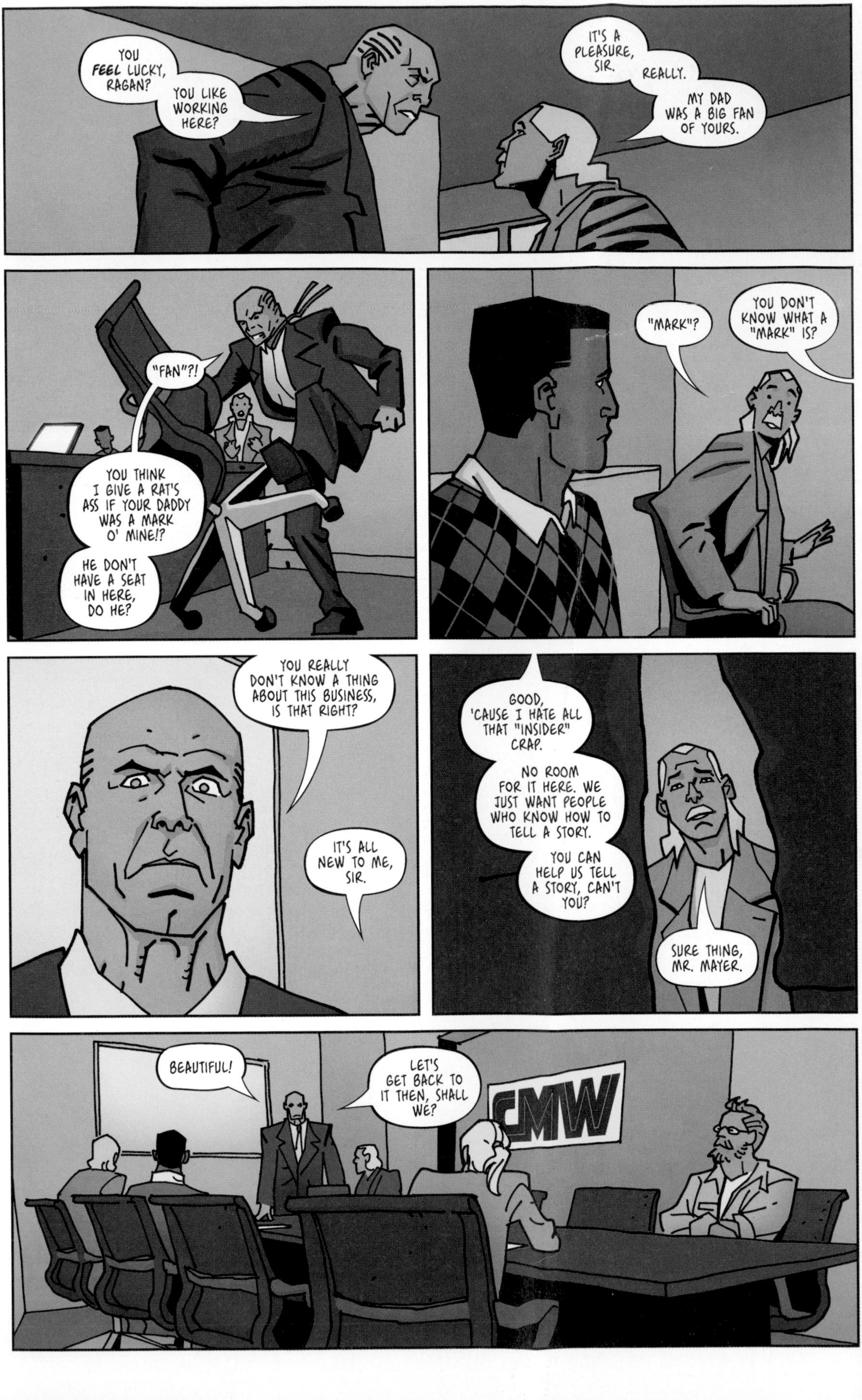
YOU FEEL LUCKY, RAGAN?
YOU LIKE WORKING HERE?
IT'S A PLEASURE, SIR.
REALLY.
MY DAD WAS A BIG FAN OF YOURS.
"FAN"?!
YOU THINK I GIVE A RAT'S ASS IF YOUR DADDY WAS A MARK O' MINE!?
HE DON'T HAVE A SEAT IN HERE, DO HE?
"MARK"?
YOU DON'T KNOW WHAT A "MARK" IS?
YOU REALLY DON'T KNOW A THING ABOUT THIS BUSINESS, IS THAT RIGHT?
IT'S ALL NEW TO ME, SIR.
GOOD, 'CAUSE I HATE ALL THAT "INSIDER" CRAP.
NO ROOM FOR IT HERE. WE JUST WANT PEOPLE WHO KNOW HOW TO TELL A STORY.
YOU CAN HELP US TELL A STORY, CAN'T YOU?
SURE THING, MR. MAYER.
BEAUTIFUL!
LET'S GET BACK TO IT THEN, SHALL WE?
CMW

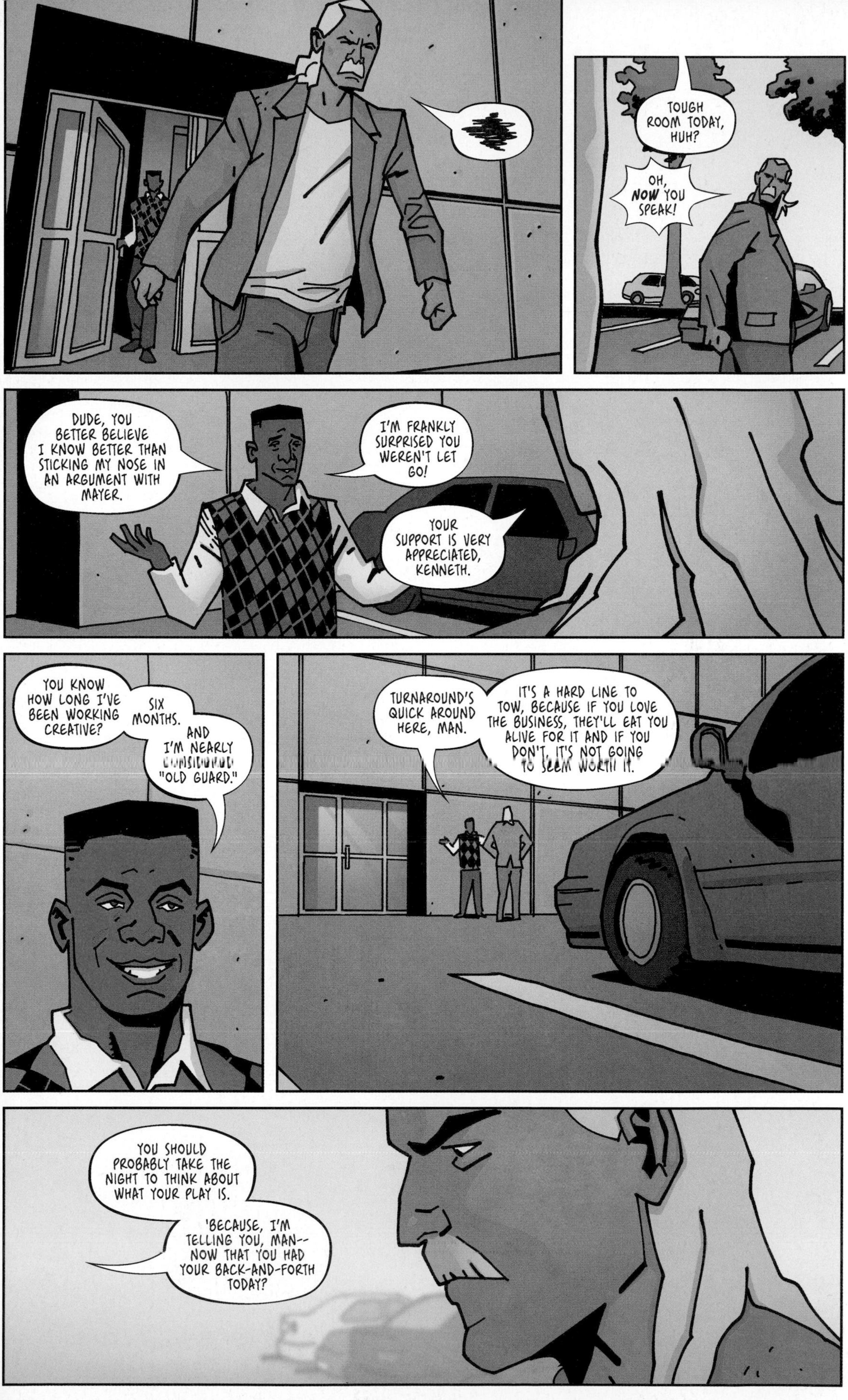
TOUGH ROOM TODAY, HUH?
OH, **NOW** YOU SPEAK!
DUDE, YOU BETTER BELIEVE I KNOW BETTER THAN STICKING MY NOSE IN AN ARGUMENT WITH MAYER.
I'M FRANKLY SURPRISED YOU WEREN'T LET GO!
YOUR SUPPORT IS VERY APPRECIATED, KENNETH.
YOU KNOW HOW LONG I'VE BEEN WORKING CREATIVE?
SIX MONTHS.
AND I'M NEARLY CONSIDERED "OLD GUARD."
TURNAROUND'S QUICK AROUND HERE, MAN.
IT'S A HARD LINE TO TOW, BECAUSE IF YOU LOVE THE BUSINESS, THEY'LL EAT YOU ALIVE FOR IT AND IF YOU DON'T, IT'S NOT GOING TO SEEM WORTH IT.
YOU SHOULD PROBABLY TAKE THE NIGHT TO THINK ABOUT WHAT YOUR PLAY IS.
'BECAUSE, I'M TELLING YOU, MAN-- NOW THAT YOU HAD YOUR BACK-AND-FORTH TODAY?

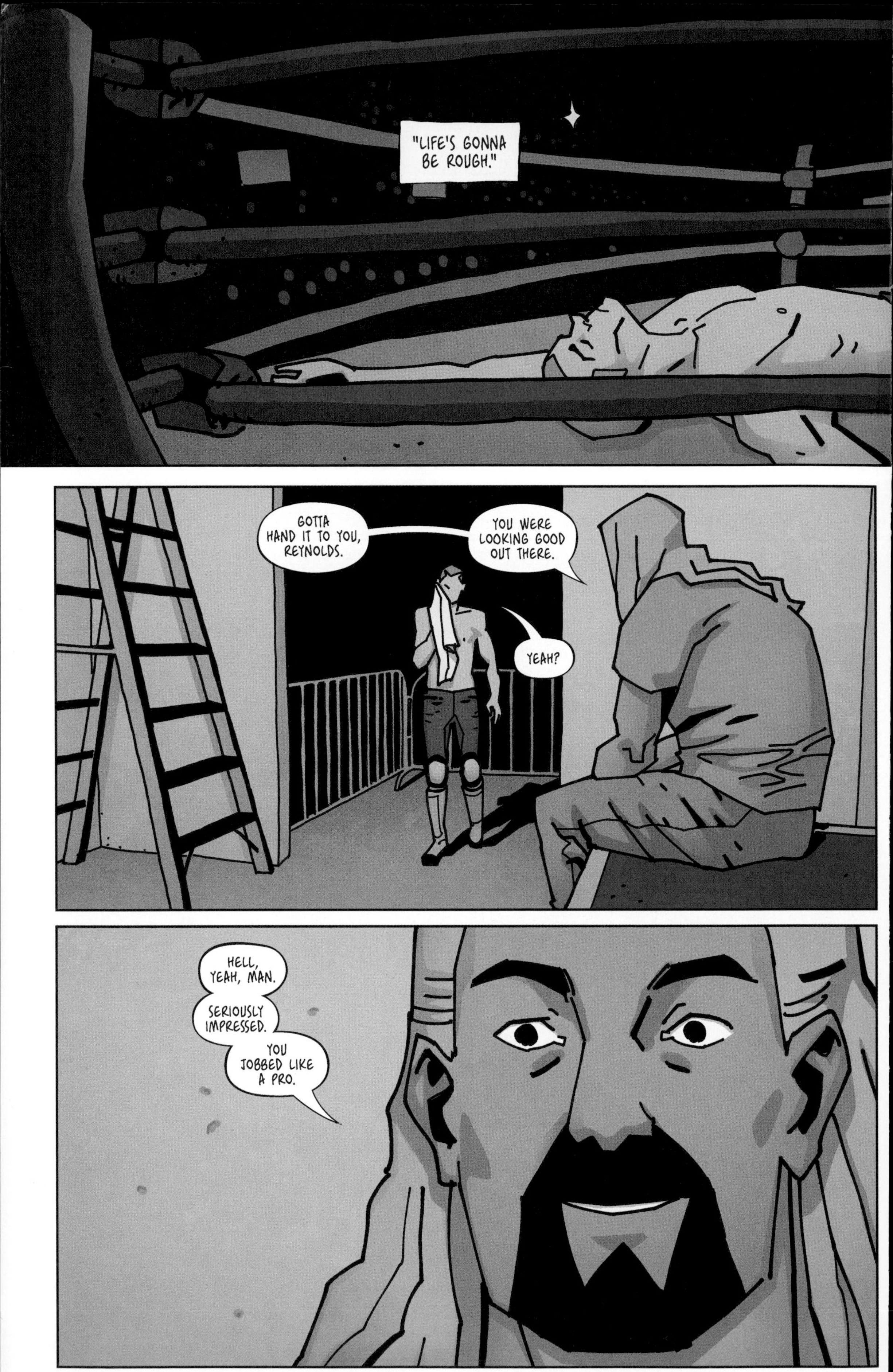
"LIFE'S GONNA BE ROUGH."
GOTTA HAND IT TO YOU, REYNOLDS.
YOU WERE LOOKING GOOD OUT THERE.
YEAH?
HELL, YEAH, MAN.
SERIOUSLY IMPRESSED.
YOU JOBBED LIKE A PRO.

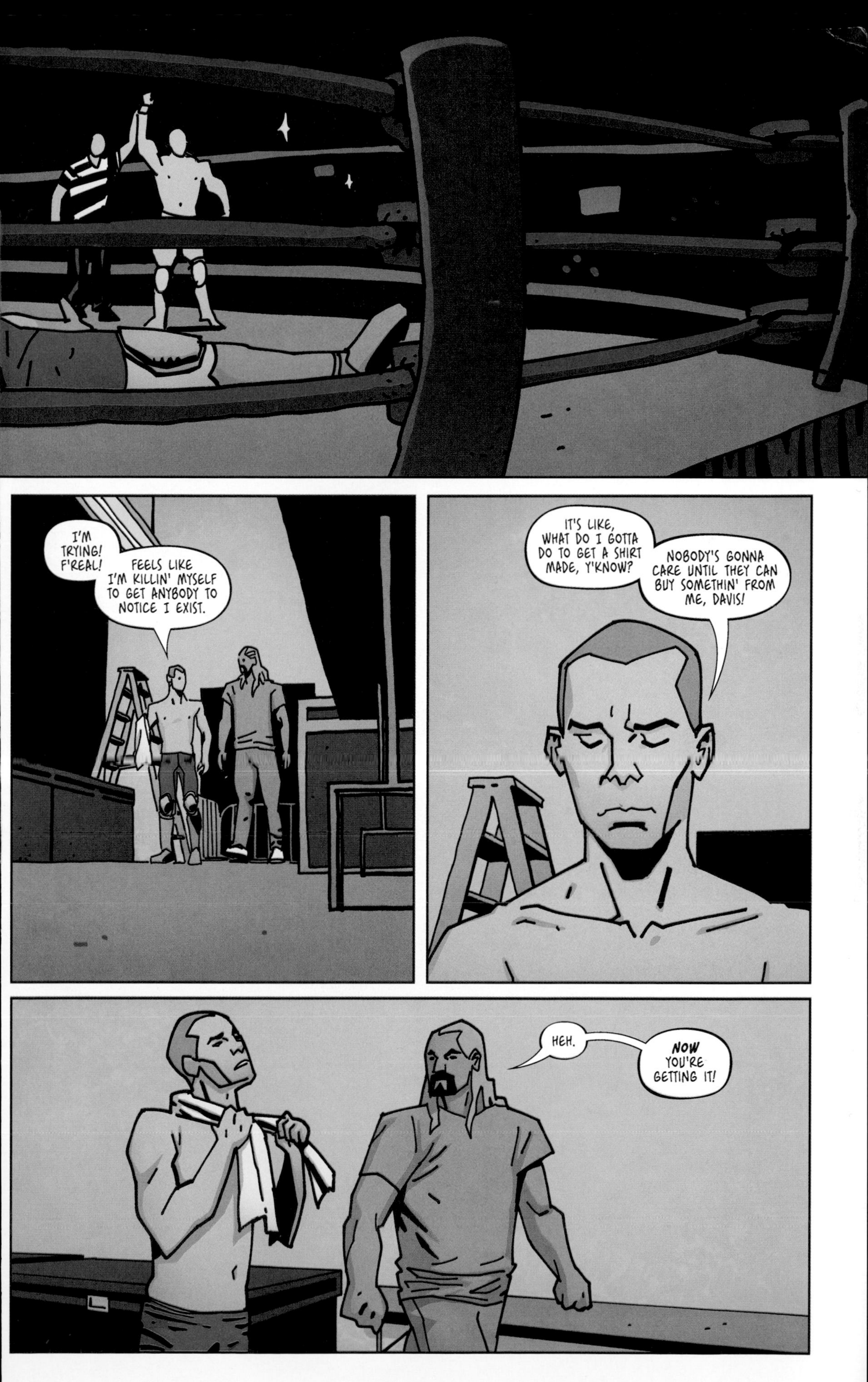
I'M TRYING! F'REAL!
FEELS LIKE I'M KILLIN' MYSELF TO GET ANYBODY TO NOTICE I EXIST.
IT'S LIKE, WHAT DO I GOTTA DO TO GET A SHIRT MADE, Y'KNOW?
NOBODY'S GONNA CARE UNTIL THEY CAN BUY SOMETHIN' FROM ME, DAVIS!
HEH.
NOW YOU'RE GETTING IT!

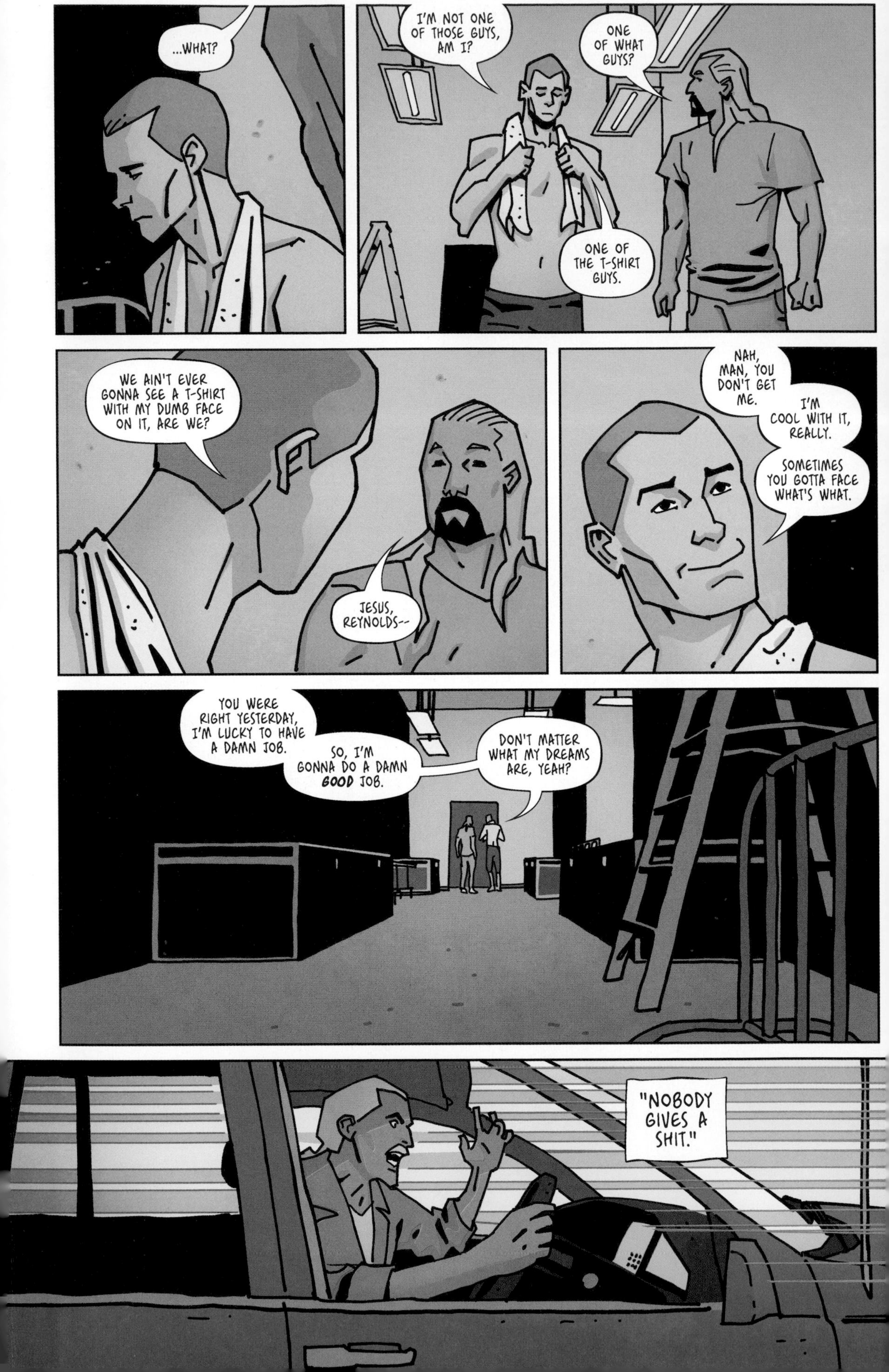
...WHAT?
I'M NOT ONE OF THOSE GUYS, AM I?
ONE OF WHAT GUYS?
ONE OF THE T-SHIRT GUYS.
WE AIN'T EVER GONNA SEE A T-SHIRT WITH MY DUMB FACE ON IT, ARE WE?
JESUS, REYNOLDS--
NAH, MAN, YOU DON'T GET ME.
I'M COOL WITH IT, REALLY.
SOMETIMES YOU GOTTA FACE WHAT'S WHAT.
YOU WERE RIGHT YESTERDAY, I'M LUCKY TO HAVE A DAMN JOB.
SO, I'M GONNA DO A DAMN **GOOD** JOB.
DON'T MATTER WHAT MY DREAMS ARE, YEAH?
"NOBODY GIVES A SHIT."

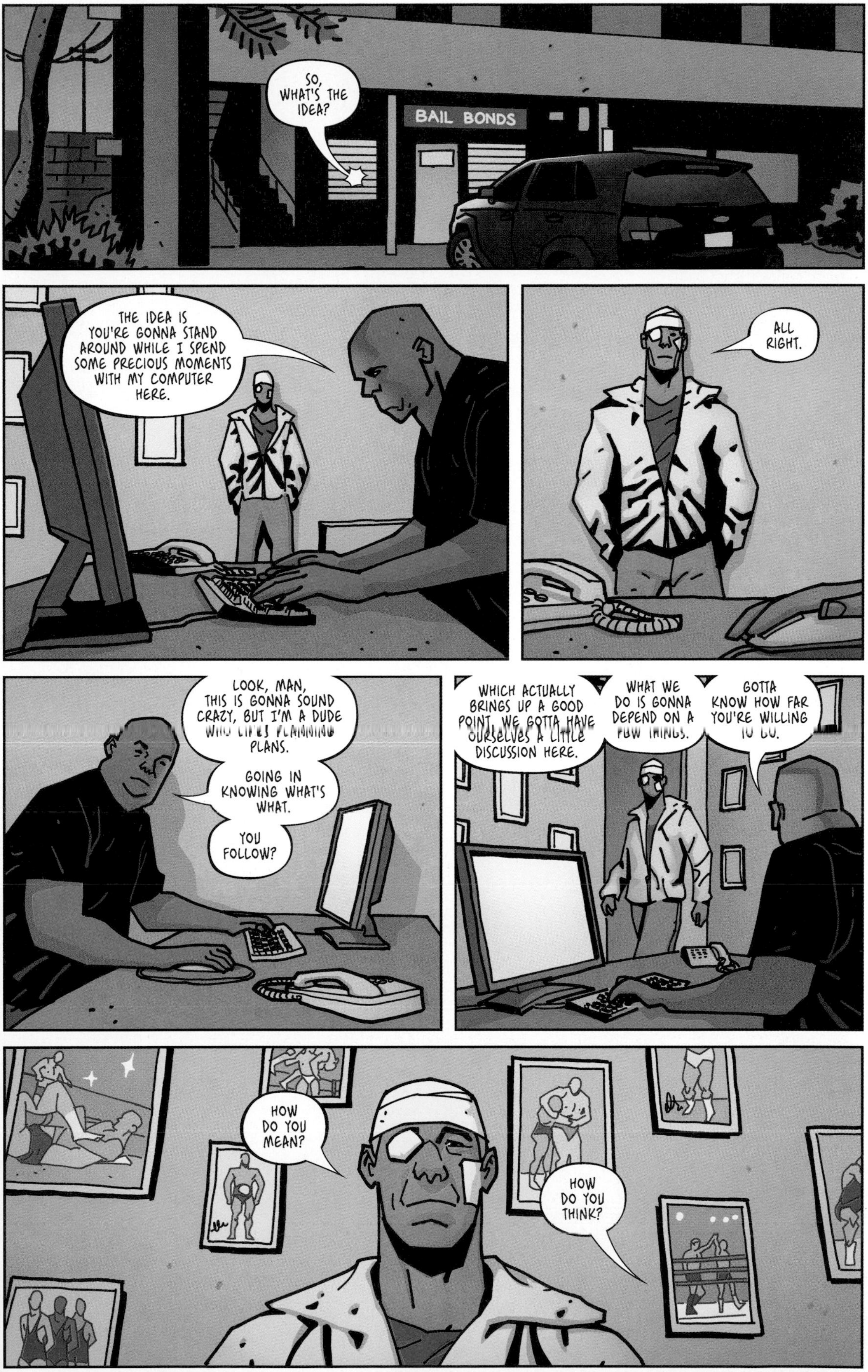
SO, WHAT'S THE IDEA?
BAIL BONDS
THE IDEA IS YOU'RE GONNA STAND AROUND WHILE I SPEND SOME PRECIOUS MOMENTS WITH MY COMPUTER HERE.
ALL RIGHT.
LOOK, MAN, THIS IS GONNA SOUND CRAZY, BUT I'M A DUDE WHO LIKES PLANNING PLANS.
GOING IN KNOWING WHAT'S WHAT.
YOU FOLLOW?
WHICH ACTUALLY BRINGS UP A GOOD POINT. WE GOTTA HAVE OURSELVES A LITTLE DISCUSSION HERE.
WHAT WE DO IS GONNA DEPEND ON A FEW THINGS.
GOTTA KNOW HOW FAR YOU'RE WILLING TO GO.
HOW DO YOU MEAN?
HOW DO YOU THINK?

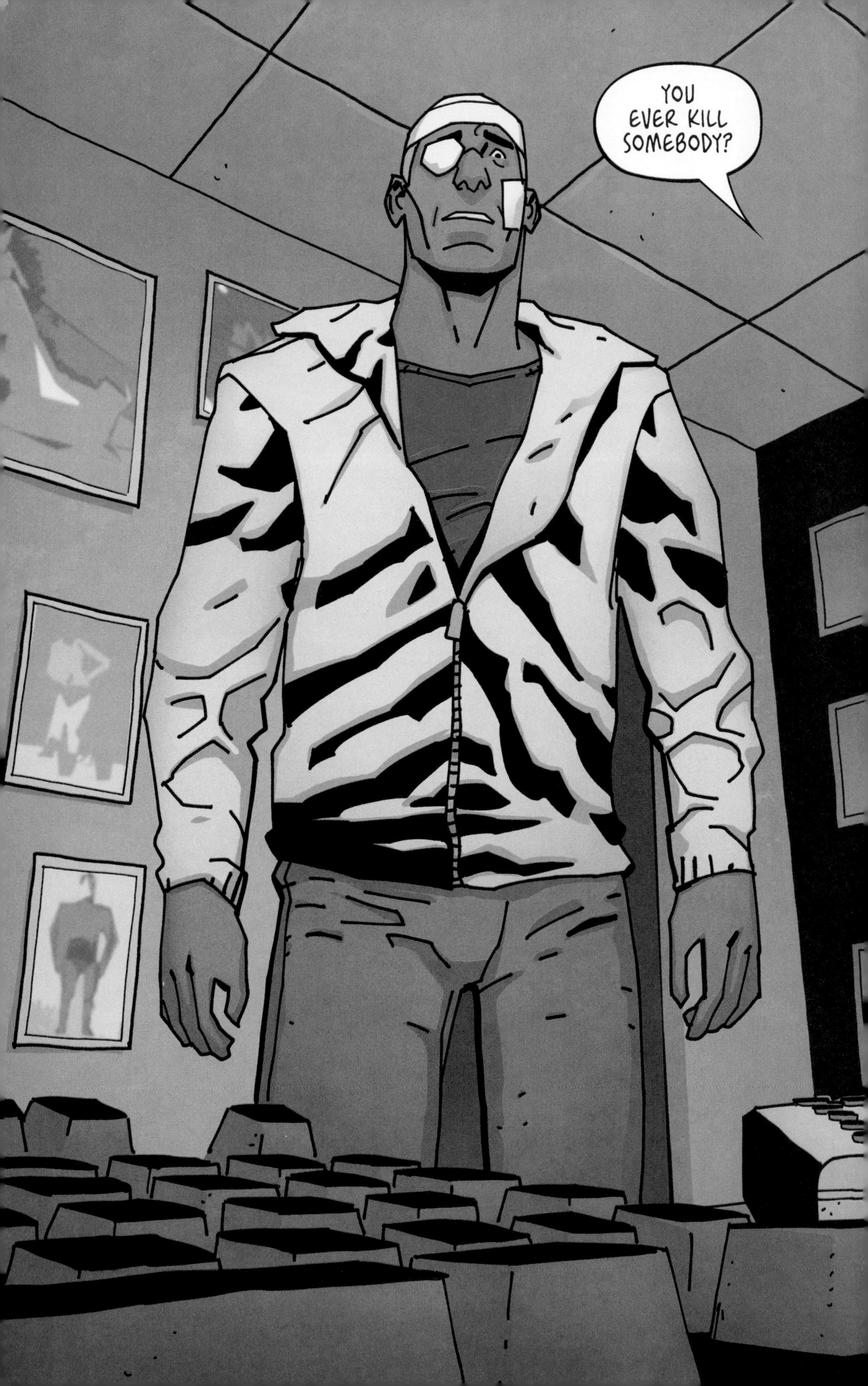
YOU EVER KILL SOMEBODY?

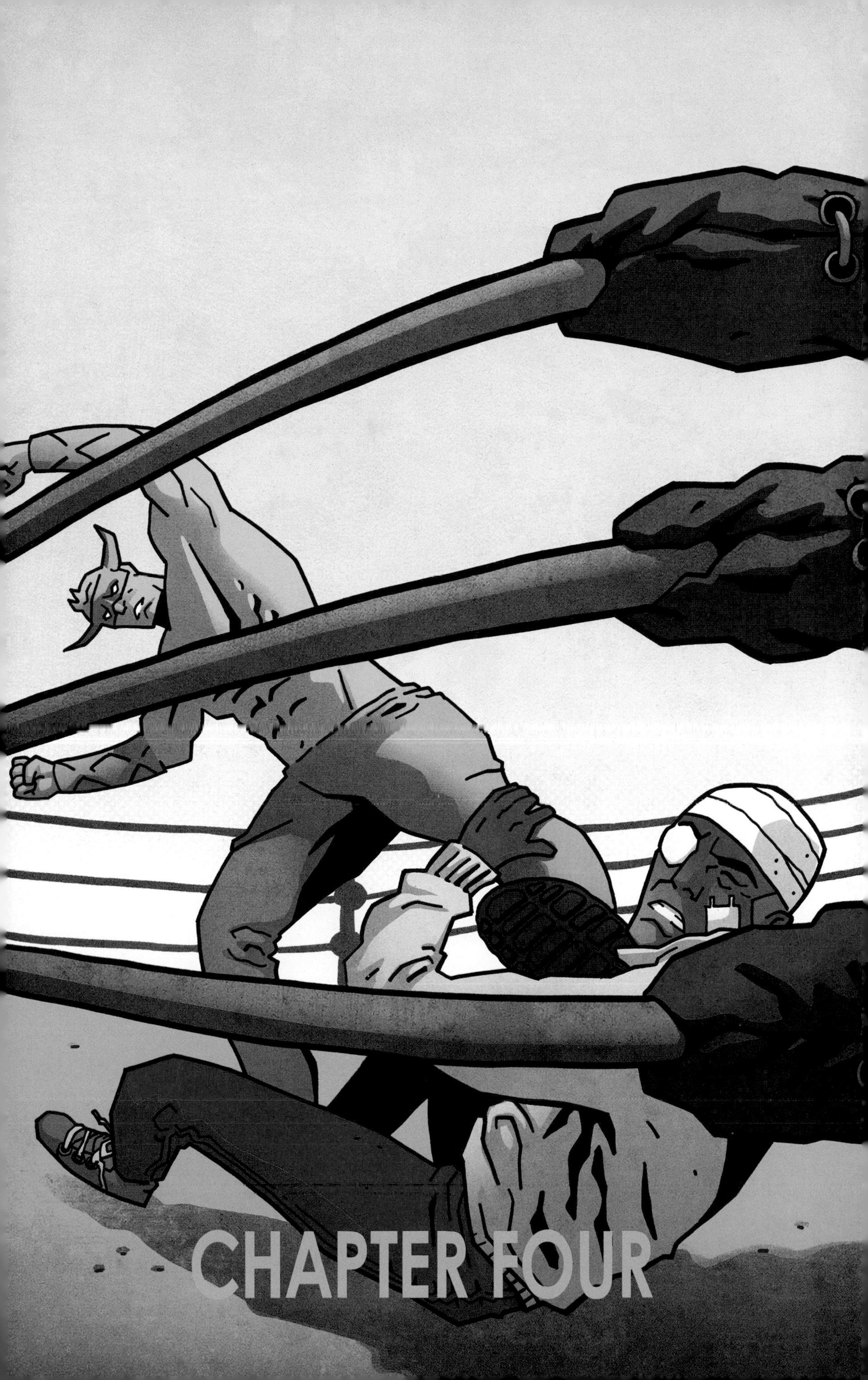
CHAPTER FOUR

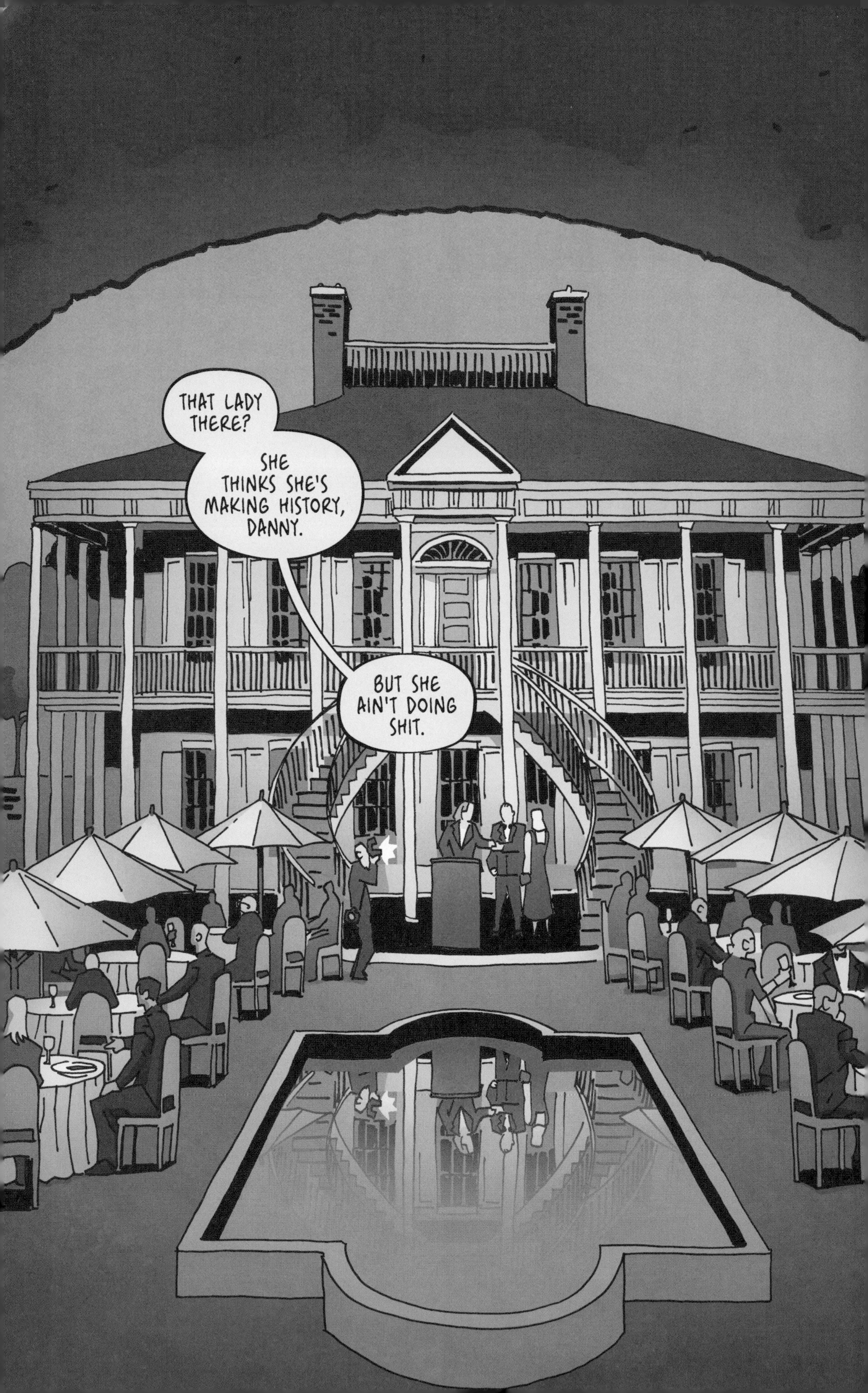
THAT LADY THERE?
SHE THINKS SHE'S MAKING HISTORY, DANNY.
BUT SHE AIN'T DOING SHIT.

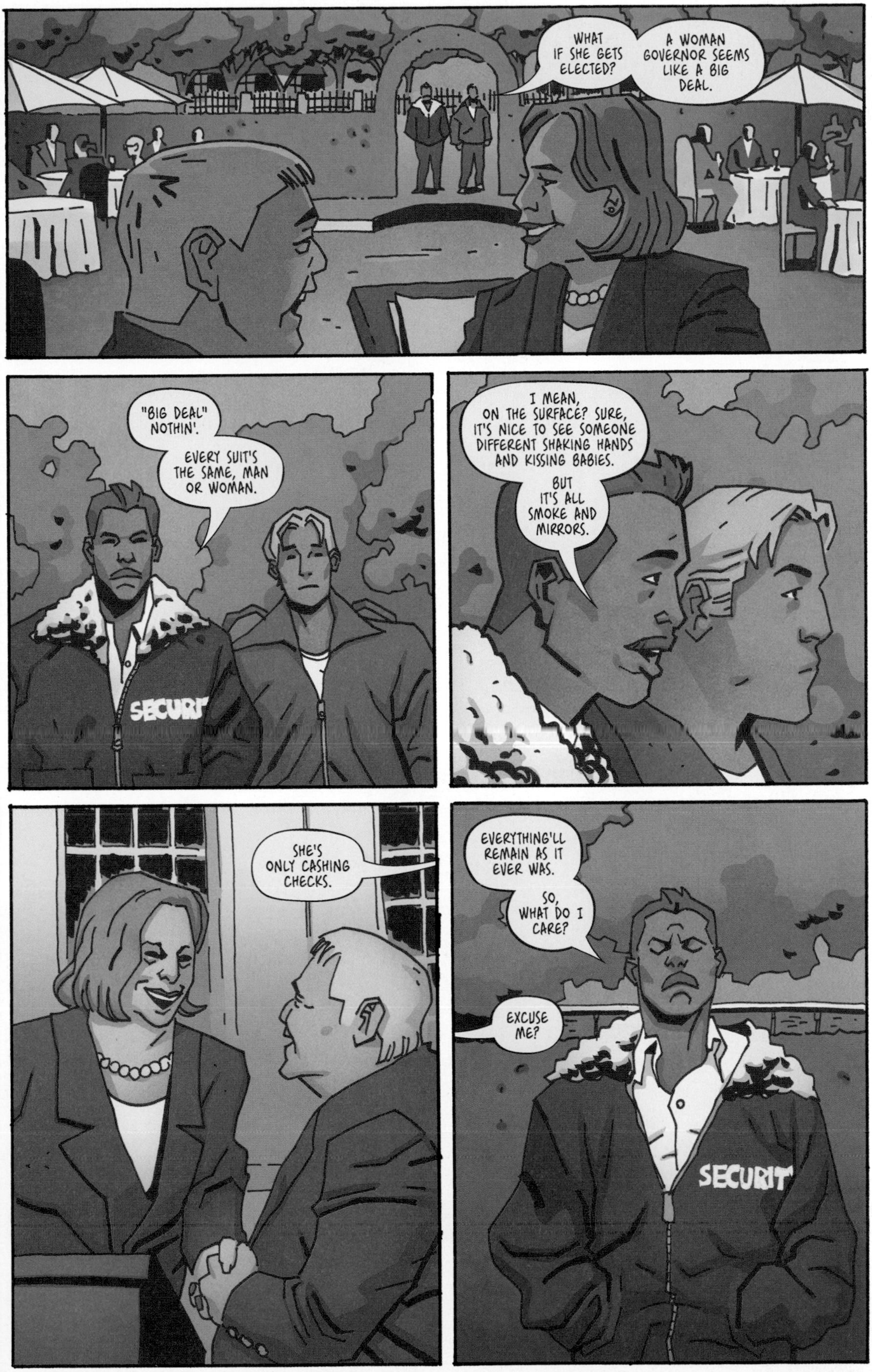

WHAT IF SHE GETS ELECTED?
A WOMAN GOVERNOR SEEMS LIKE A BIG DEAL.
"BIG DEAL" NOTHIN'.
EVERY SUIT'S THE SAME, MAN OR WOMAN.
SECURIT
I MEAN, ON THE SURFACE? SURE, IT'S NICE TO SEE SOMEONE DIFFERENT SHAKING HANDS AND KISSING BABIES.
BUT IT'S ALL SMOKE AND MIRRORS.
SHE'S ONLY CASHING CHECKS.
EVERYTHING'LL REMAIN AS IT EVER WAS.
SO, WHAT DO I CARE?
EXCUSE ME?
SECURIT

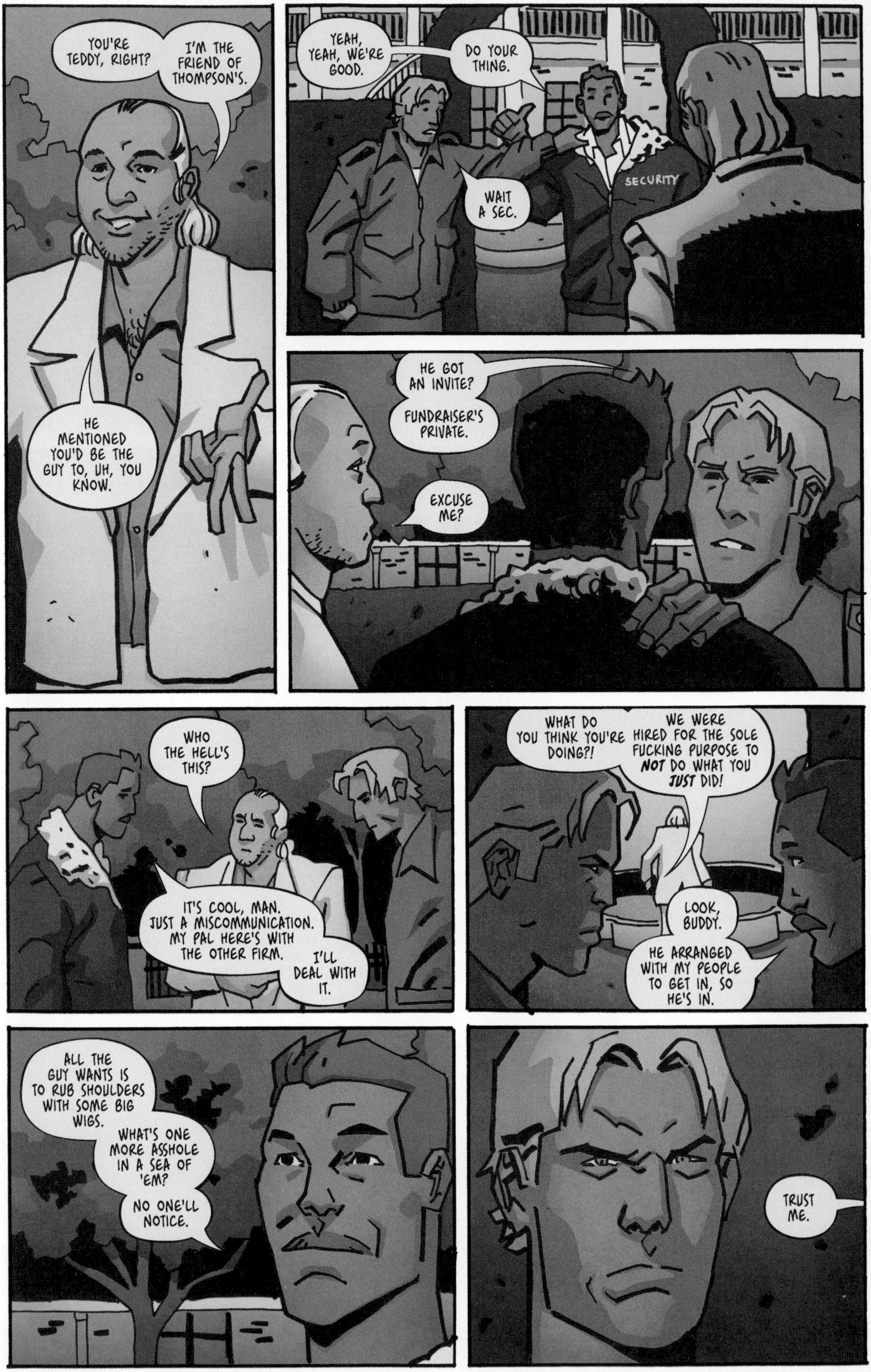
YOU'RE TEDDY, RIGHT?
I'M THE FRIEND OF THOMPSON'S.
HE MENTIONED YOU'D BE THE GUY TO, UH, YOU KNOW.
YEAH, YEAH, WE'RE GOOD.
DO YOUR THING.
SECURITY
WAIT A SEC.
HE GOT AN INVITE?
FUNDRAISER'S PRIVATE.
EXCUSE ME?
WHO THE HELL'S THIS?
IT'S COOL, MAN. JUST A MISCOMMUNICATION. MY PAL HERE'S WITH THE OTHER FIRM.
I'LL DEAL WITH IT.
WHAT DO YOU THINK YOU'RE DOING?!
WE WERE HIRED FOR THE SOLE FUCKING PURPOSE TO **NOT** DO WHAT YOU ***JUST*** DID!
LOOK, BUDDY.
HE ARRANGED WITH MY PEOPLE TO GET IN, SO HE'S IN.
ALL THE GUY WANTS IS TO RUB SHOULDERS WITH SOME BIG WIGS.
WHAT'S ONE MORE ASSHOLE IN A SEA OF 'EM?
NO ONE'LL NOTICE.
TRUST ME.

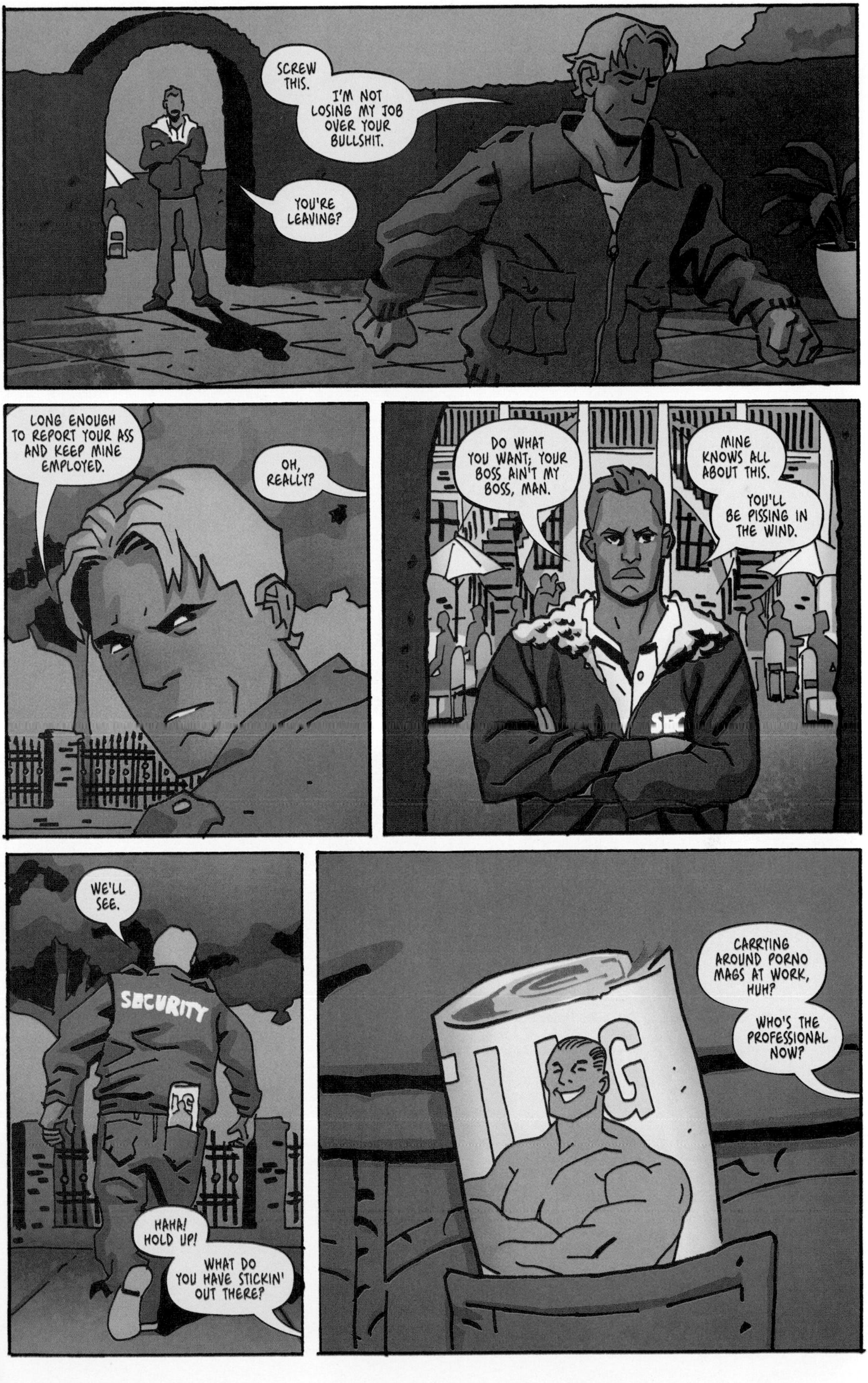
SCREW THIS.
I'M NOT LOSING MY JOB OVER YOUR BULLSHIT.
YOU'RE LEAVING?
LONG ENOUGH TO REPORT YOUR ASS AND KEEP MINE EMPLOYED.
OH, REALLY?
DO WHAT YOU WANT; YOUR BOSS AIN'T MY BOSS, MAN.
MINE KNOWS ALL ABOUT THIS.
YOU'LL BE PISSING IN THE WIND.
WE'LL SEE.
SECURITY
HAHA! HOLD UP!
WHAT DO YOU HAVE STICKIN' OUT THERE?
CARRYING AROUND PORNO MAGS AT WORK, HUH?
WHO'S THE PROFESSIONAL NOW?

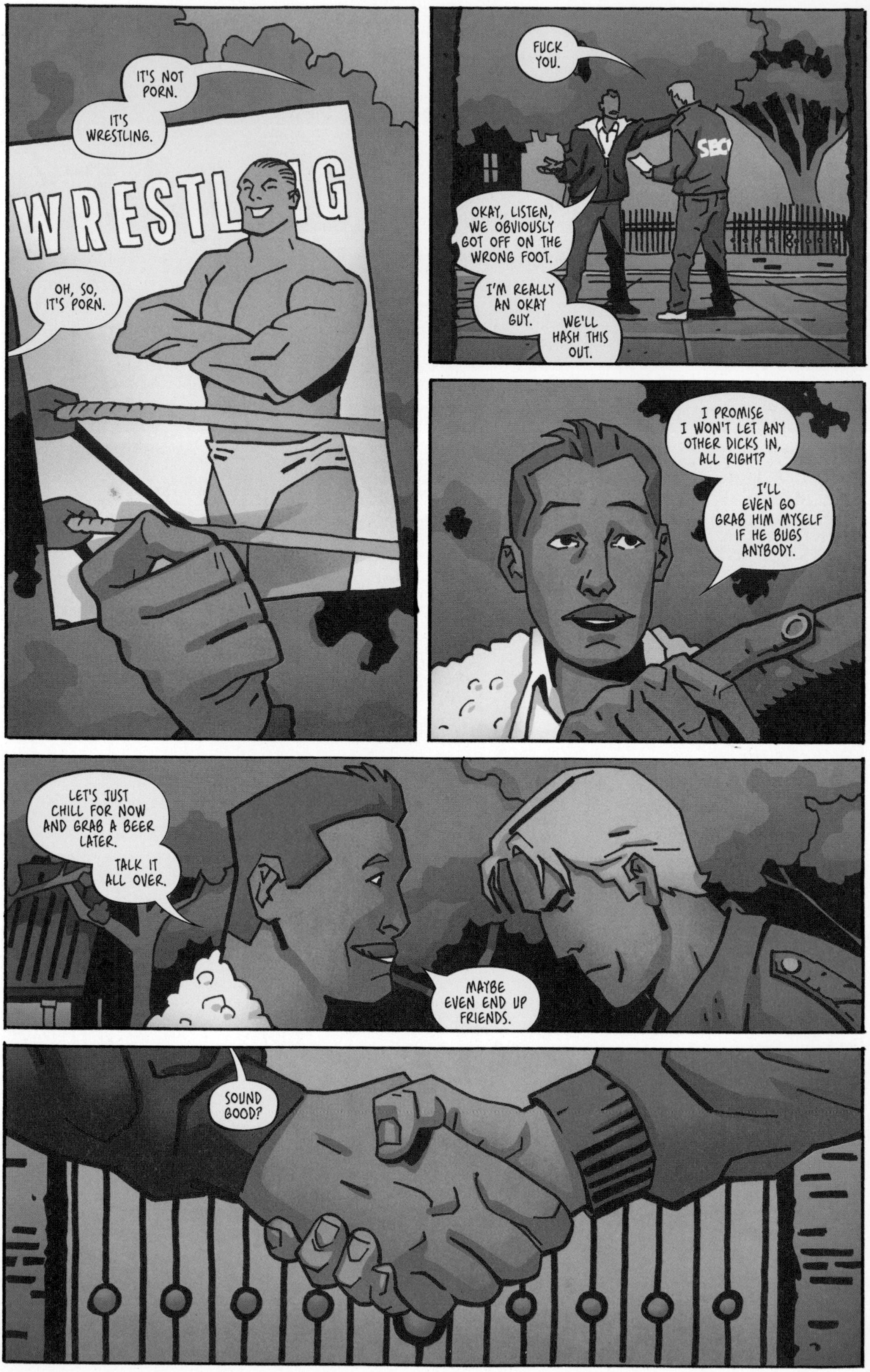
IT'S NOT PORN.
IT'S WRESTLING.
WRESTLING
OH, SO, IT'S PORN.
FUCK YOU.
SEC
OKAY, LISTEN, WE OBVIOUSLY GOT OFF ON THE WRONG FOOT.
I'M REALLY AN OKAY GUY.
WE'LL HASH THIS OUT.
I PROMISE I WON'T LET ANY OTHER DICKS IN, ALL RIGHT?
I'LL EVEN GO GRAB HIM MYSELF IF HE BUGS ANYBODY.
LET'S JUST CHILL FOR NOW AND GRAB A BEER LATER.
TALK IT ALL OVER.
MAYBE EVEN END UP FRIENDS.
SOUND GOOD?

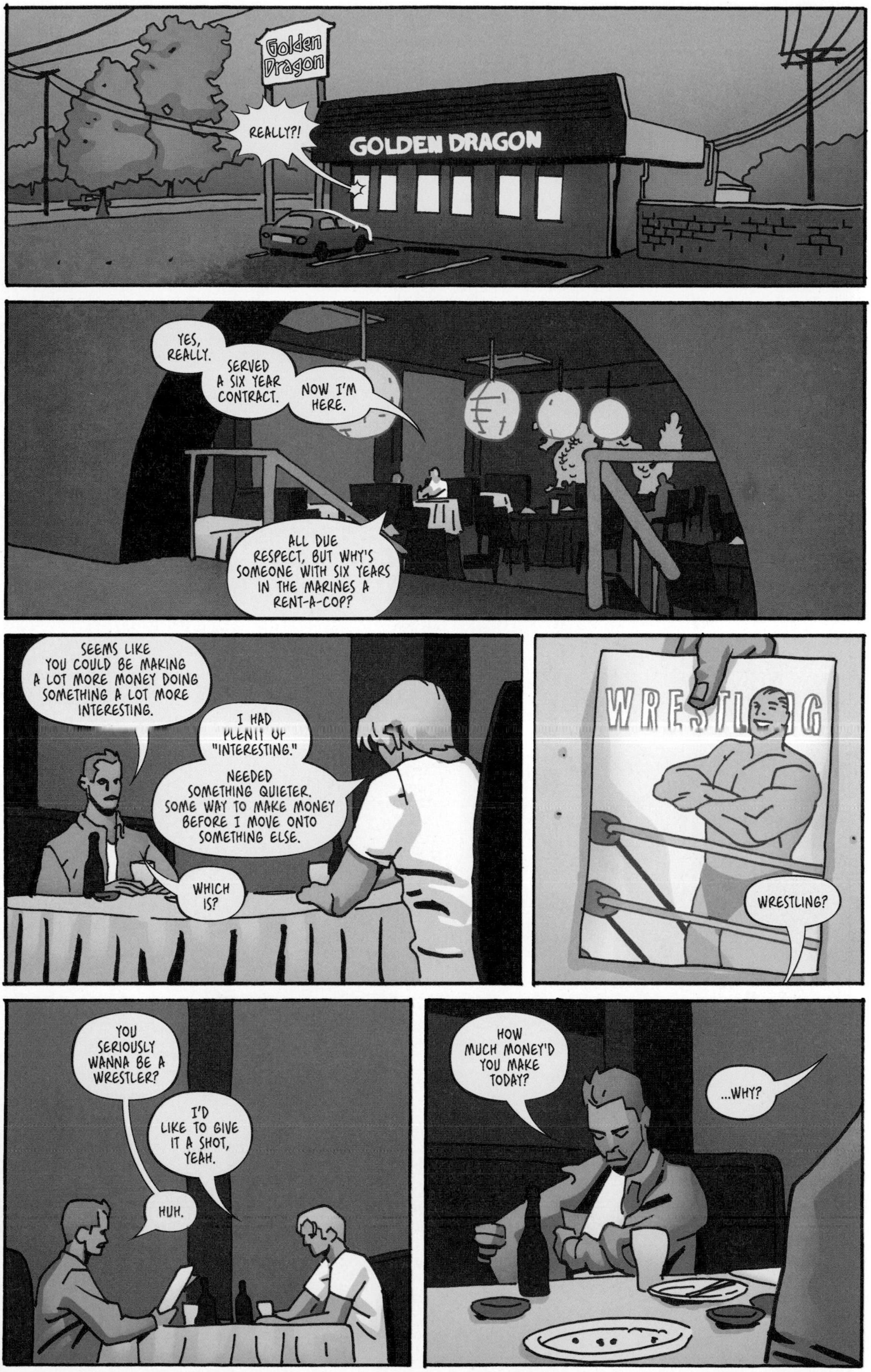
Golden Dragon
GOLDEN DRAGON
REALLY?!
YES, REALLY.
SERVED A SIX YEAR CONTRACT.
NOW I'M HERE.
ALL DUE RESPECT, BUT WHY'S SOMEONE WITH SIX YEARS IN THE MARINES A RENT-A-COP?
SEEMS LIKE YOU COULD BE MAKING A LOT MORE MONEY DOING SOMETHING A LOT MORE INTERESTING.
I HAD PLENTY OF "INTERESTING."
NEEDED SOMETHING QUIETER. SOME WAY TO MAKE MONEY BEFORE I MOVE ONTO SOMETHING ELSE.
WHICH IS?
WRESTLING
WRESTLING?
YOU SERIOUSLY WANNA BE A WRESTLER?
I'D LIKE TO GIVE IT A SHOT, YEAH.
HUH.
HOW MUCH MONEY'D YOU MAKE TODAY?
...WHY?

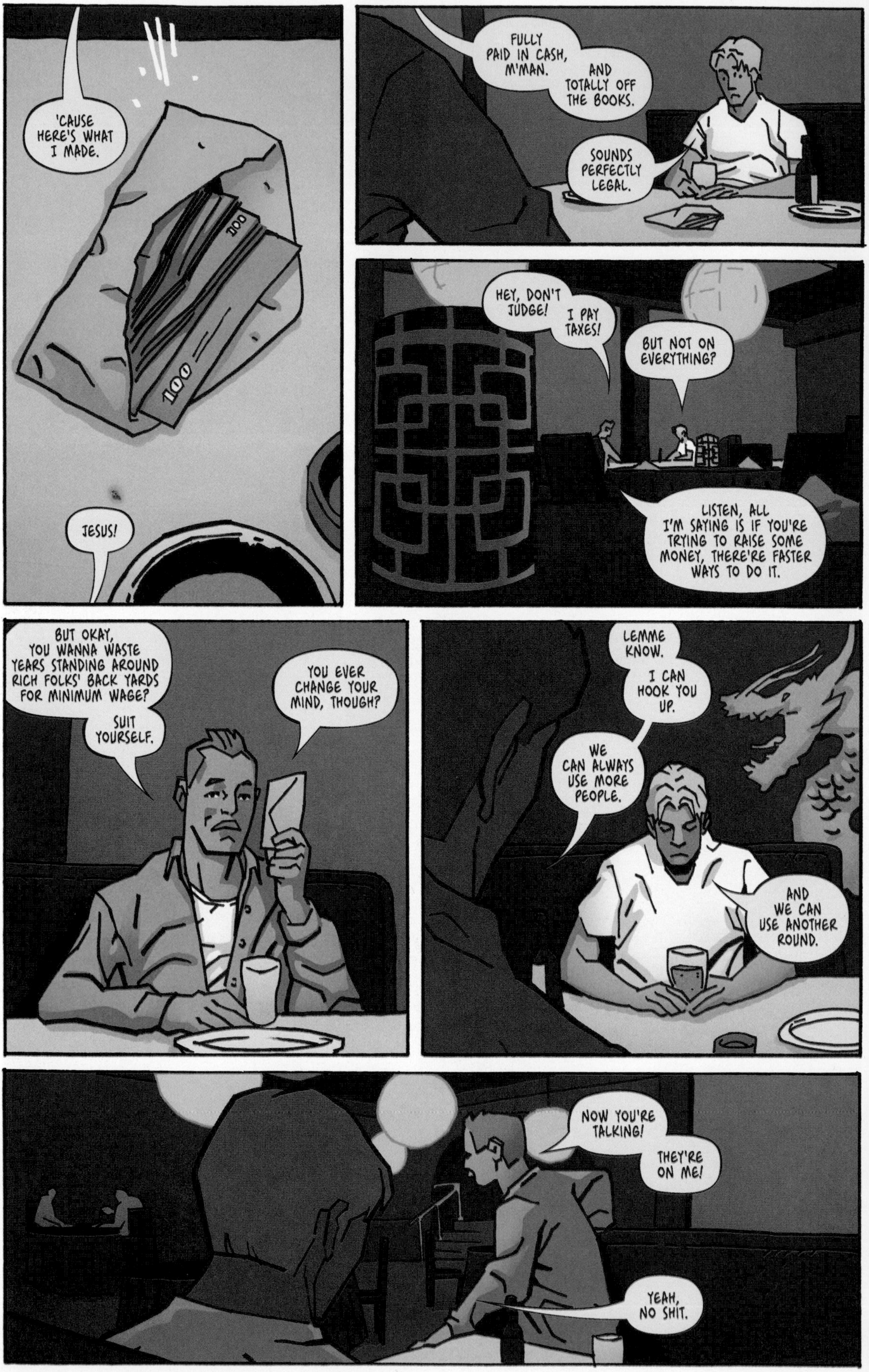
'CAUSE HERE'S WHAT I MADE.
100
100
JESUS!
FULLY PAID IN CASH, M'MAN.
AND TOTALLY OFF THE BOOKS.
SOUNDS PERFECTLY LEGAL.
HEY, DON'T JUDGE!
I PAY TAXES!
BUT NOT ON EVERYTHING?
LISTEN, ALL I'M SAYING IS IF YOU'RE TRYING TO RAISE SOME MONEY, THERE'RE FASTER WAYS TO DO IT.
BUT OKAY, YOU WANNA WASTE YEARS STANDING AROUND RICH FOLKS' BACK YARDS FOR MINIMUM WAGE?
SUIT YOURSELF.
YOU EVER CHANGE YOUR MIND, THOUGH?
LEMME KNOW.
I CAN HOOK YOU UP.
WE CAN ALWAYS USE MORE PEOPLE.
AND WE CAN USE ANOTHER ROUND.
NOW YOU'RE TALKING!
THEY'RE ON ME!
YEAH, NO SHIT.

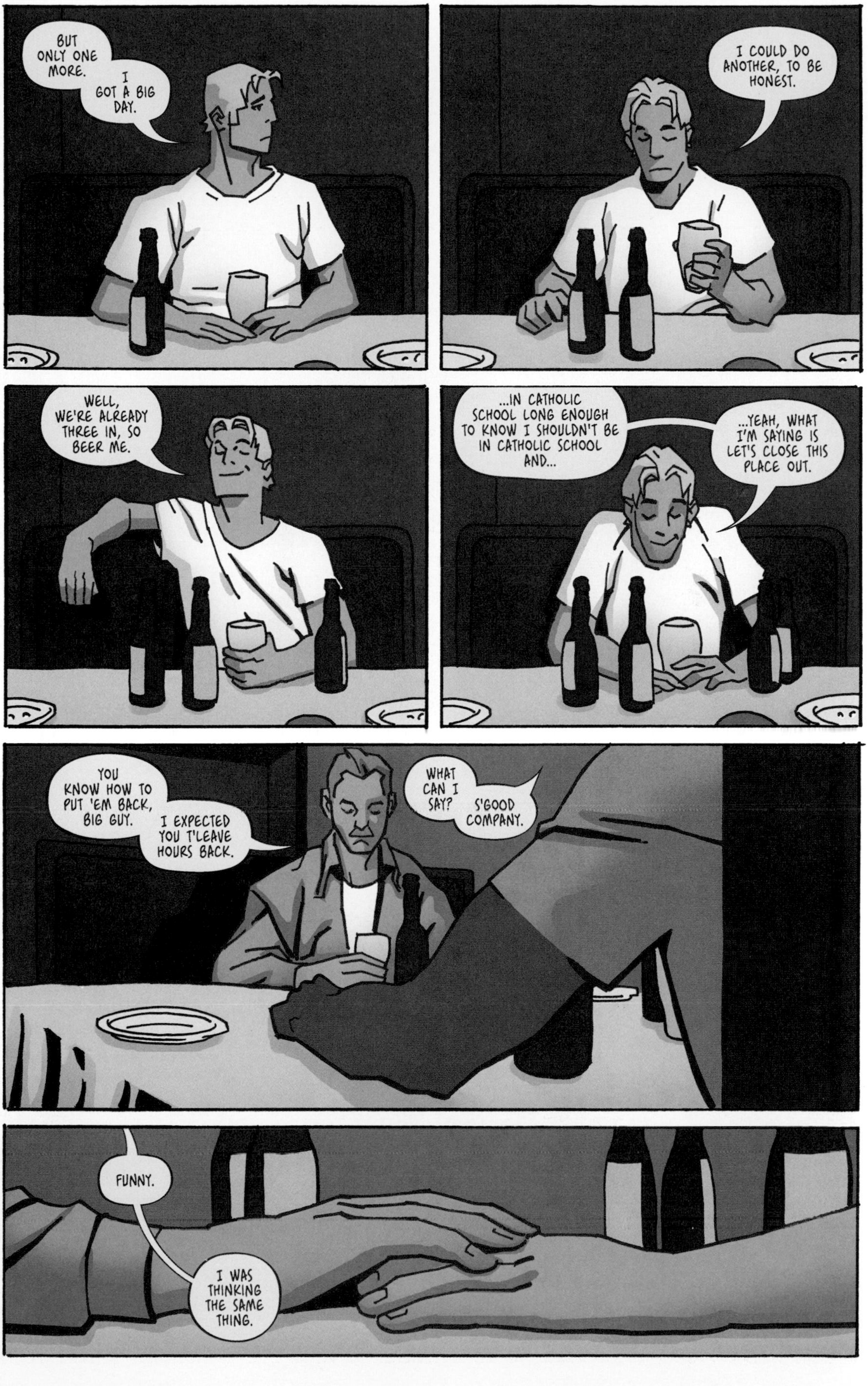
BUT ONLY ONE MORE.
I GOT A BIG DAY.
I COULD DO ANOTHER, TO BE HONEST.
WELL, WE'RE ALREADY THREE IN, SO BEER ME.
...IN CATHOLIC SCHOOL LONG ENOUGH TO KNOW I SHOULDN'T BE IN CATHOLIC SCHOOL AND...
...YEAH, WHAT I'M SAYING IS LET'S CLOSE THIS PLACE OUT.
YOU KNOW HOW TO PUT 'EM BACK, BIG GUY.
I EXPECTED YOU T'LEAVE HOURS BACK.
WHAT CAN I SAY?
S'GOOD COMPANY.
FUNNY.
I WAS THINKING THE SAME THING.

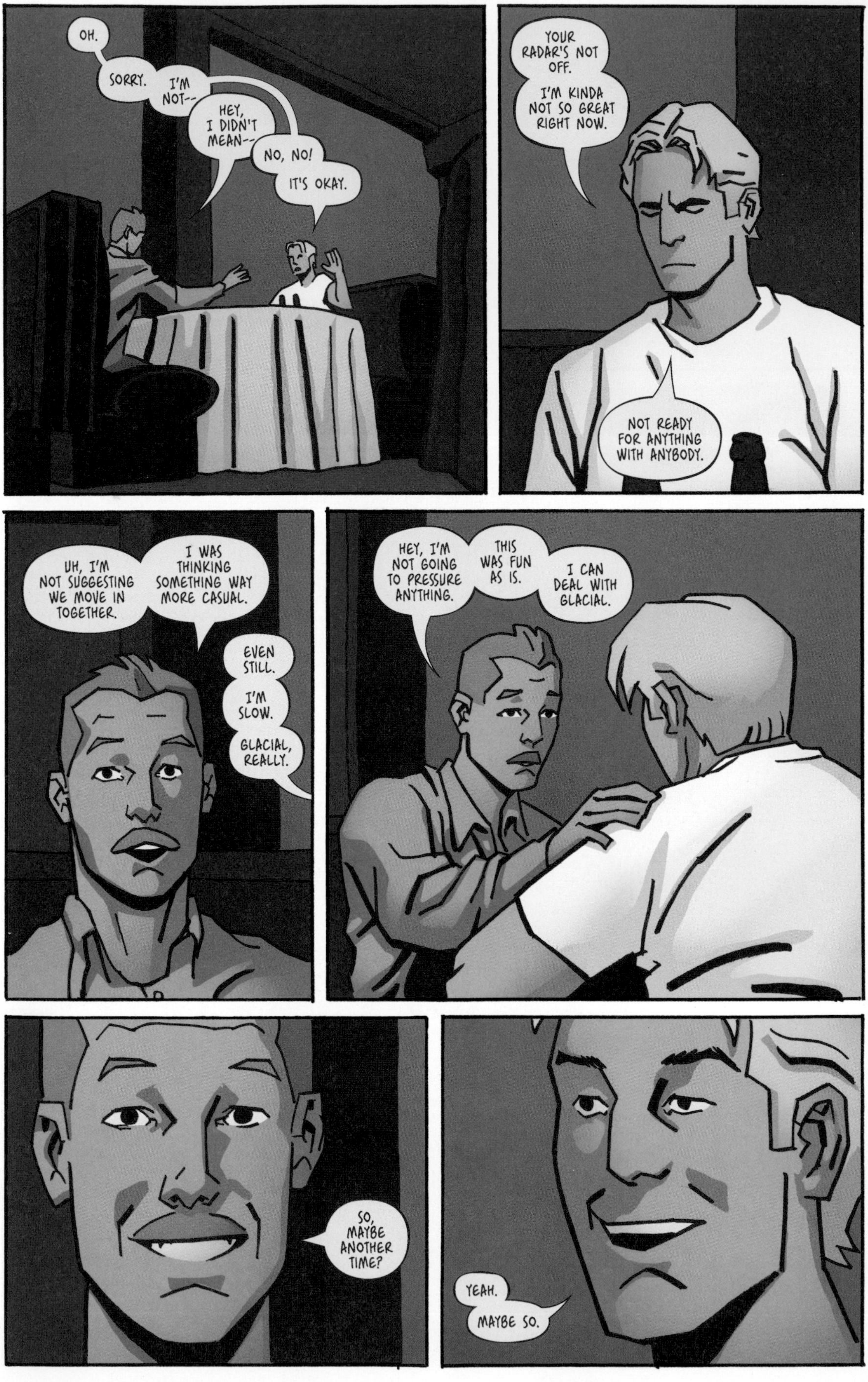
OH.
SORRY.
I'M NOT--
HEY, I DIDN'T MEAN--
NO, NO!
IT'S OKAY.
YOUR RADAR'S NOT OFF.
I'M KINDA NOT SO GREAT RIGHT NOW.
NOT READY FOR ANYTHING WITH ANYBODY.
UH, I'M NOT SUGGESTING WE MOVE IN TOGETHER.
I WAS THINKING SOMETHING WAY MORE CASUAL.
EVEN STILL.
I'M SLOW.
GLACIAL, REALLY.
HEY, I'M NOT GOING TO PRESSURE ANYTHING.
THIS WAS FUN AS IS.
I CAN DEAL WITH GLACIAL.
SO, MAYBE ANOTHER TIME?
YEAH.
MAYBE SO.

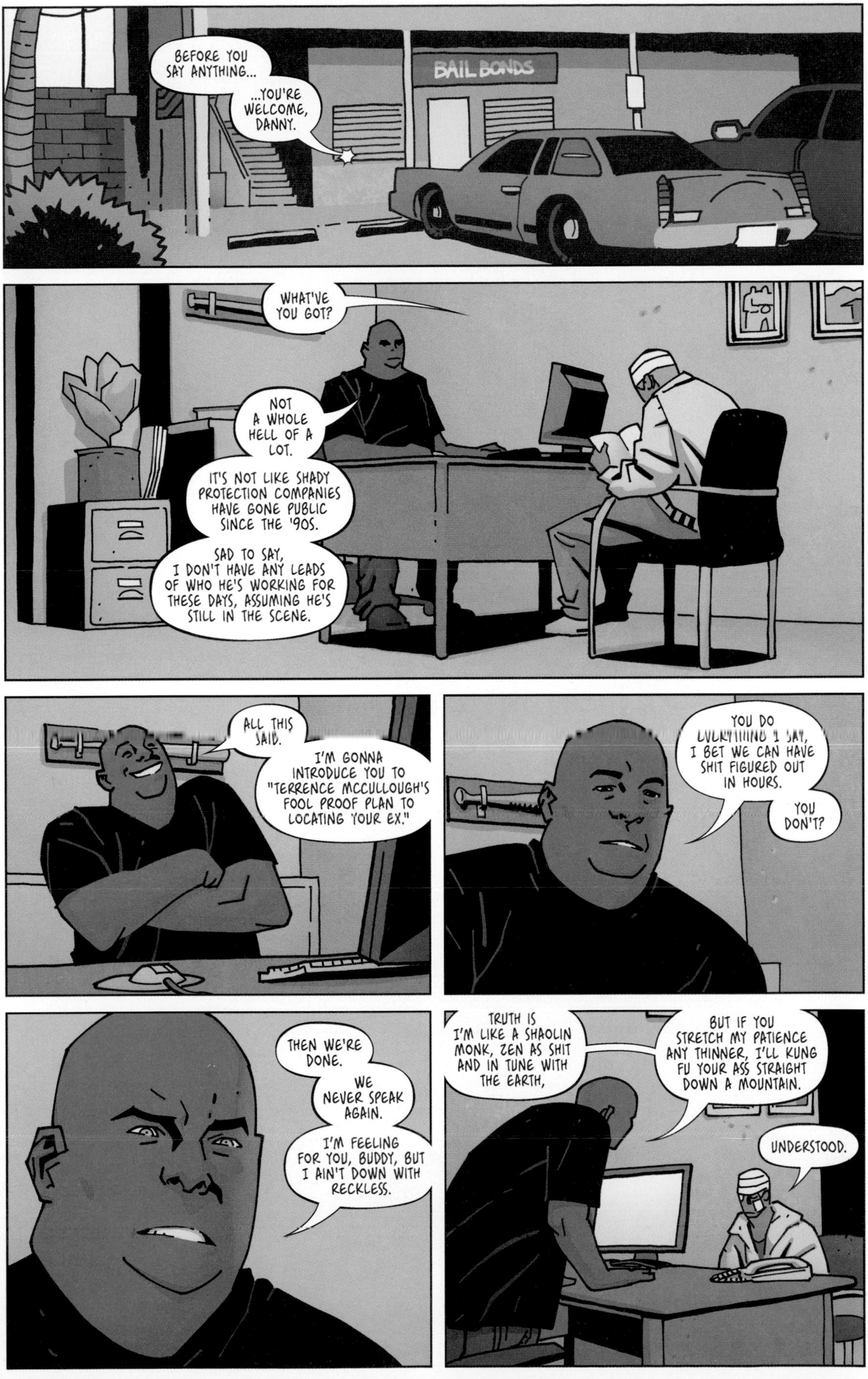
BEFORE YOU SAY ANYTHING...
...YOU'RE WELCOME, DANNY.
BAIL BONDS
WHAT'VE YOU GOT?
NOT A WHOLE HELL OF A LOT.
IT'S NOT LIKE SHADY PROTECTION COMPANIES HAVE GONE PUBLIC SINCE THE '90S.
SAD TO SAY, I DON'T HAVE ANY LEADS OF WHO HE'S WORKING FOR THESE DAYS, ASSUMING HE'S STILL IN THE SCENE.
ALL THIS SAID.
I'M GONNA INTRODUCE YOU TO "TERRENCE McCULLOUGH'S FOOL PROOF PLAN TO LOCATING YOUR EX."
YOU DO EVERYTHING I SAY, I BET WE CAN HAVE SHIT FIGURED OUT IN HOURS.
YOU DON'T?
THEN WE'RE DONE.
WE NEVER SPEAK AGAIN.
I'M FEELING FOR YOU, BUDDY, BUT I AIN'T DOWN WITH RECKLESS.
TRUTH IS I'M LIKE A SHAOLIN MONK, ZEN AS SHIT AND IN TUNE WITH THE EARTH,
BUT IF YOU STRETCH MY PATIENCE ANY THINNER, I'LL KUNG FU YOUR ASS STRAIGHT DOWN A MOUNTAIN.
UNDERSTOOD.

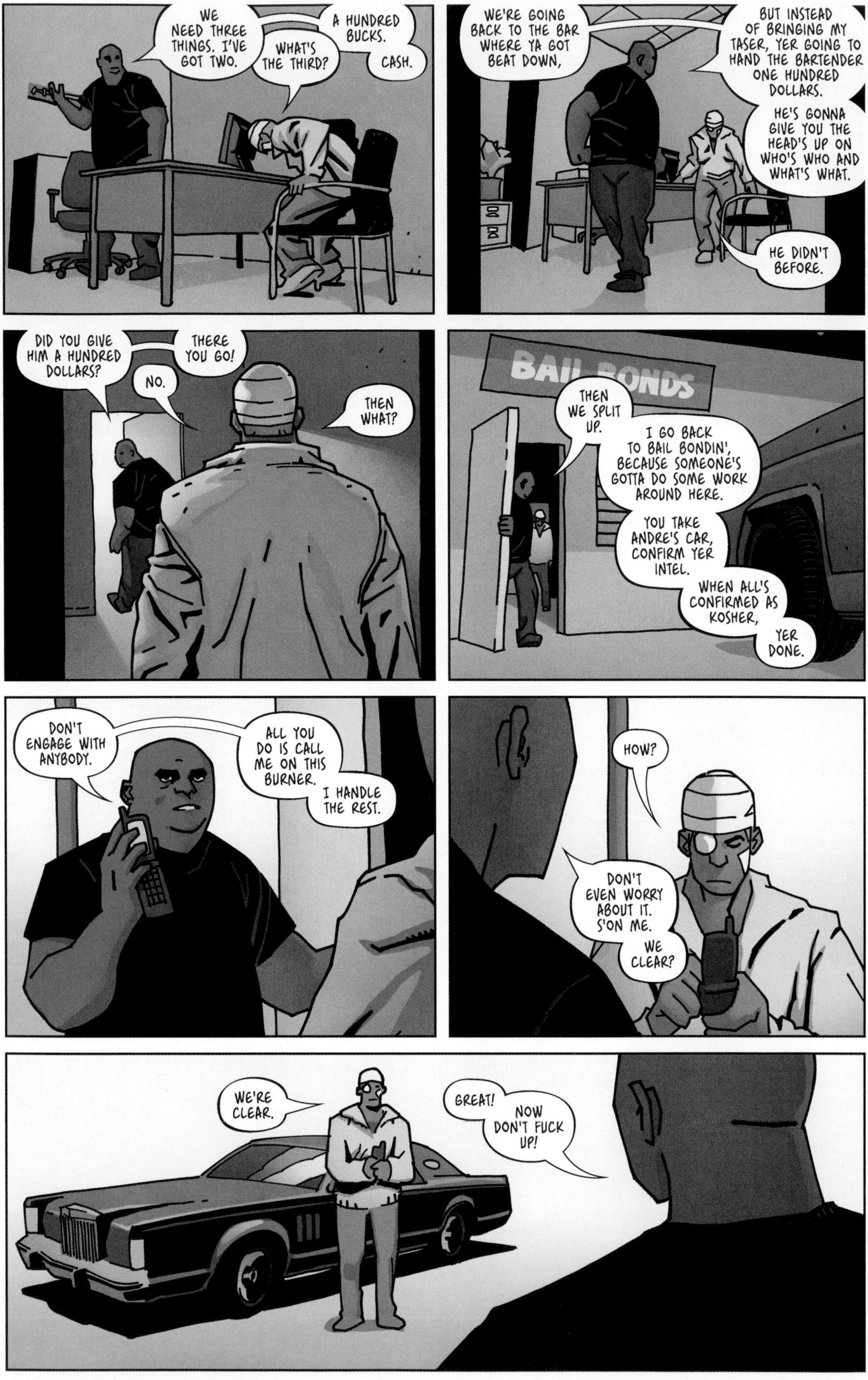

WE NEED THREE THINGS. I'VE GOT TWO.
WHAT'S THE THIRD?
A HUNDRED BUCKS.
CASH.
WE'RE GOING BACK TO THE BAR WHERE YA GOT BEAT DOWN,
BUT INSTEAD OF BRINGING MY TASER, YER GOING TO HAND THE BARTENDER ONE HUNDRED DOLLARS.
HE'S GONNA GIVE YOU THE HEAD'S UP ON WHO'S WHO AND WHAT'S WHAT.
HE DIDN'T BEFORE.
DID YOU GIVE HIM A HUNDRED DOLLARS?
NO.
THERE YOU GO!
THEN WHAT?
BAIL BONDS
THEN WE SPLIT UP.
I GO BACK TO BAIL BONDIN', BECAUSE SOMEONE'S GOTTA DO SOME WORK AROUND HERE.
YOU TAKE ANDRE'S CAR, CONFIRM YER INTEL.
WHEN ALL'S CONFIRMED AS KOSHER,
YER DONE.
DON'T ENGAGE WITH ANYBODY.
ALL YOU DO IS CALL ME ON THIS BURNER.
I HANDLE THE REST.
HOW?
DON'T EVEN WORRY ABOUT IT. S'ON ME.
WE CLEAR?
WE'RE CLEAR.
GREAT!
NOW DON'T FUCK UP!

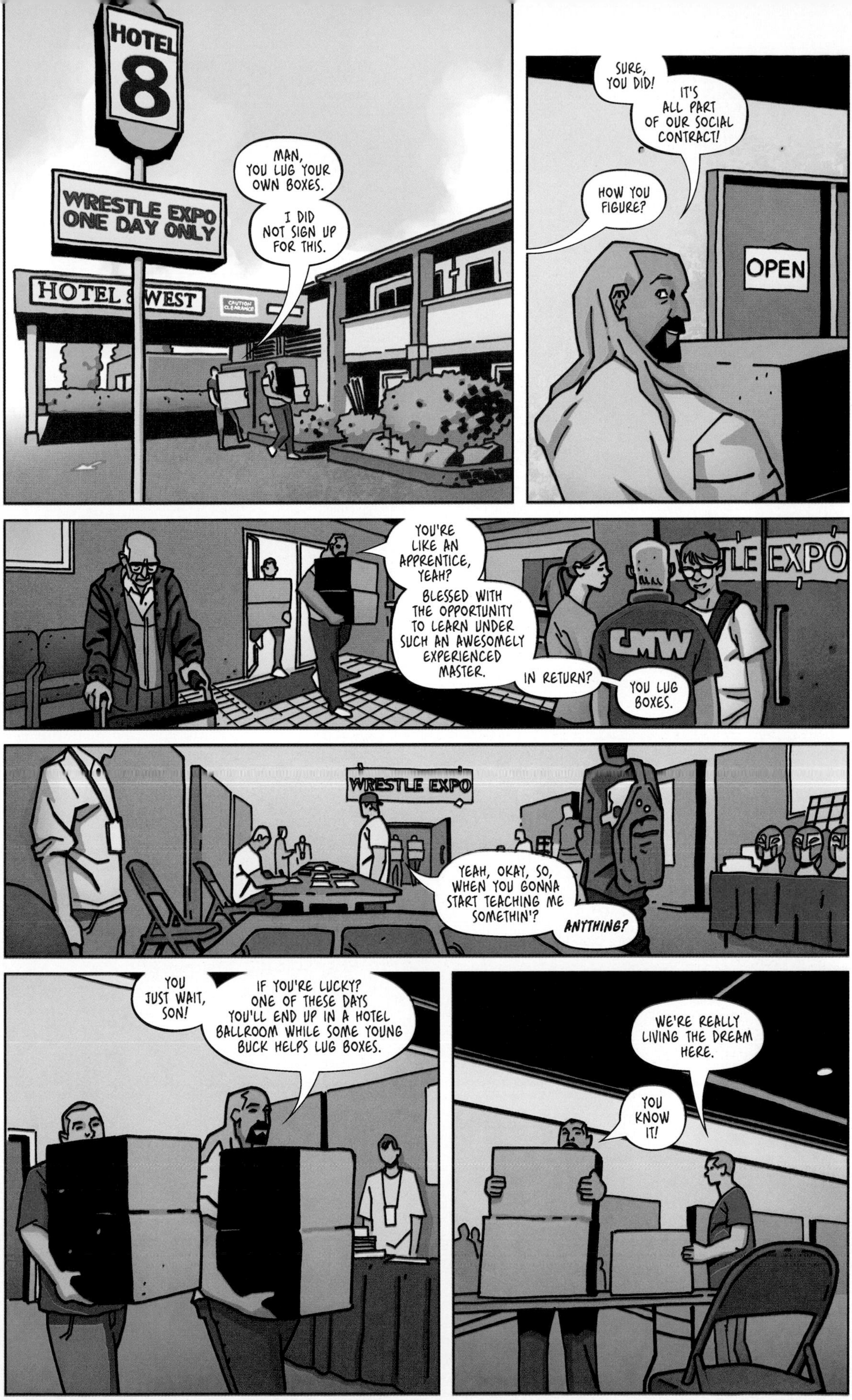
HOTEL 8
WRESTLE EXPO ONE DAY ONLY
HOTEL 8 WEST
MAN, YOU LUG YOUR OWN BOXES.
I DID NOT SIGN UP FOR THIS.
SURE, YOU DID!
IT'S ALL PART OF OUR SOCIAL CONTRACT!
HOW YOU FIGURE?
OPEN
YOU'RE LIKE AN APPRENTICE, YEAH?
BLESSED WITH THE OPPORTUNITY TO LEARN UNDER SUCH AN AWESOMELY EXPERIENCED MASTER.
IN RETURN?
YOU LUG BOXES.
CMW
WRESTLE EXPO
YEAH, OKAY, SO, WHEN YOU GONNA START TEACHING ME SOMETHIN'?
ANYTHING?
YOU JUST WAIT, SON!
IF YOU'RE LUCKY? ONE OF THESE DAYS YOU'LL END UP IN A HOTEL BALLROOM WHILE SOME YOUNG BUCK HELPS LUG BOXES.
WE'RE REALLY LIVING THE DREAM HERE.
YOU KNOW IT!

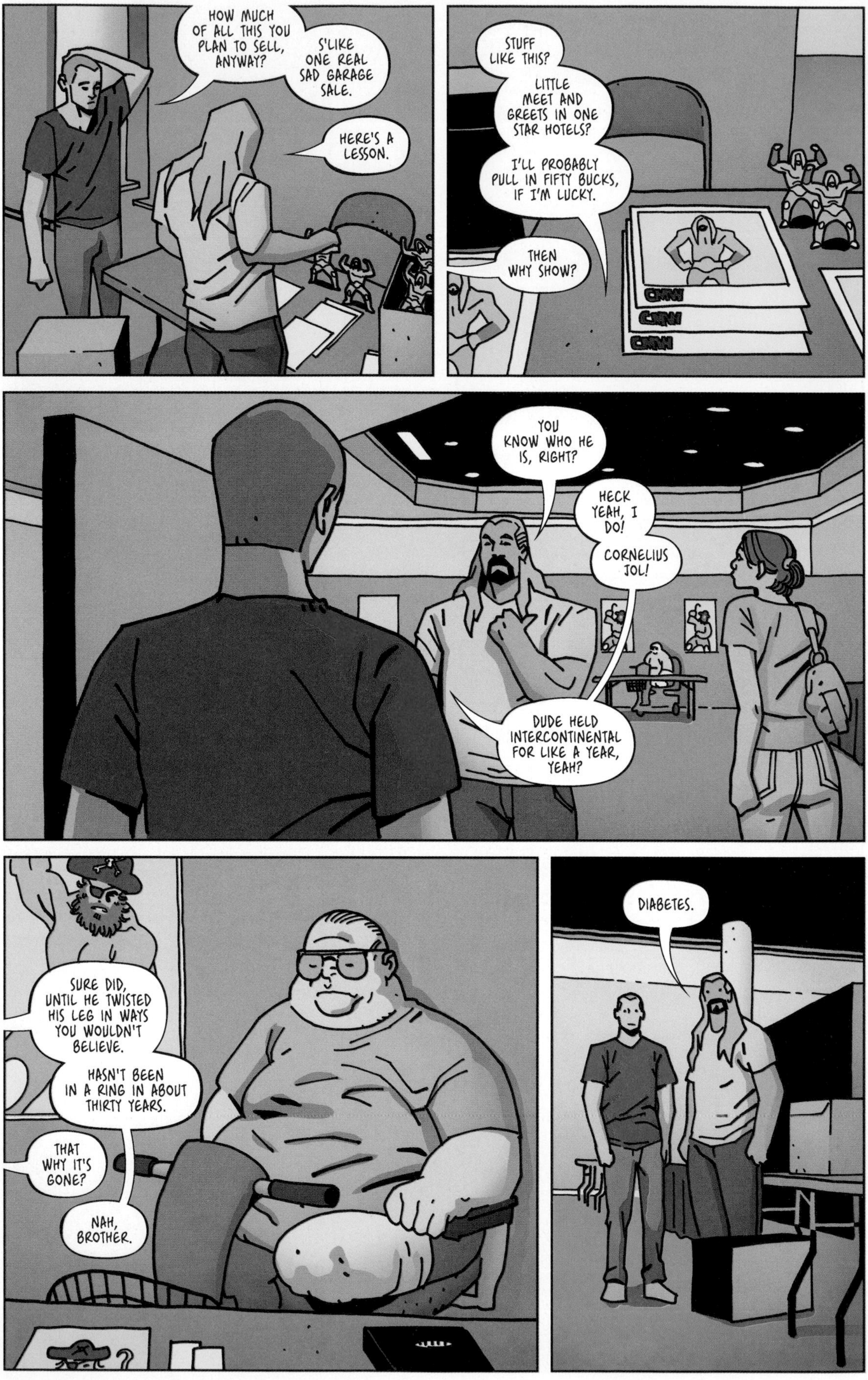
HOW MUCH OF ALL THIS YOU PLAN TO SELL, ANYWAY?
S'LIKE ONE REAL SAD GARAGE SALE.
HERE'S A LESSON.
STUFF LIKE THIS?
LITTLE MEET AND GREETS IN ONE STAR HOTELS?
I'LL PROBABLY PULL IN FIFTY BUCKS, IF I'M LUCKY.
THEN WHY SHOW?
YOU KNOW WHO HE IS, RIGHT?
HECK YEAH, I DO!
CORNELIUS JOL!
DUDE HELD INTERCONTINENTAL FOR LIKE A YEAR, YEAH?
SURE DID, UNTIL HE TWISTED HIS LEG IN WAYS YOU WOULDN'T BELIEVE.
HASN'T BEEN IN A RING IN ABOUT THIRTY YEARS.
THAT WHY IT'S GONE?
NAH, BROTHER.
DIABETES.

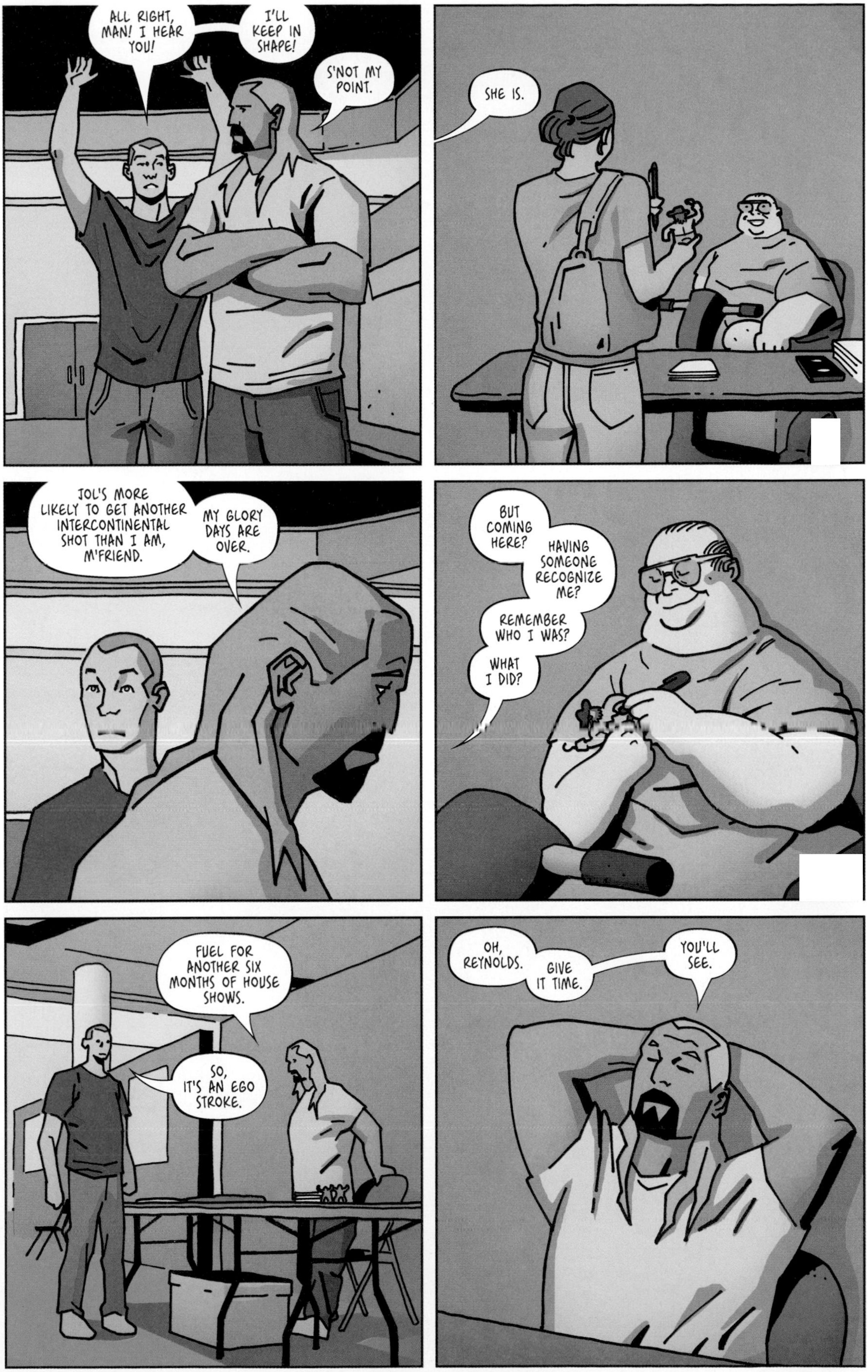
ALL RIGHT, MAN! I HEAR YOU!
I'LL KEEP IN SHAPE!
S'NOT MY POINT.
SHE IS.
JOL'S MORE LIKELY TO GET ANOTHER INTERCONTINENTAL SHOT THAN I AM, M'FRIEND.
MY GLORY DAYS ARE OVER.
BUT COMING HERE?
HAVING SOMEONE RECOGNIZE ME?
REMEMBER WHO I WAS?
WHAT I DID?
FUEL FOR ANOTHER SIX MONTHS OF HOUSE SHOWS.
SO, IT'S AN EGO STROKE.
OH, REYNOLDS.
GIVE IT TIME.
YOU'LL SEE.

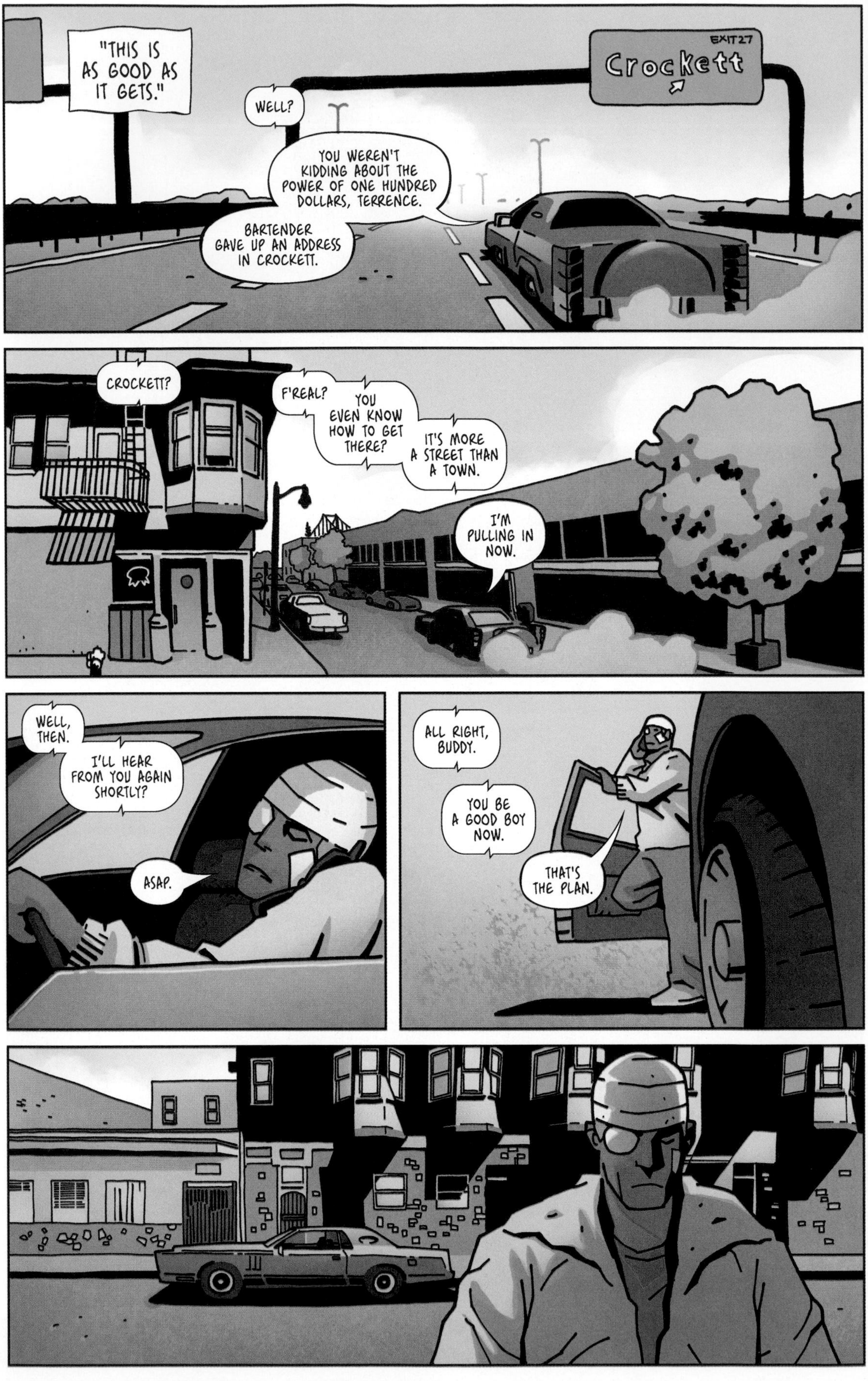
"THIS IS AS GOOD AS IT GETS."
EXIT27
Crockett
WELL?
YOU WEREN'T KIDDING ABOUT THE POWER OF ONE HUNDRED DOLLARS, TERRENCE.
BARTENDER GAVE UP AN ADDRESS IN CROCKETT.
CROCKETT?
F'REAL?
YOU EVEN KNOW HOW TO GET THERE?
IT'S MORE A STREET THAN A TOWN.
I'M PULLING IN NOW.
WELL, THEN.
I'LL HEAR FROM YOU AGAIN SHORTLY?
ASAP.
ALL RIGHT, BUDDY.
YOU BE A GOOD BOY NOW.
THAT'S THE PLAN.

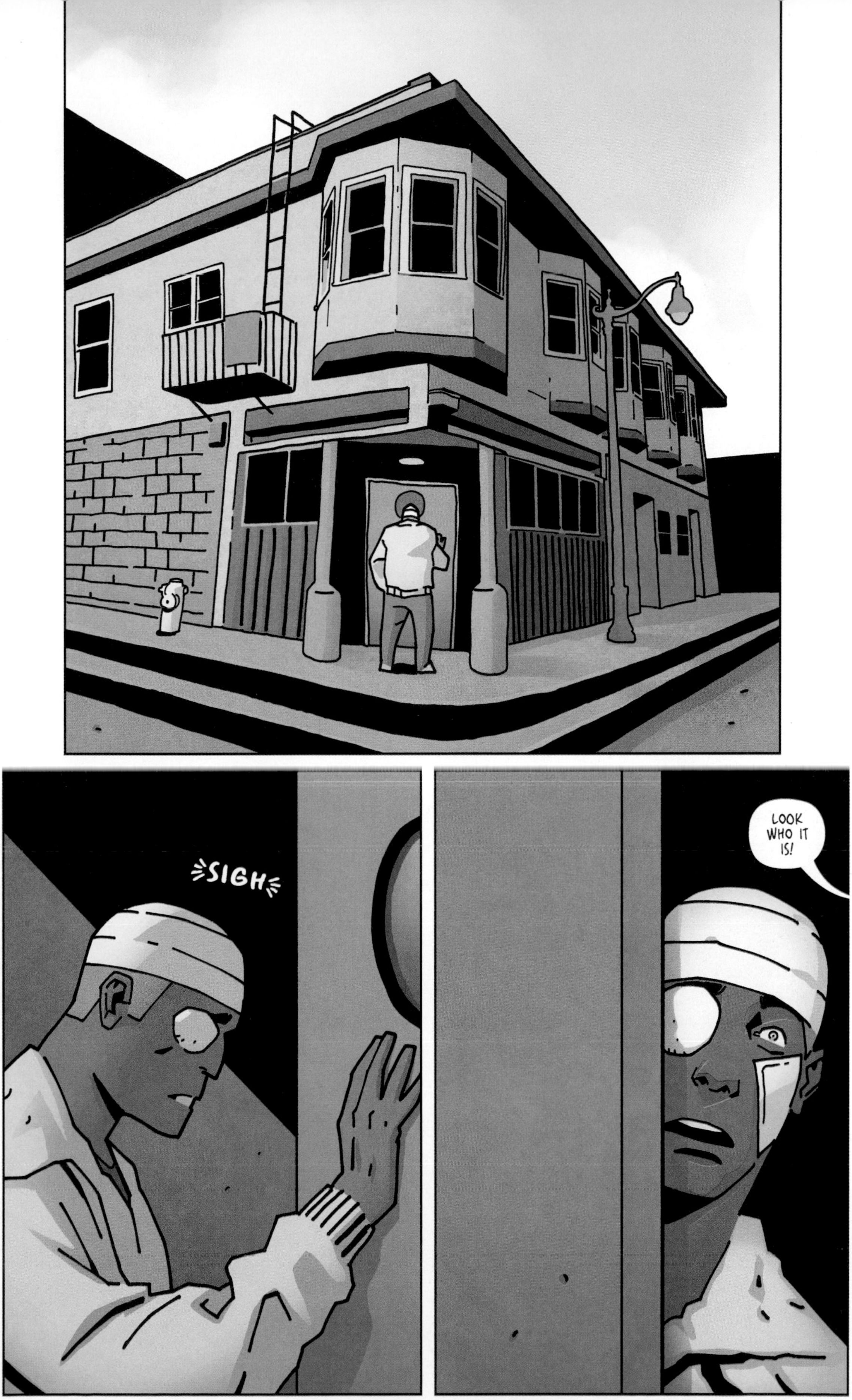
SIGH
LOOK WHO IT IS!

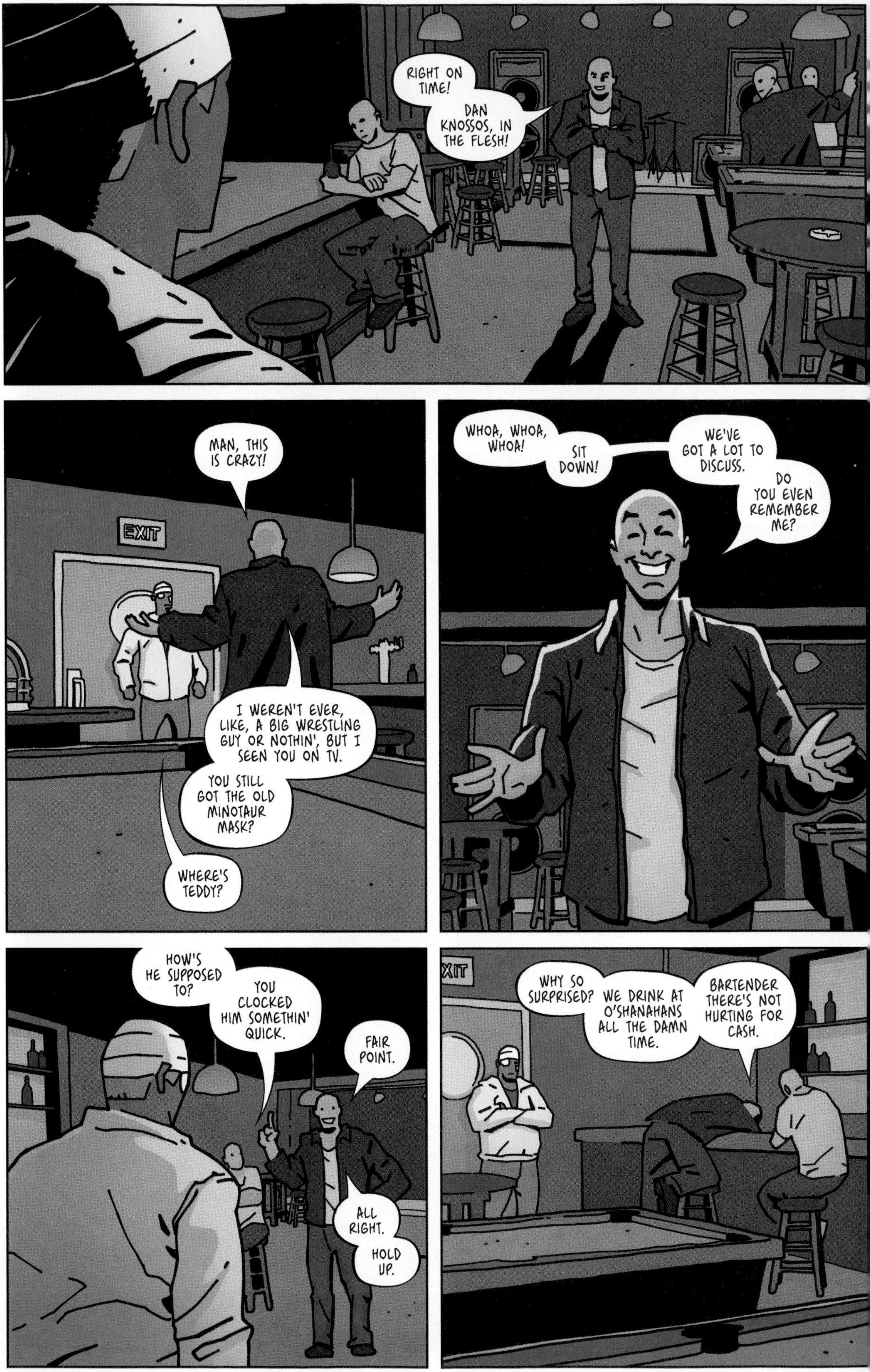

RIGHT ON TIME!
DAN KNOSSOS, IN THE FLESH!
MAN, THIS IS CRAZY!
I WEREN'T EVER, LIKE, A BIG WRESTLING GUY OR NOTHIN', BUT I SEEN YOU ON TV.
YOU STILL GOT THE OLD MINOTAUR MASK?
WHERE'S TEDDY?
WHOA, WHOA, WHOA!
SIT DOWN!
WE'VE GOT A LOT TO DISCUSS.
DO YOU EVEN REMEMBER ME?
HOW'S HE SUPPOSED TO?
YOU CLOCKED HIM SOMETHIN' QUICK.
FAIR POINT.
ALL RIGHT.
HOLD UP.
EXIT
WHY SO SURPRISED?
WE DRINK AT O'SHANAHANS ALL THE DAMN TIME.
BARTENDER THERE'S NOT HURTING FOR CASH.

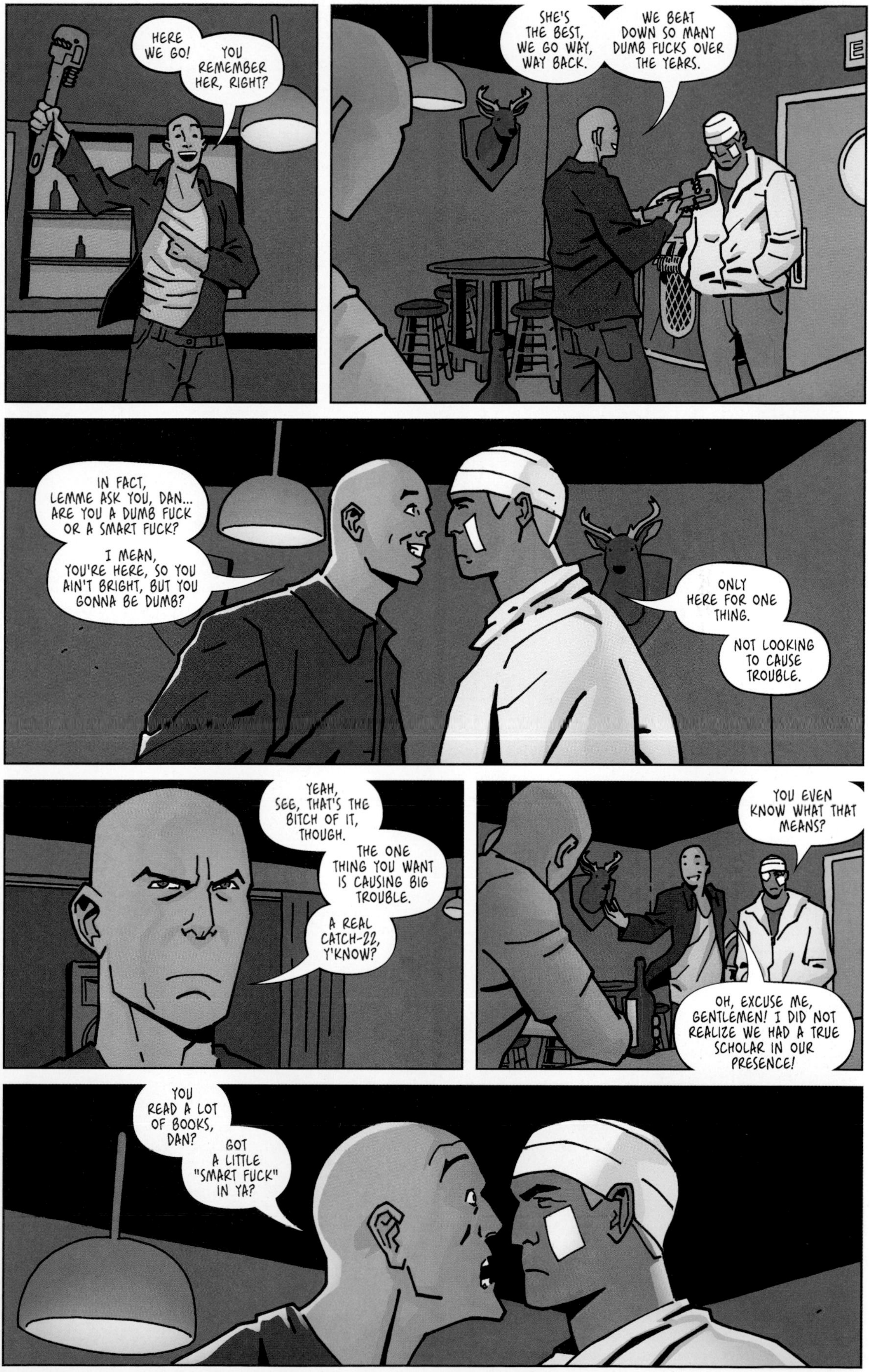
HERE WE GO!
YOU REMEMBER HER, RIGHT?
SHE'S THE BEST, WE GO WAY, WAY BACK.
WE BEAT DOWN SO MANY DUMB FUCKS OVER THE YEARS.
IN FACT, LEMME ASK YOU, DAN... ARE YOU A DUMB FUCK OR A SMART FUCK?
I MEAN, YOU'RE HERE, SO YOU AIN'T BRIGHT, BUT YOU GONNA BE DUMB?
ONLY HERE FOR ONE THING.
NOT LOOKING TO CAUSE TROUBLE.
YEAH, SEE, THAT'S THE BITCH OF IT, THOUGH.
THE ONE THING YOU WANT IS CAUSING BIG TROUBLE.
A REAL CATCH-22, Y'KNOW?
YOU EVEN KNOW WHAT THAT MEANS?
OH, EXCUSE ME, GENTLEMEN! I DID NOT REALIZE WE HAD A TRUE SCHOLAR IN OUR PRESENCE!
YOU READ A LOT OF BOOKS, DAN?
GOT A LITTLE "SMART FUCK" IN YA?

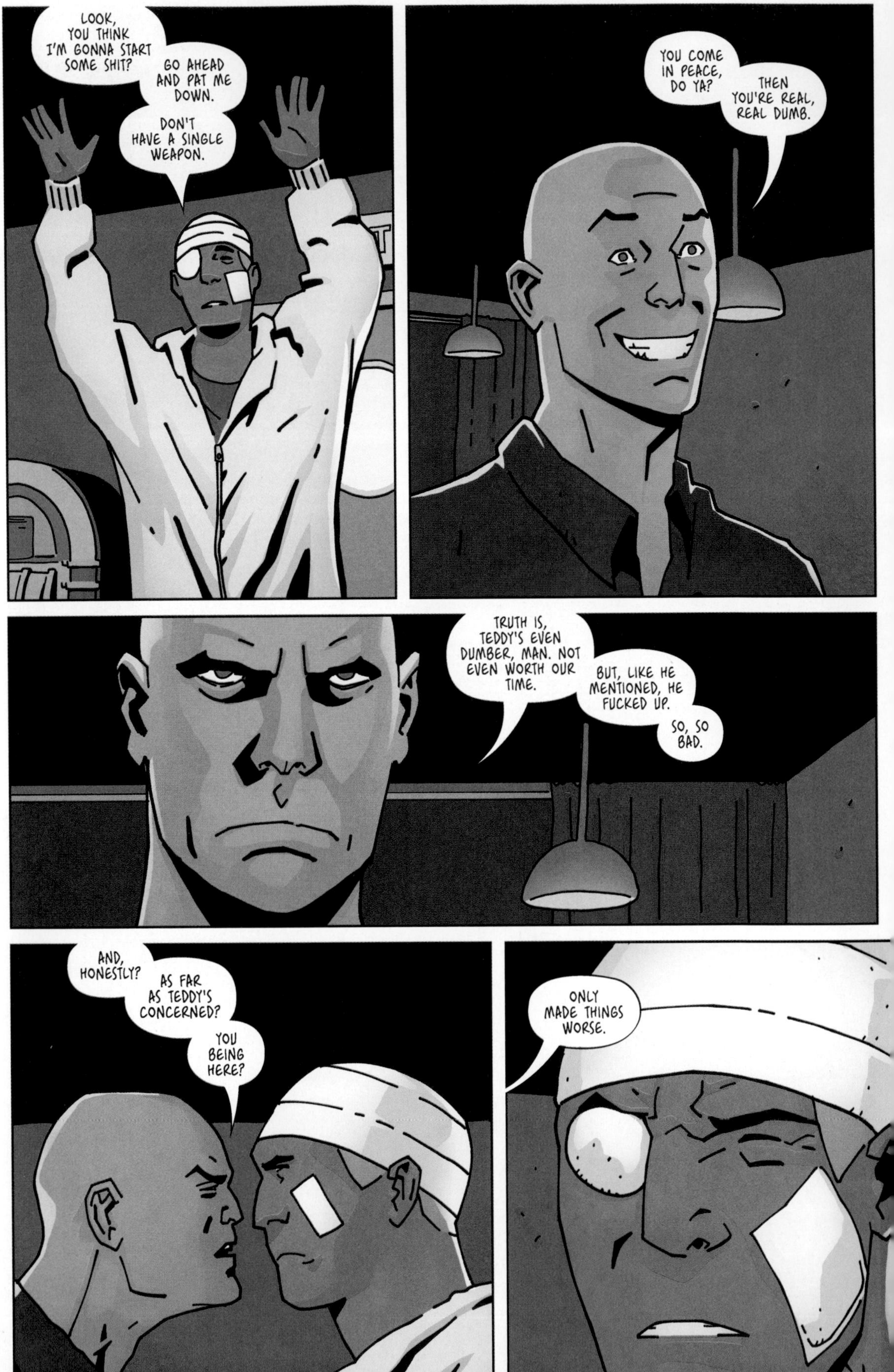
LOOK, YOU THINK I'M GONNA START SOME SHIT?
GO AHEAD AND PAT ME DOWN.
DON'T HAVE A SINGLE WEAPON.
YOU COME IN PEACE, DO YA?
THEN YOU'RE REAL, REAL DUMB.
TRUTH IS, TEDDY'S EVEN DUMBER, MAN. NOT EVEN WORTH OUR TIME.
BUT, LIKE HE MENTIONED, HE FUCKED UP.
SO, SO BAD.
AND, HONESTLY?
AS FAR AS TEDDY'S CONCERNED?
YOU BEING HERE?
ONLY MADE THINGS WORSE.

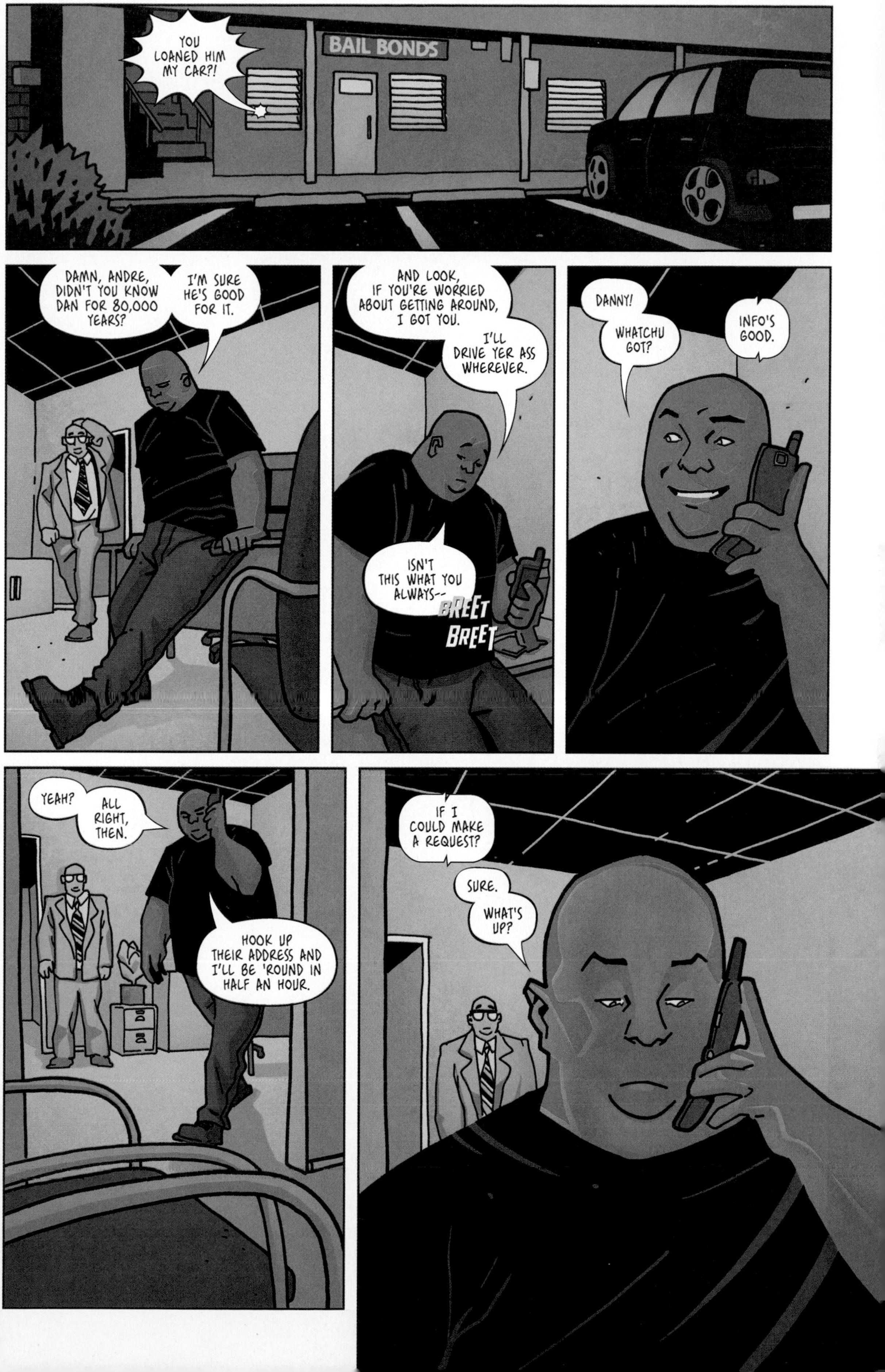
YOU LOANED HIM MY CAR?!
BAIL BONDS
DAMN, ANDRE, DIDN'T YOU KNOW DAN FOR 80,000 YEARS?
I'M SURE HE'S GOOD FOR IT.
AND LOOK, IF YOU'RE WORRIED ABOUT GETTING AROUND, I GOT YOU.
I'LL DRIVE YER ASS WHEREVER.
ISN'T THIS WHAT YOU ALWAYS--
BREET BREET
DANNY!
WHATCHU GOT?
INFO'S GOOD.
YEAH?
ALL RIGHT, THEN.
HOOK UP THEIR ADDRESS AND I'LL BE 'ROUND IN HALF AN HOUR.
IF I COULD MAKE A REQUEST?
SURE.
WHAT'S UP?

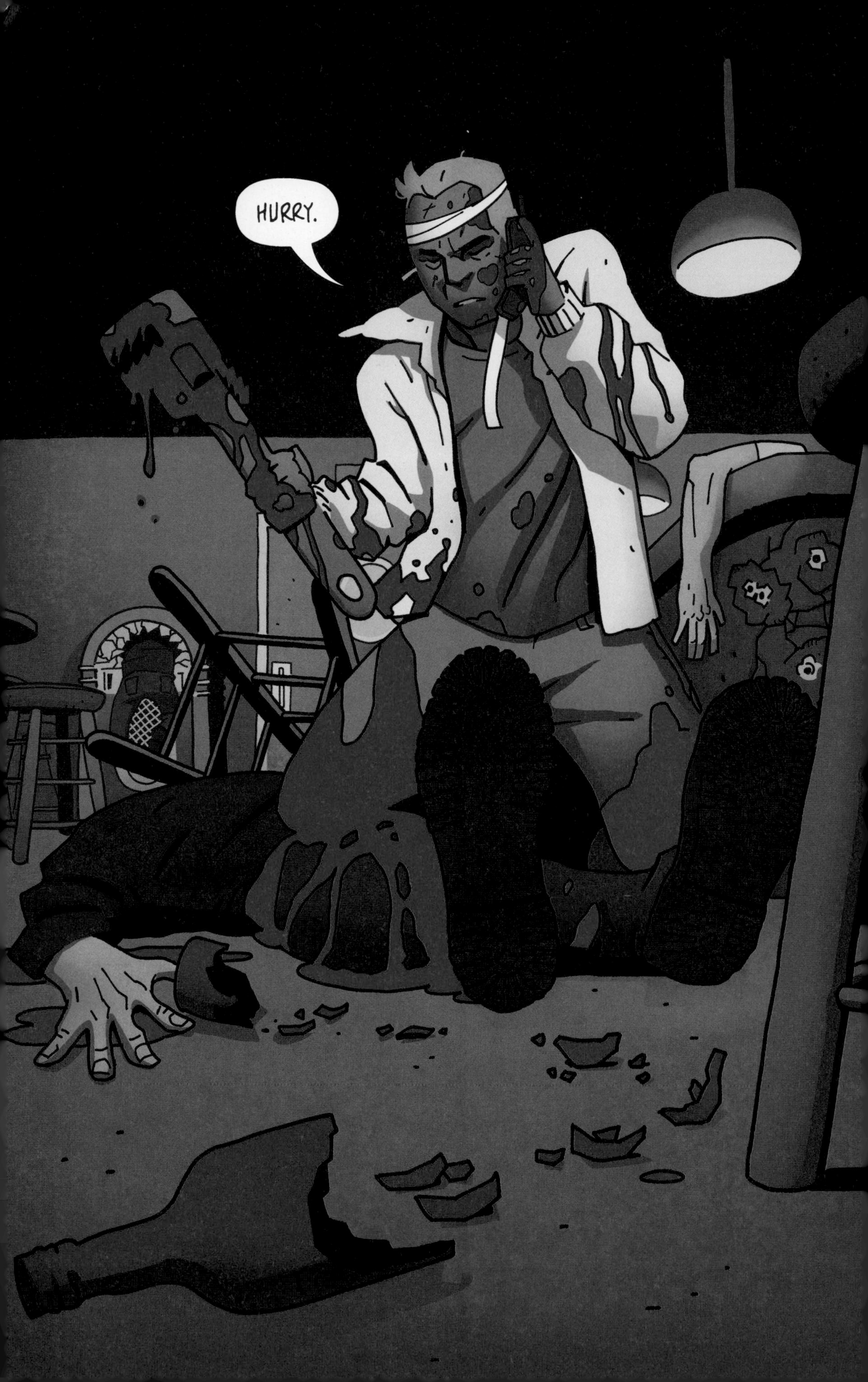
HURRY.

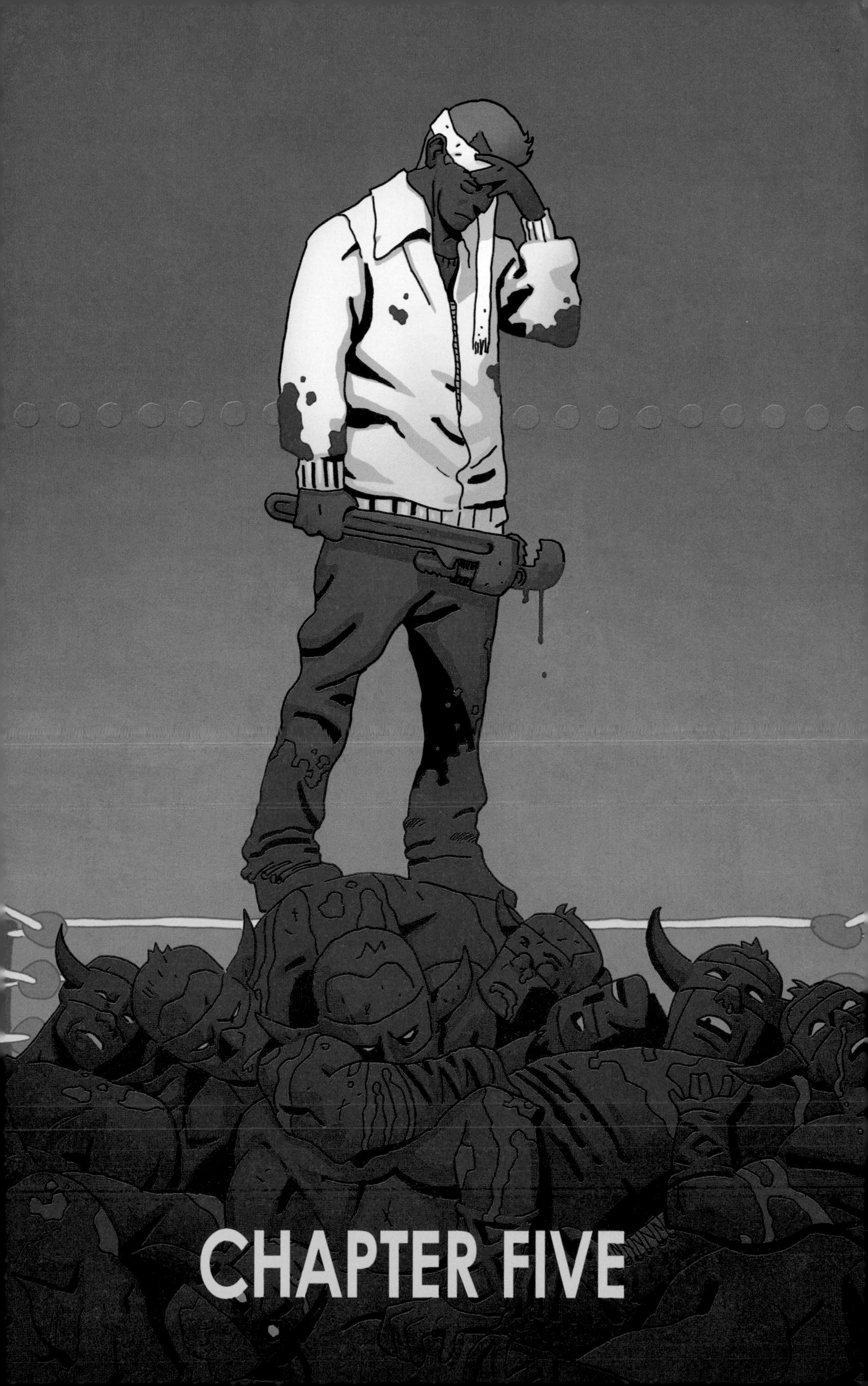
CHAPTER FIVE

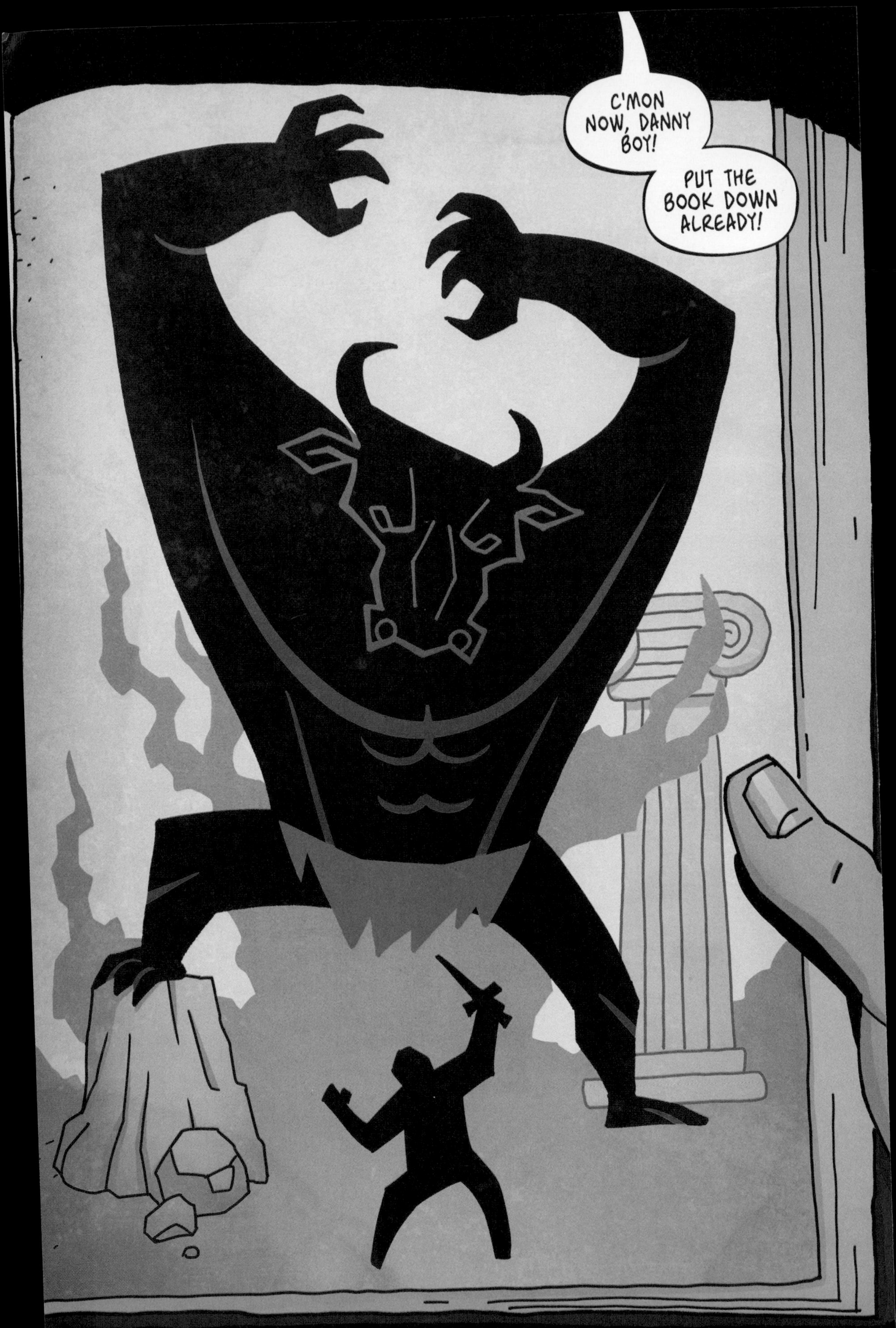
C'MON NOW, DANNY BOY!
PUT THE BOOK DOWN ALREADY!

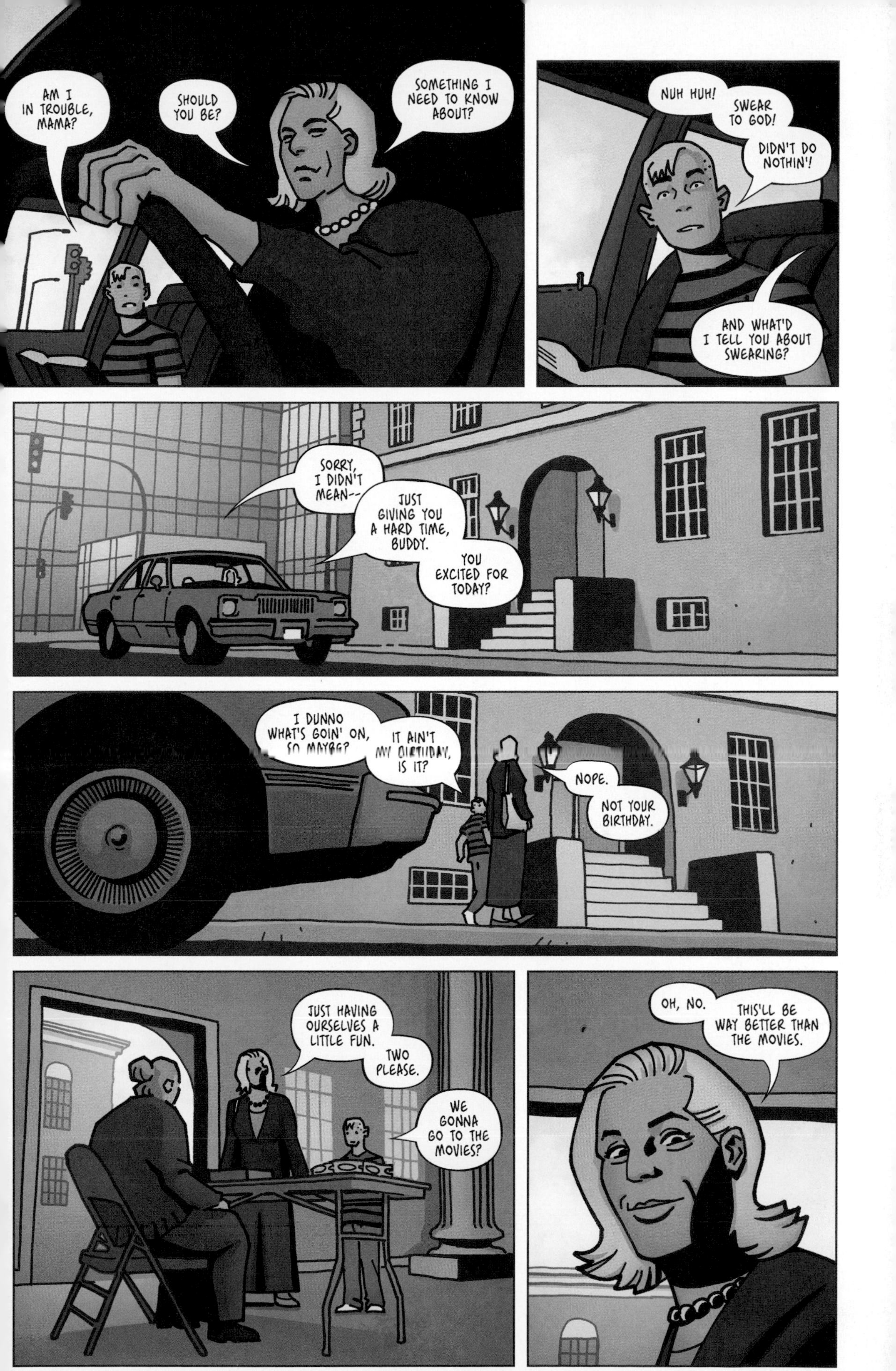
AM I IN TROUBLE, MAMA?
SHOULD YOU BE?
SOMETHING I NEED TO KNOW ABOUT?
NUH HUH!
SWEAR TO GOD!
DIDN'T DO NOTHIN'!
AND WHAT'D I TELL YOU ABOUT SWEARING?
SORRY, I DIDN'T MEAN--
JUST GIVING YOU A HARD TIME, BUDDY.
YOU EXCITED FOR TODAY?
I DUNNO WHAT'S GOIN' ON, SO MAYBE?
IT AIN'T MY BIRTHDAY, IS IT?
NOPE.
NOT YOUR BIRTHDAY.
JUST HAVING OURSELVES A LITTLE FUN.
TWO PLEASE.
WE GONNA GO TO THE MOVIES?
OH, NO.
THIS'LL BE WAY BETTER THAN THE MOVIES.

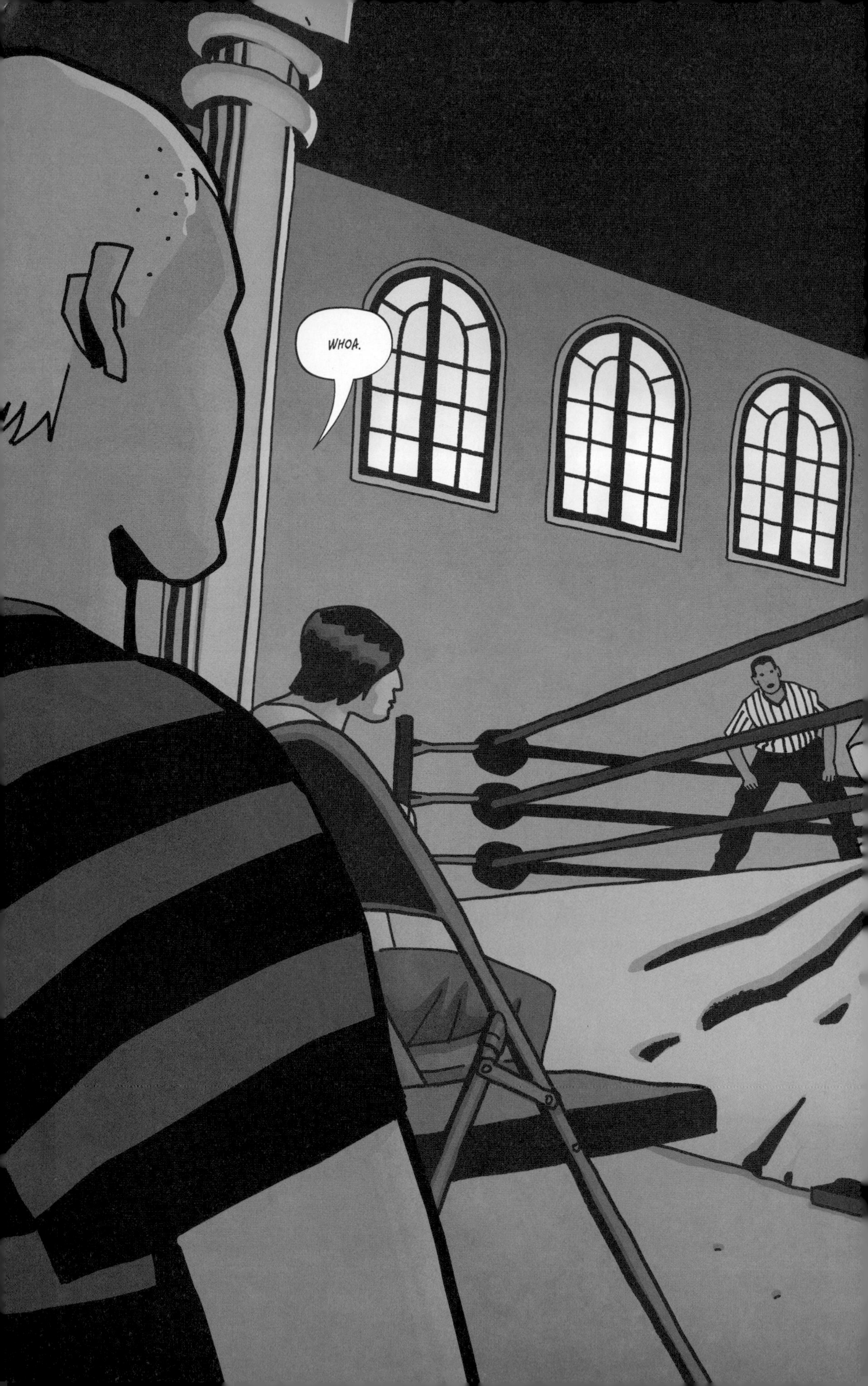
WHOA.

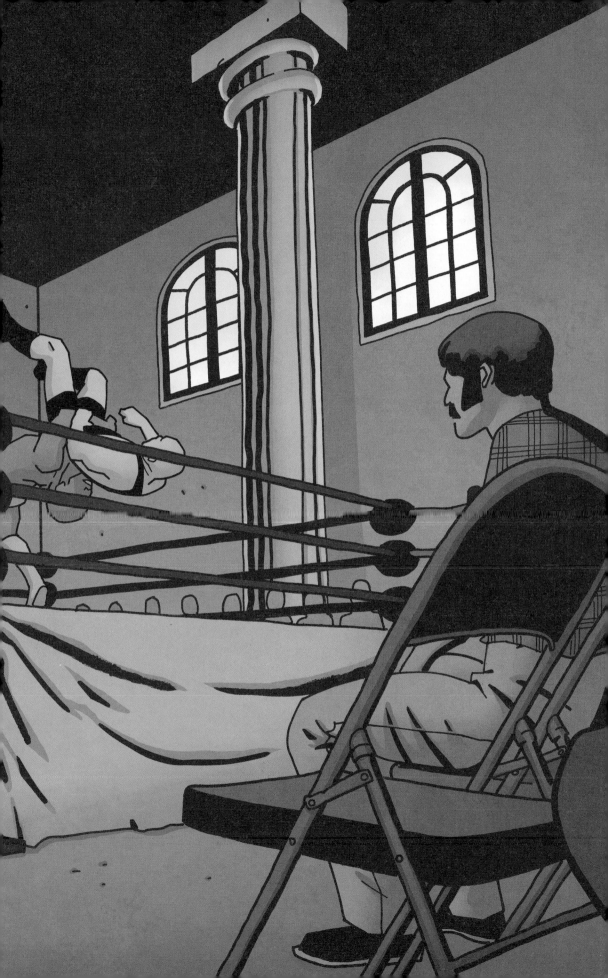

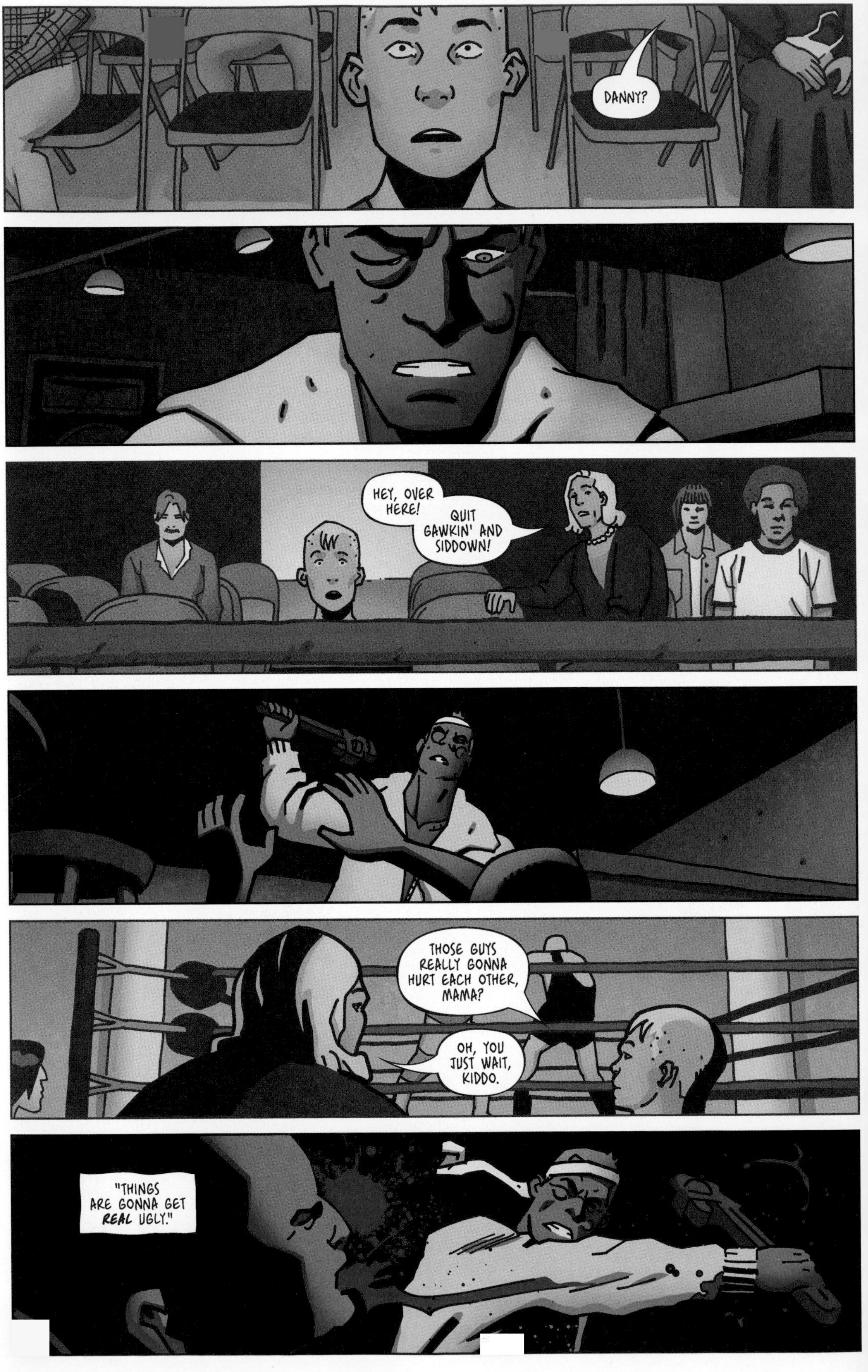
DANNY?
HEY, OVER HERE!
QUIT GAWKIN' AND SIDDOWN!
THOSE GUYS REALLY GONNA HURT EACH OTHER, MAMA?
OH, YOU JUST WAIT, KIDDO.
"THINGS ARE GONNA GET **REAL** UGLY."

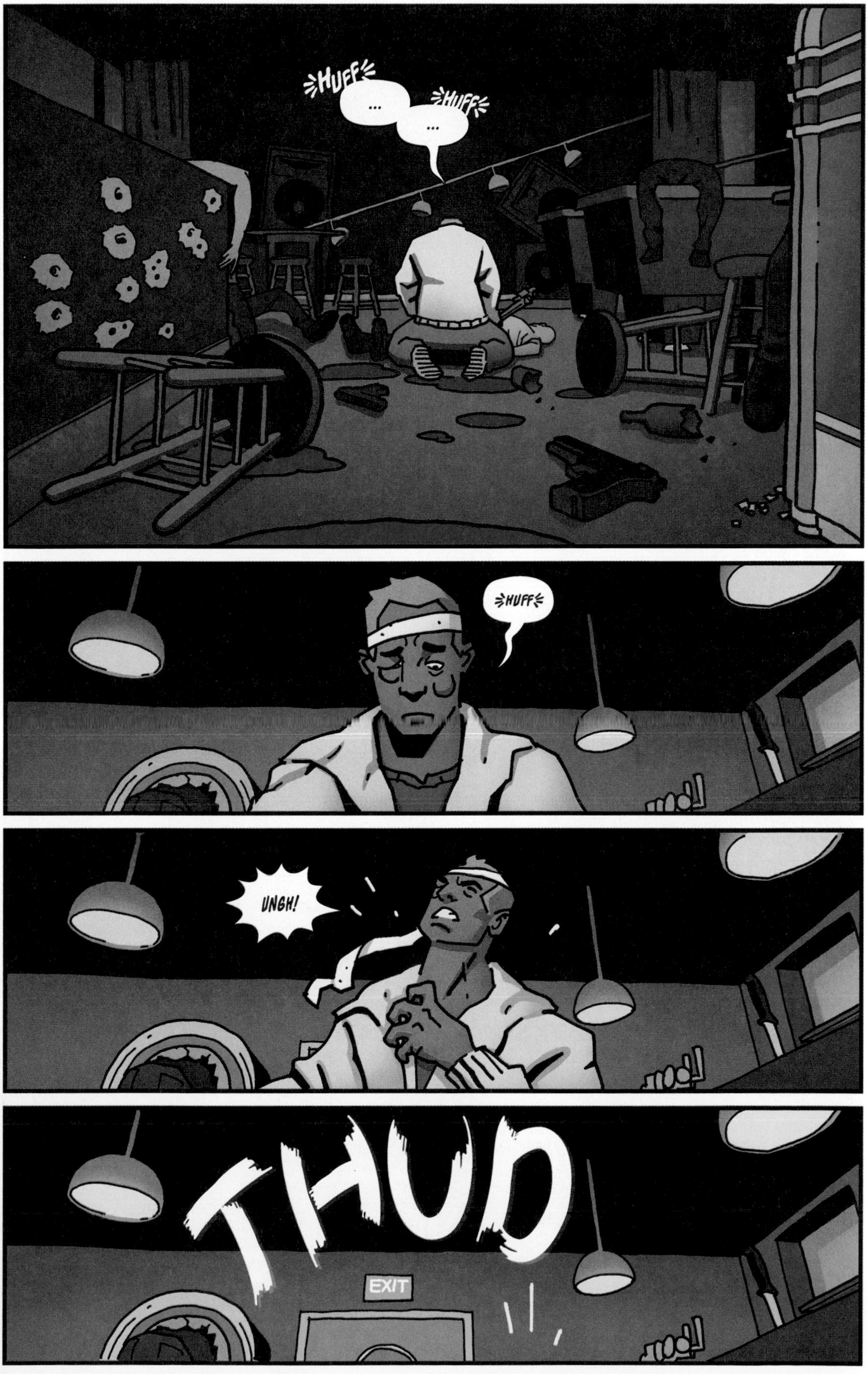
HUFF
...
HUFF
...
HUFF
UNGH!
THUD
EXIT

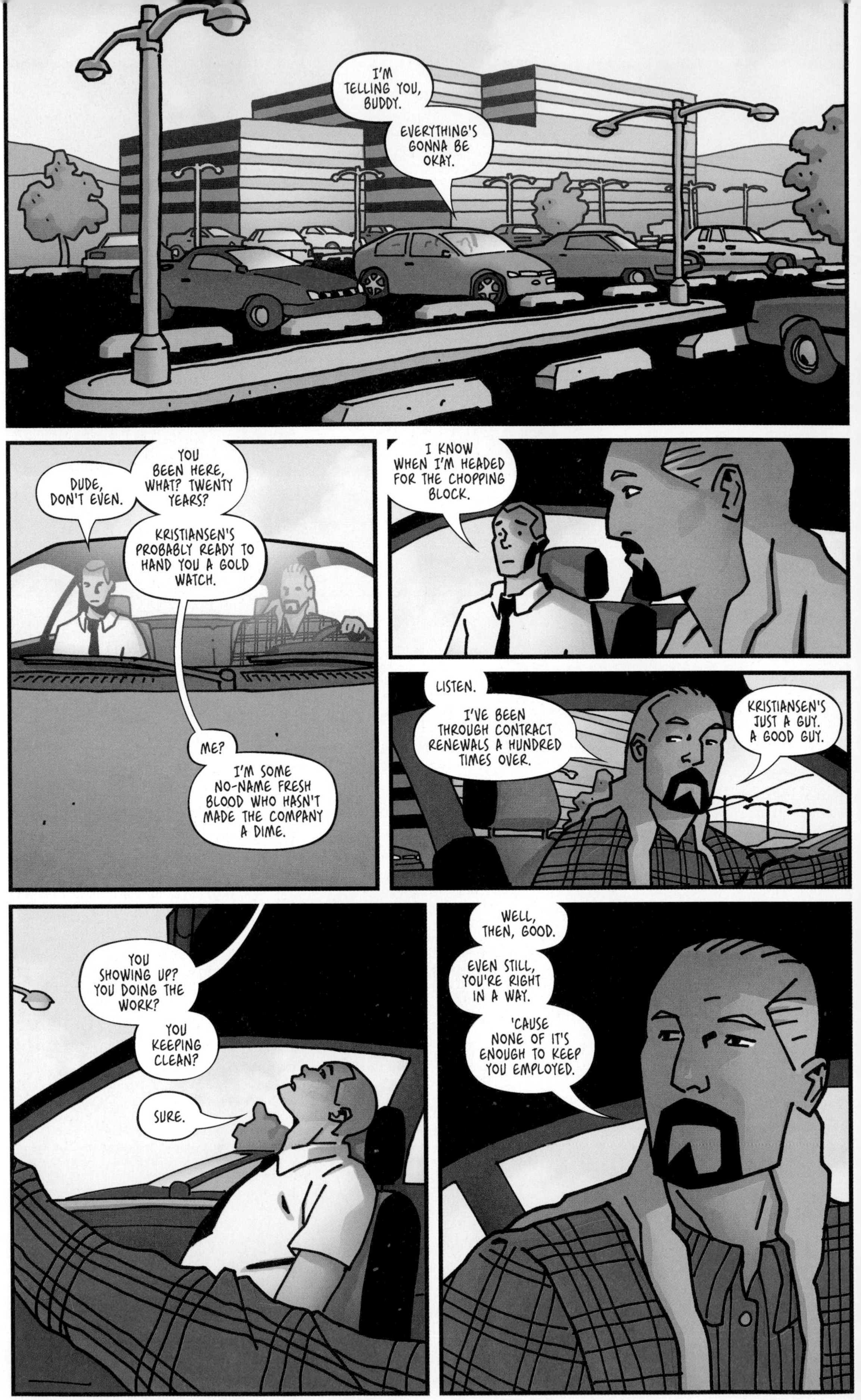
I'M TELLING YOU, BUDDY.
EVERYTHING'S GONNA BE OKAY.
DUDE, DON'T EVEN.
YOU BEEN HERE, WHAT? TWENTY YEARS?
KRISTIANSEN'S PROBABLY READY TO HAND YOU A GOLD WATCH.
ME?
I'M SOME NO-NAME FRESH BLOOD WHO HASN'T MADE THE COMPANY A DIME.
I KNOW WHEN I'M HEADED FOR THE CHOPPING BLOCK.
LISTEN.
I'VE BEEN THROUGH CONTRACT RENEWALS A HUNDRED TIMES OVER.
KRISTIANSEN'S JUST A GUY. A GOOD GUY.
YOU SHOWING UP? YOU DOING THE WORK?
YOU KEEPING CLEAN?
SURE.
WELL, THEN, GOOD.
EVEN STILL, YOU'RE RIGHT IN A WAY.
'CAUSE NONE OF IT'S ENOUGH TO KEEP YOU EMPLOYED.

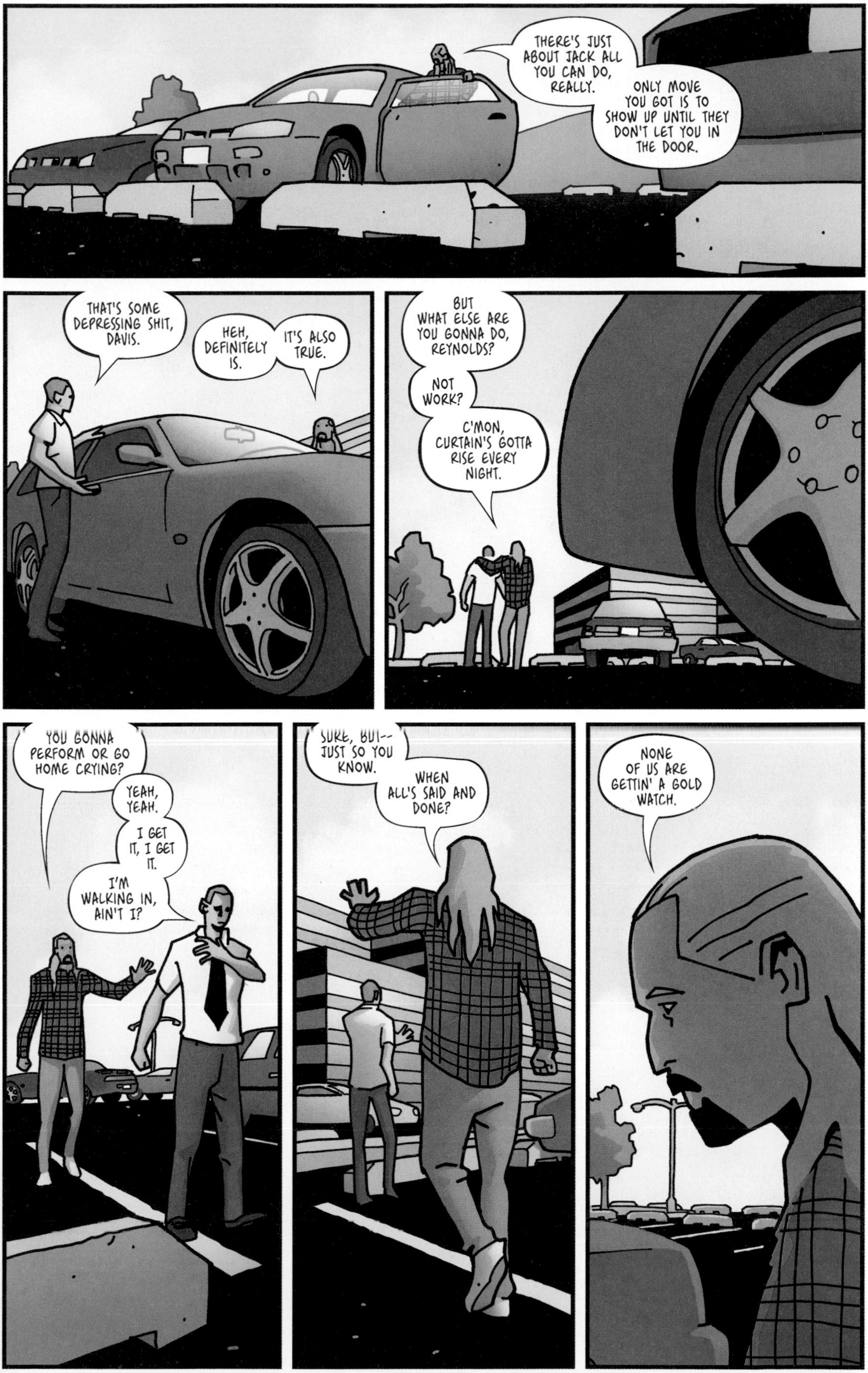
THERE'S JUST ABOUT JACK ALL YOU CAN DO, REALLY.
ONLY MOVE YOU GOT IS TO SHOW UP UNTIL THEY DON'T LET YOU IN THE DOOR.
THAT'S SOME DEPRESSING SHIT, DAVIS.
HEH, DEFINITELY IS.
IT'S ALSO TRUE.
BUT WHAT ELSE ARE YOU GONNA DO, REYNOLDS?
NOT WORK?
C'MON, CURTAIN'S GOTTA RISE EVERY NIGHT.
YOU GONNA PERFORM OR GO HOME CRYING?
YEAH, YEAH.
I GET IT, I GET IT.
I'M WALKING IN, AIN'T I?
SURE, BUT-- JUST SO YOU KNOW.
WHEN ALL'S SAID AND DONE?
NONE OF US ARE GETTIN' A GOLD WATCH.

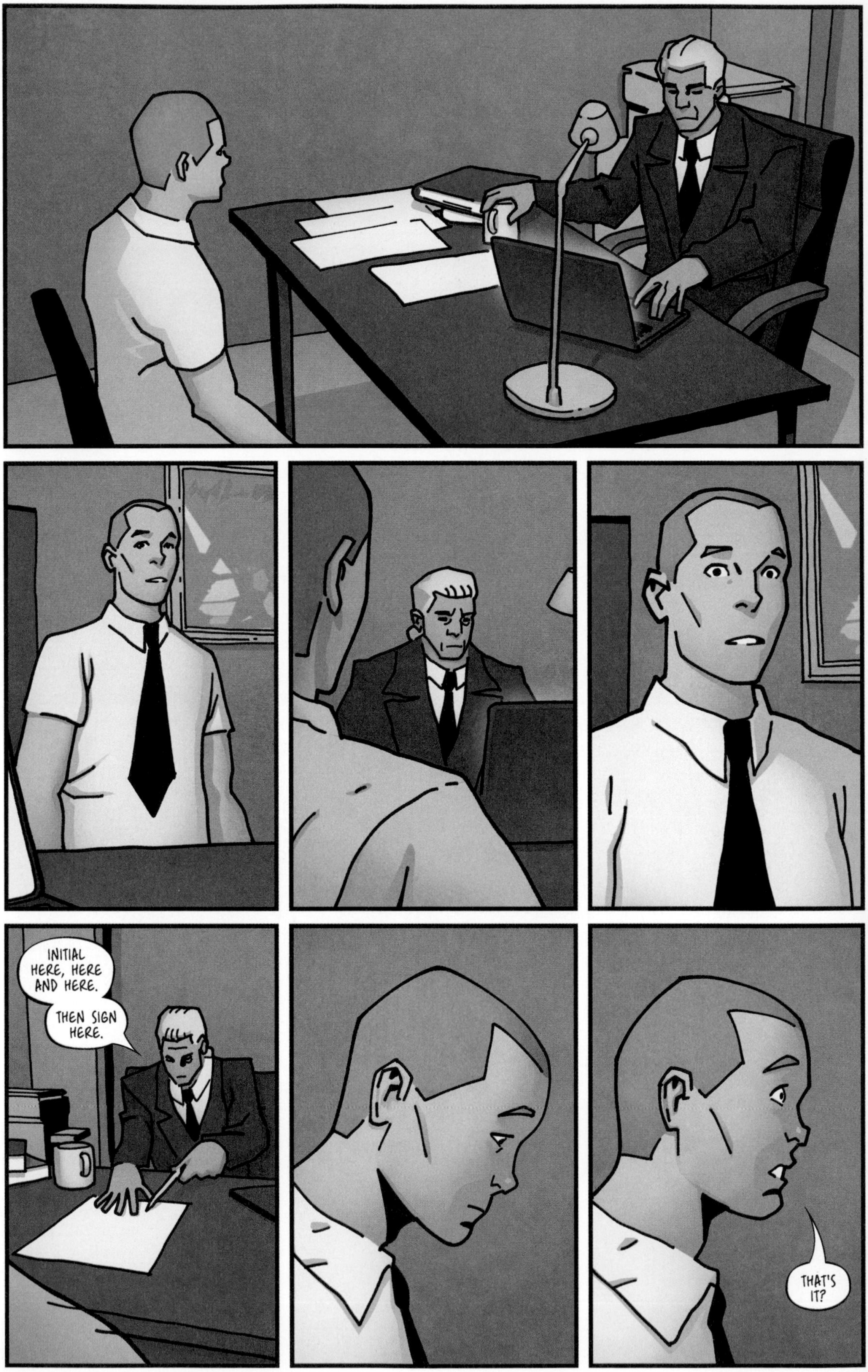
INITIAL HERE, HERE AND HERE.
THEN SIGN HERE.
THAT'S IT?

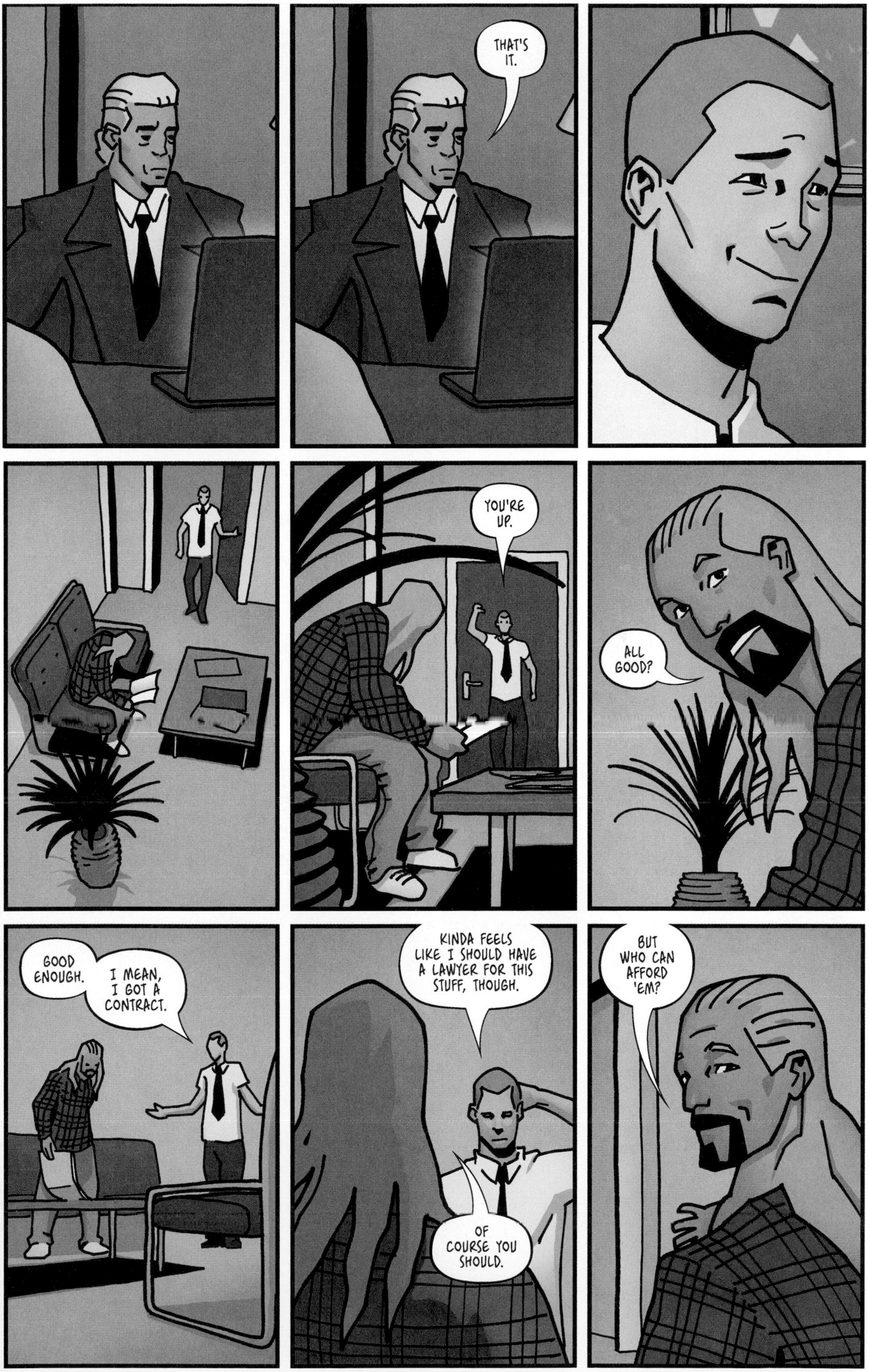
THAT'S IT.
YOU'RE UP.
ALL GOOD?
GOOD ENOUGH.
I MEAN, I GOT A CONTRACT.
KINDA FEELS LIKE I SHOULD HAVE A LAWYER FOR THIS STUFF, THOUGH.
OF COURSE YOU SHOULD.
BUT WHO CAN AFFORD 'EM?

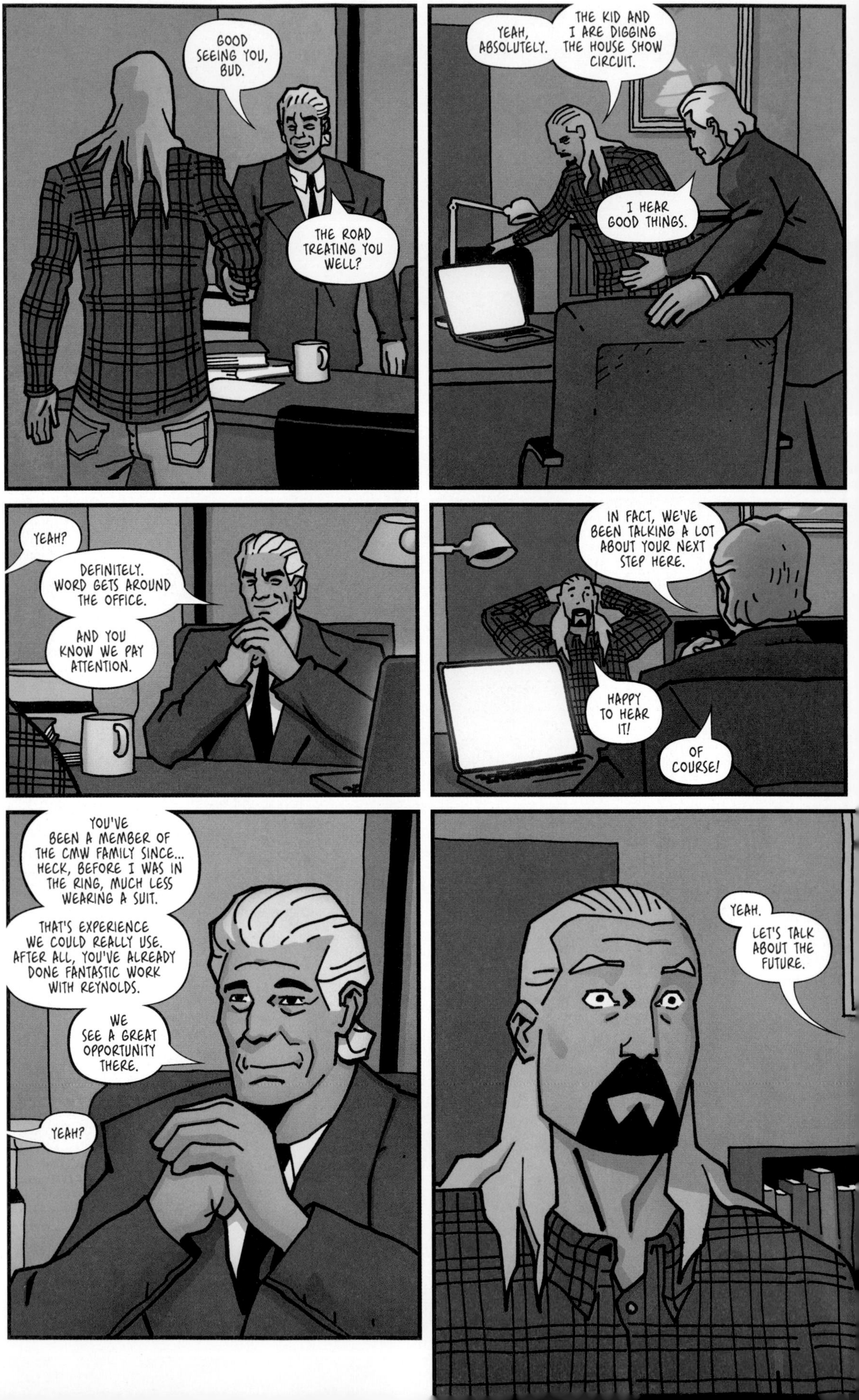

GOOD SEEING YOU, BUD.
THE ROAD TREATING YOU WELL?
YEAH, ABSOLUTELY.
THE KID AND I ARE DIGGING THE HOUSE SHOW CIRCUIT.
I HEAR GOOD THINGS.
YEAH?
DEFINITELY. WORD GETS AROUND THE OFFICE.
AND YOU KNOW WE PAY ATTENTION.
IN FACT, WE'VE BEEN TALKING A LOT ABOUT YOUR NEXT STEP HERE.
HAPPY TO HEAR IT!
OF COURSE!
YOU'VE BEEN A MEMBER OF THE CMW FAMILY SINCE... HECK, BEFORE I WAS IN THE RING, MUCH LESS WEARING A SUIT.
THAT'S EXPERIENCE WE COULD REALLY USE. AFTER ALL, YOU'VE ALREADY DONE FANTASTIC WORK WITH REYNOLDS.
WE SEE A GREAT OPPORTUNITY THERE.
YEAH?
YEAH.
LET'S TALK ABOUT THE FUTURE.

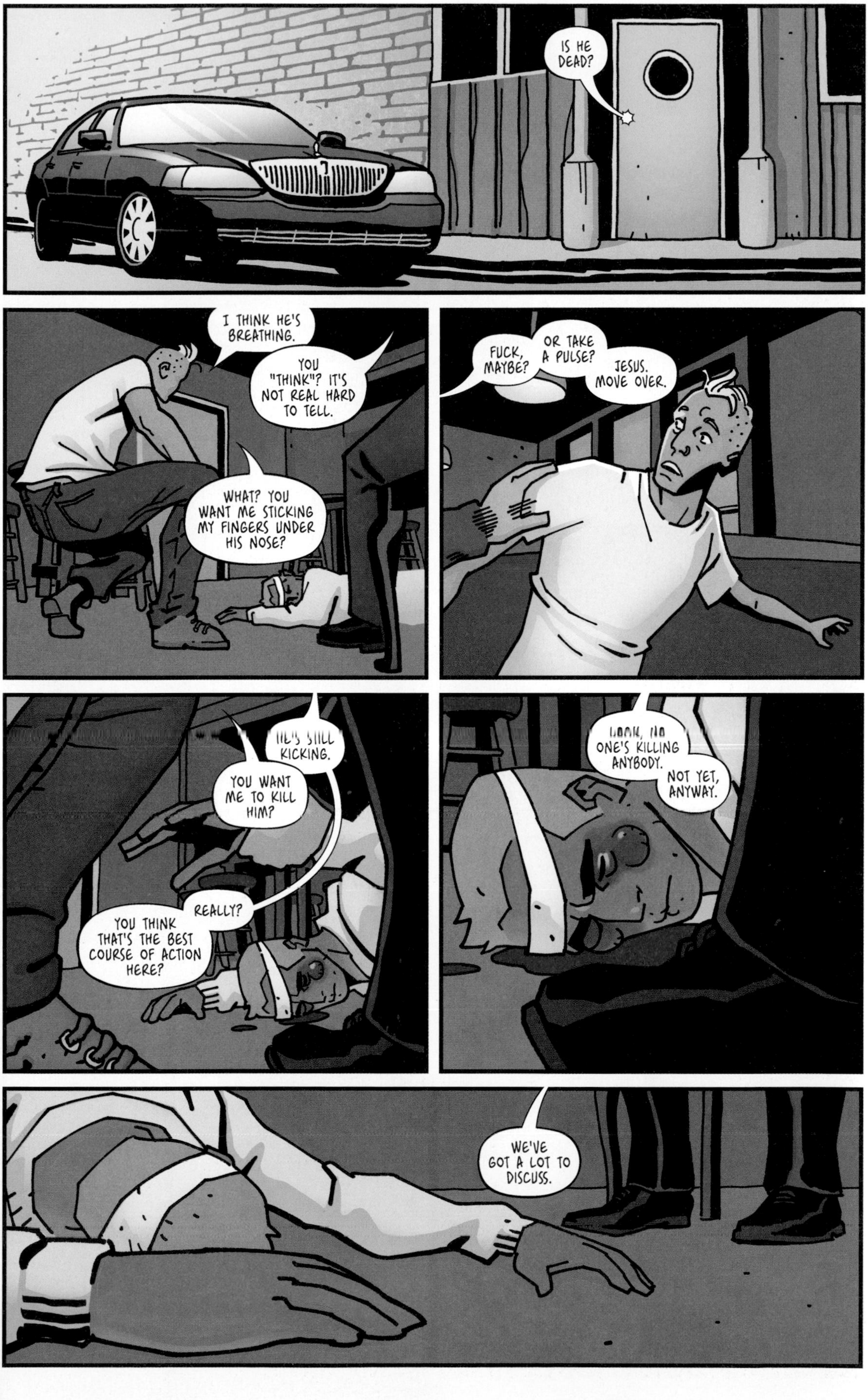
IS HE DEAD?
I THINK HE'S BREATHING.
YOU "THINK"? IT'S NOT REAL HARD TO TELL.
WHAT? YOU WANT ME STICKING MY FINGERS UNDER HIS NOSE?
FUCK, MAYBE?
OR TAKE A PULSE?
JESUS. MOVE OVER.
KICKING.
YOU WANT ME TO KILL HIM?
REALLY?
YOU THINK THAT'S THE BEST COURSE OF ACTION HERE?
ONE'S KILLING ANYBODY.
NOT YET, ANYWAY.
WE'VE GOT A LOT TO DISCUSS.

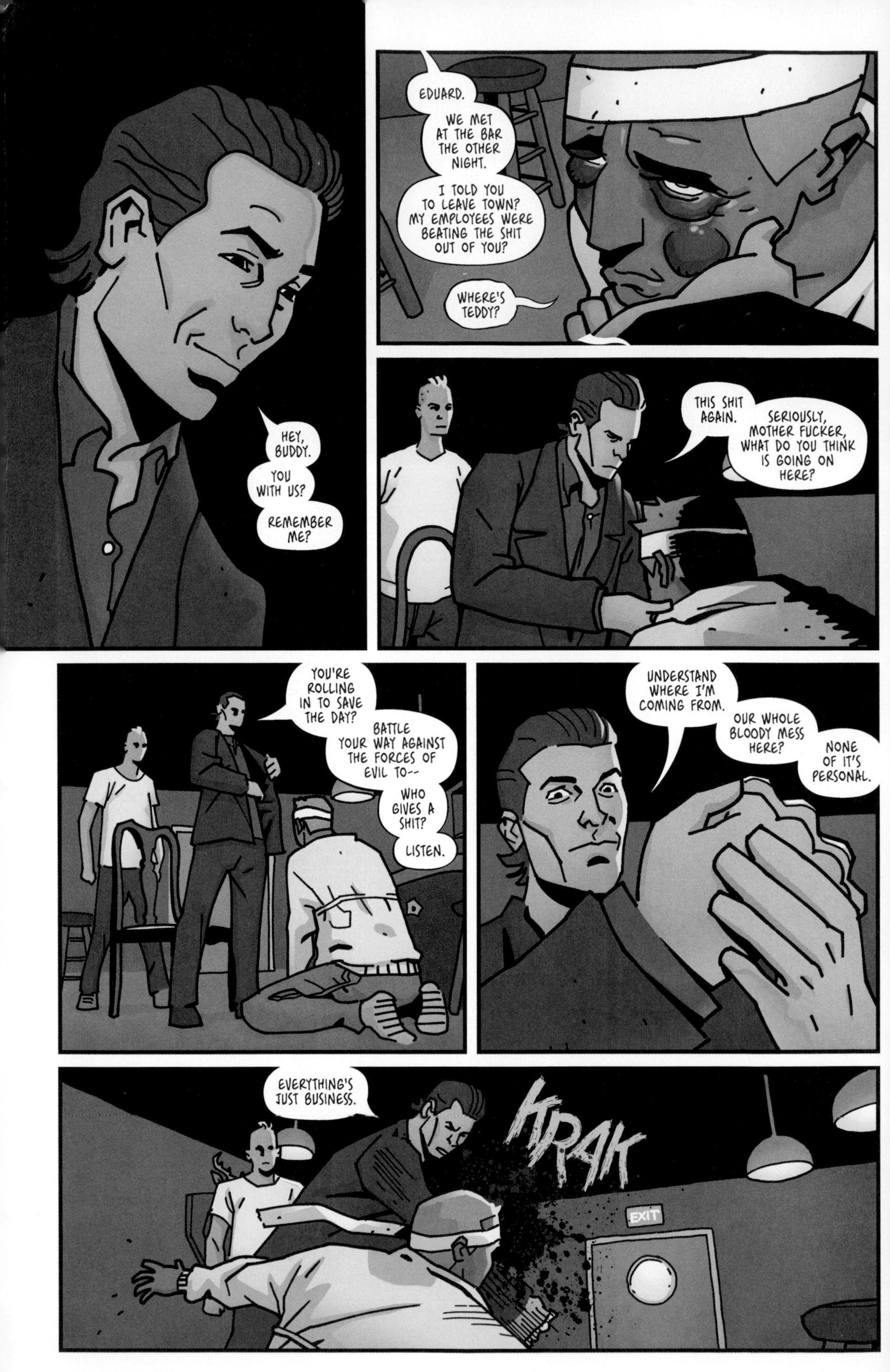
HEY, BUDDY.
YOU WITH US?
REMEMBER ME?
EDUARD.
WE MET AT THE BAR THE OTHER NIGHT.
I TOLD YOU TO LEAVE TOWN? MY EMPLOYEES WERE BEATING THE SHIT OUT OF YOU?
WHERE'S TEDDY?
THIS SHIT AGAIN.
SERIOUSLY, MOTHER FUCKER, WHAT DO YOU THINK IS GOING ON HERE?
YOU'RE ROLLING IN TO SAVE THE DAY?
BATTLE YOUR WAY AGAINST THE FORCES OF EVIL TO--
WHO GIVES A SHIT?
LISTEN.
UNDERSTAND WHERE I'M COMING FROM.
OUR WHOLE BLOODY MESS HERE?
NONE OF IT'S PERSONAL.
EVERYTHING'S JUST BUSINESS.
KRAK
EXIT

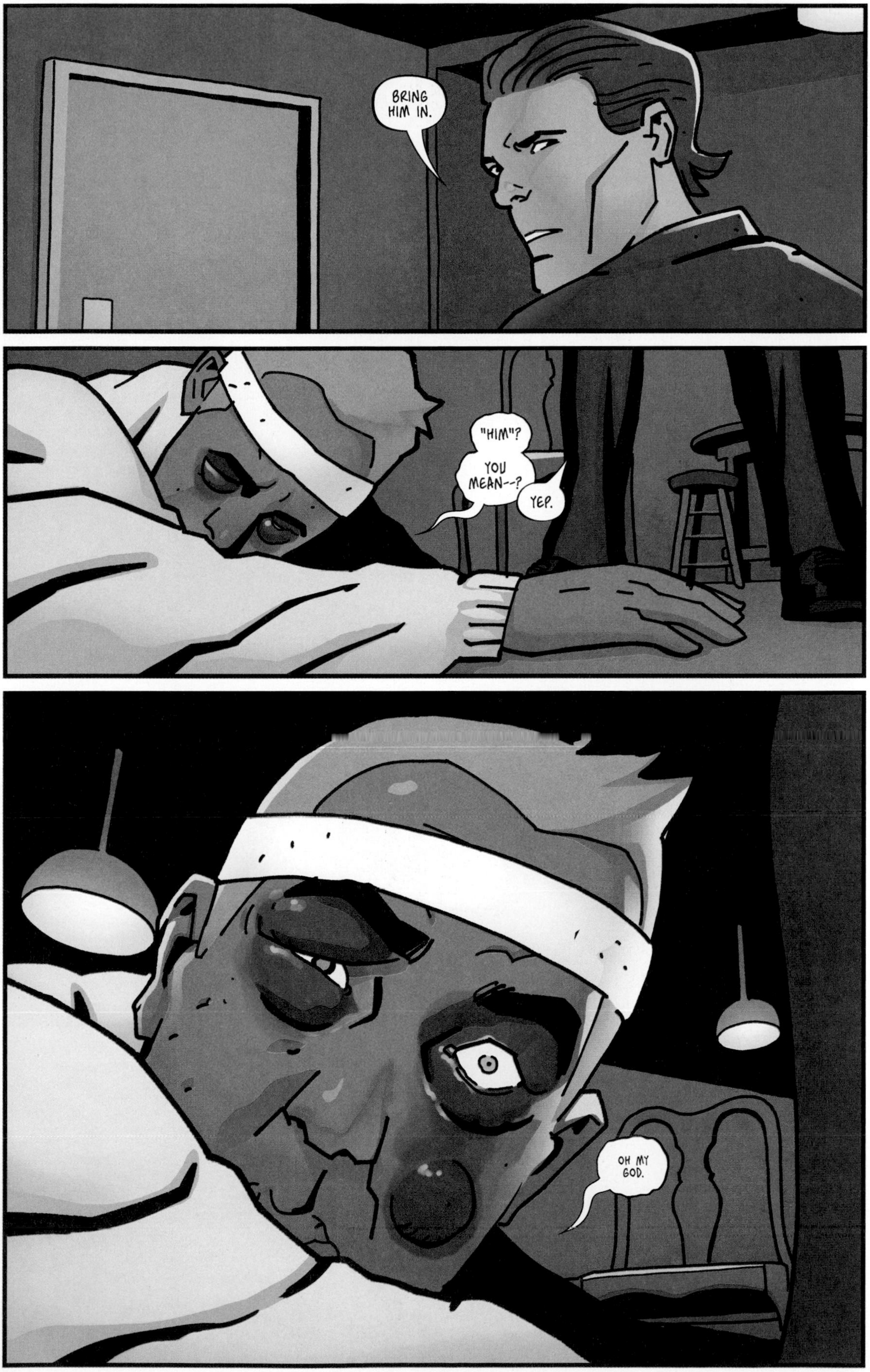
BRING HIM IN.
"HIM"?
YOU MEAN--?
YEP.
OH MY GOD.

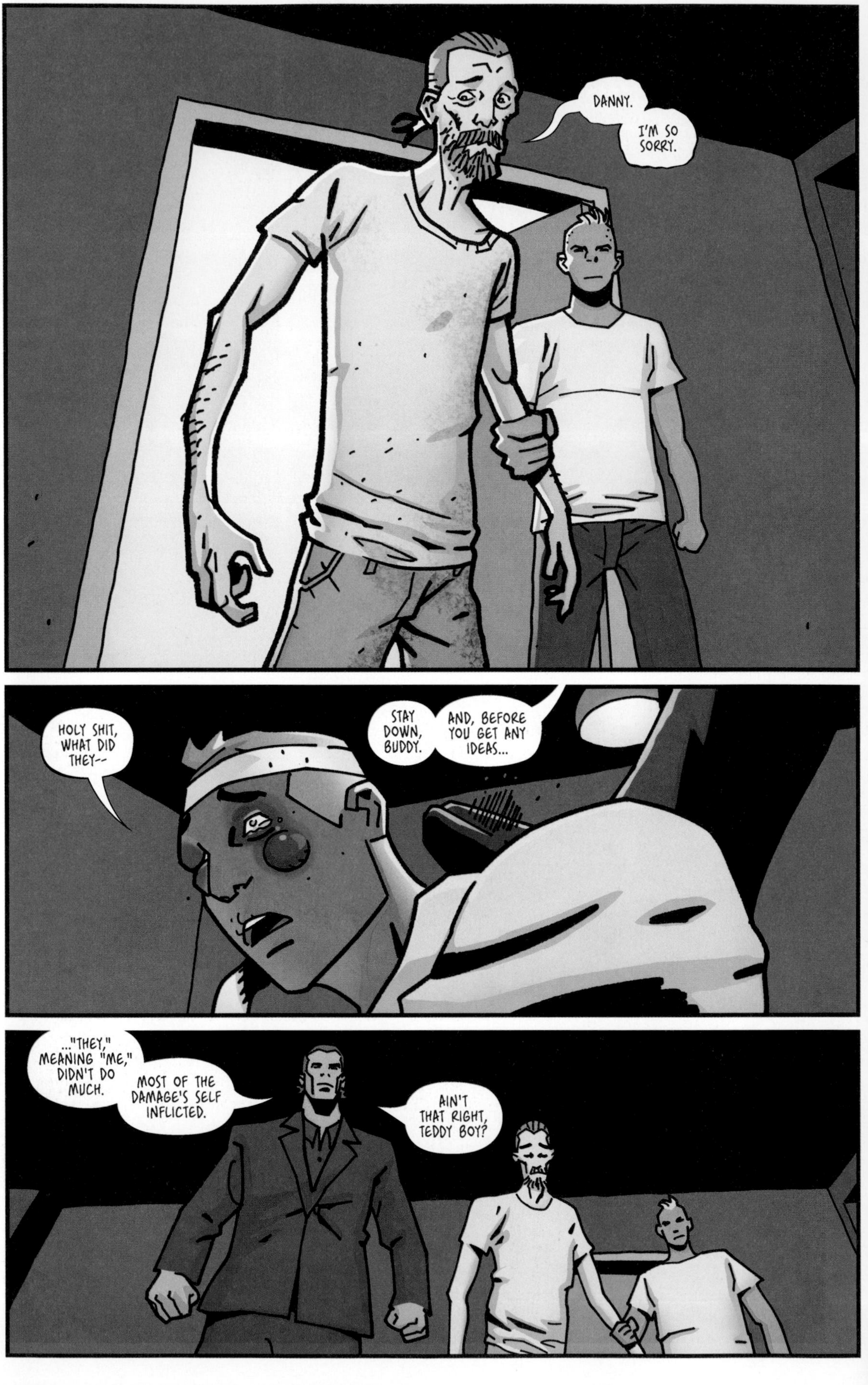
DANNY.
I'M SO SORRY.
HOLY SHIT, WHAT DID THEY--
STAY DOWN, BUDDY.
AND, BEFORE YOU GET ANY IDEAS...
..."THEY," MEANING "ME," DIDN'T DO MUCH.
MOST OF THE DAMAGE'S SELF INFLICTED.
AIN'T THAT RIGHT, TEDDY BOY?

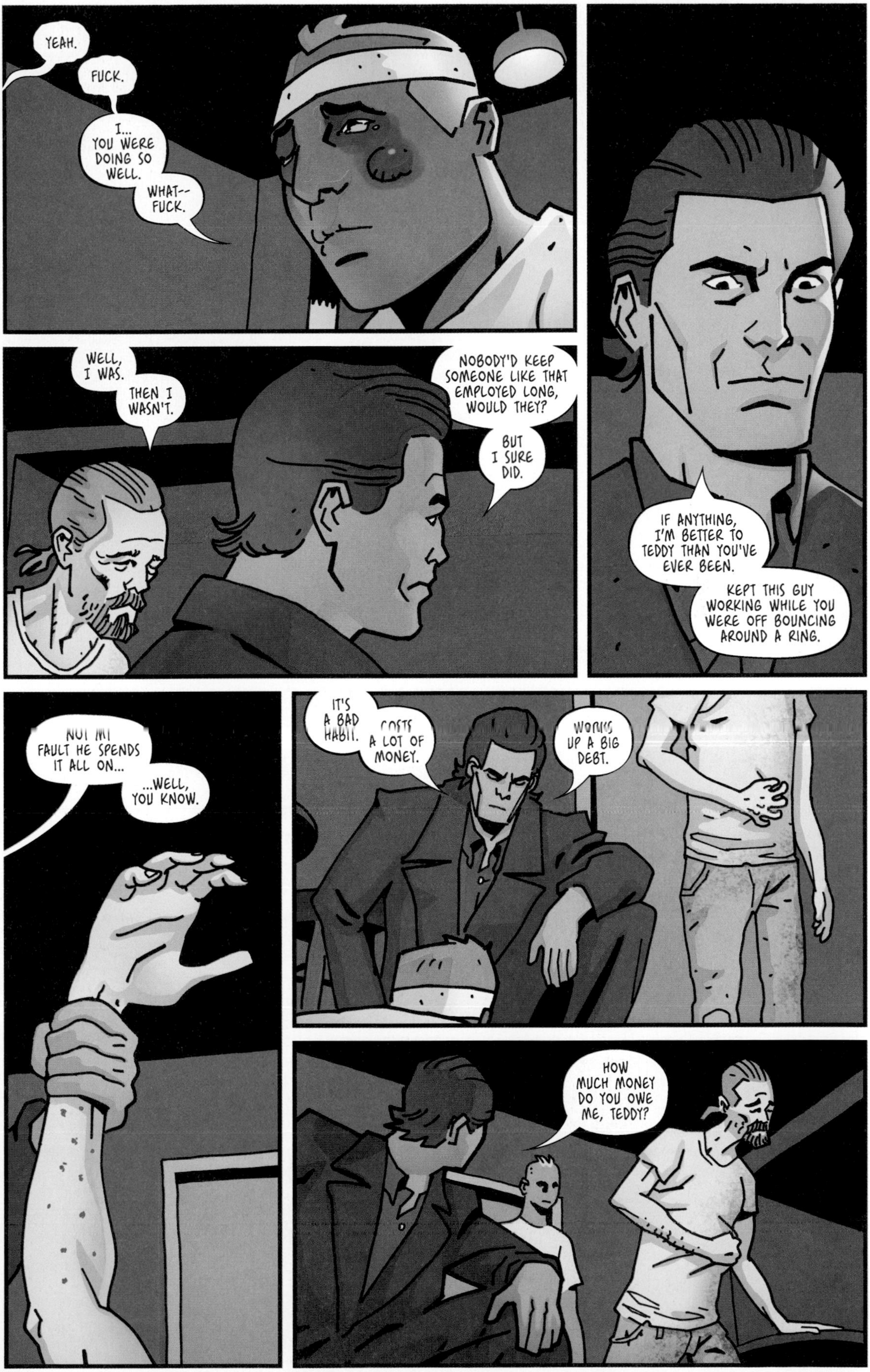
YEAH.
FUCK.
I... YOU WERE DOING SO WELL.
WHAT-- FUCK.
WELL, I WAS.
THEN I WASN'T.
NOBODY'D KEEP SOMEONE LIKE THAT EMPLOYED LONG, WOULD THEY?
BUT I SURE DID.
IF ANYTHING, I'M BETTER TO TEDDY THAN YOU'VE EVER BEEN.
KEPT THIS GUY WORKING WHILE YOU WERE OFF BOUNCING AROUND A RING.
NOT MY FAULT HE SPENDS IT ALL ON...
...WELL, YOU KNOW.
IT'S A BAD HABIT.
COSTS A LOT OF MONEY.
WORKS UP A BIG DEBT.
HOW MUCH MONEY DO YOU OWE ME, TEDDY?

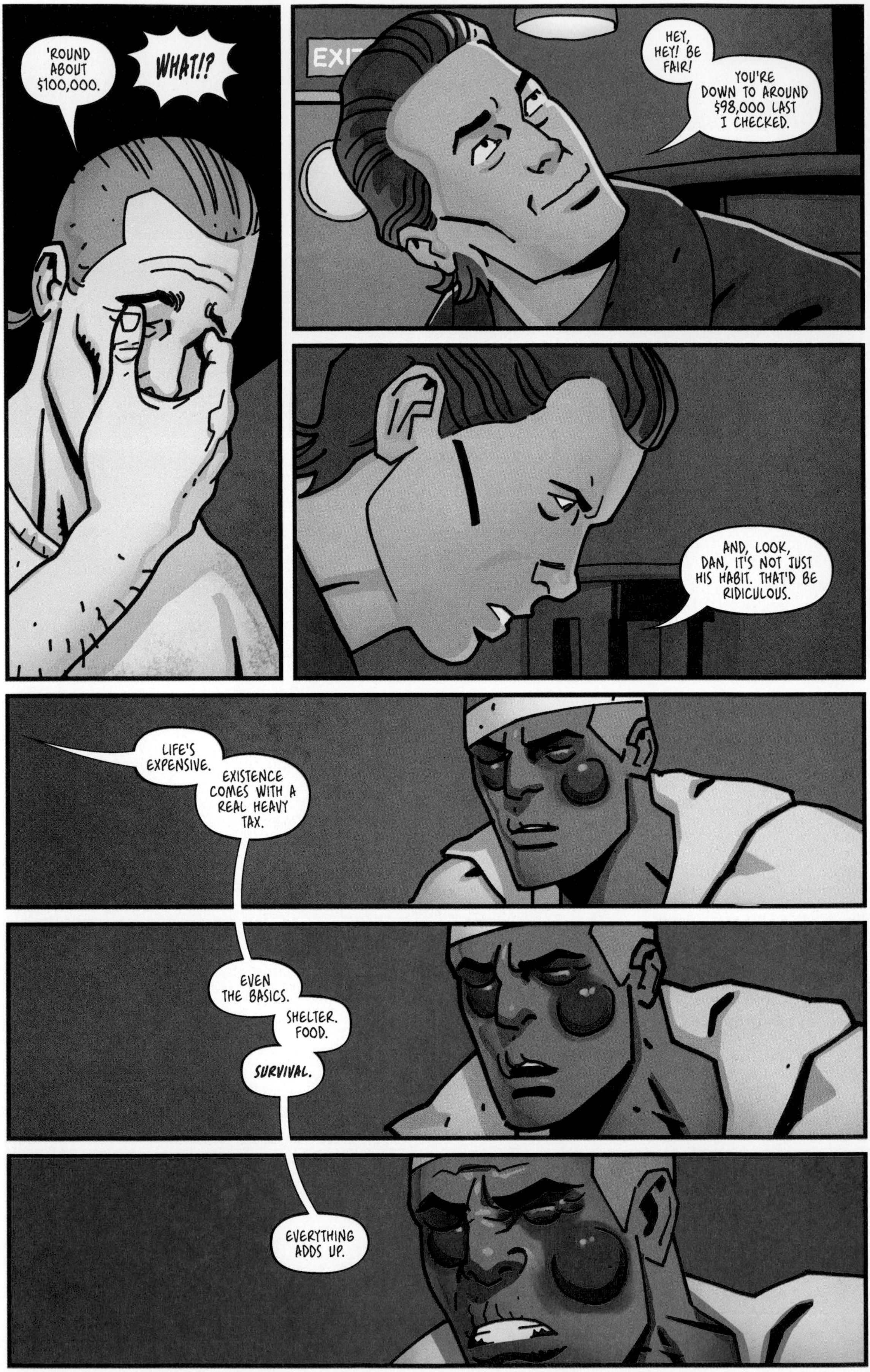
'ROUND ABOUT $100,000.
WHAT!?
HEY, HEY! BE FAIR!
YOU'RE DOWN TO AROUND $98,000 LAST I CHECKED.
AND, LOOK, DAN, IT'S NOT JUST HIS HABIT. THAT'D BE RIDICULOUS.
LIFE'S EXPENSIVE.
EXISTENCE COMES WITH A REAL HEAVY TAX.
EVEN THE BASICS.
SHELTER. FOOD.
SURVIVAL.
EVERYTHING ADDS UP.

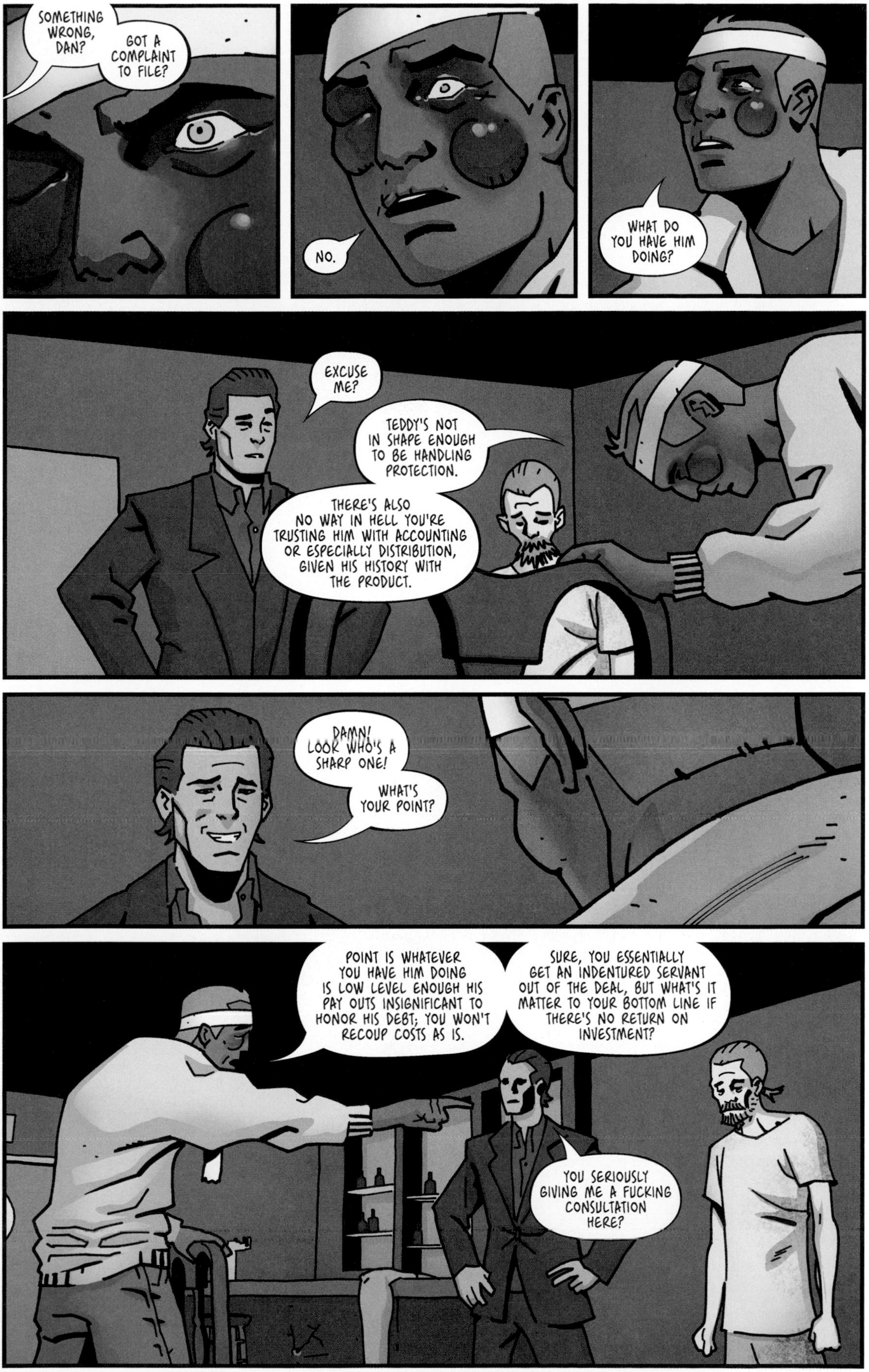
SOMETHING WRONG, DAN?
GOT A COMPLAINT TO FILE?
NO.
WHAT DO YOU HAVE HIM DOING?
EXCUSE ME?
TEDDY'S NOT IN SHAPE ENOUGH TO BE HANDLING PROTECTION.
THERE'S ALSO NO WAY IN HELL YOU'RE TRUSTING HIM WITH ACCOUNTING OR ESPECIALLY DISTRIBUTION, GIVEN HIS HISTORY WITH THE PRODUCT.
DAMN! LOOK WHO'S A SHARP ONE!
WHAT'S YOUR POINT?
POINT IS WHATEVER YOU HAVE HIM DOING IS LOW LEVEL ENOUGH HIS PAY OUTS INSIGNIFICANT TO HONOR HIS DEBT; YOU WON'T RECOUP COSTS AS IS.
SURE, YOU ESSENTIALLY GET AN INDENTURED SERVANT OUT OF THE DEAL, BUT WHAT'S IT MATTER TO YOUR BOTTOM LINE IF THERE'S NO RETURN ON INVESTMENT?
YOU SERIOUSLY GIVING ME A FUCKING CONSULTATION HERE?

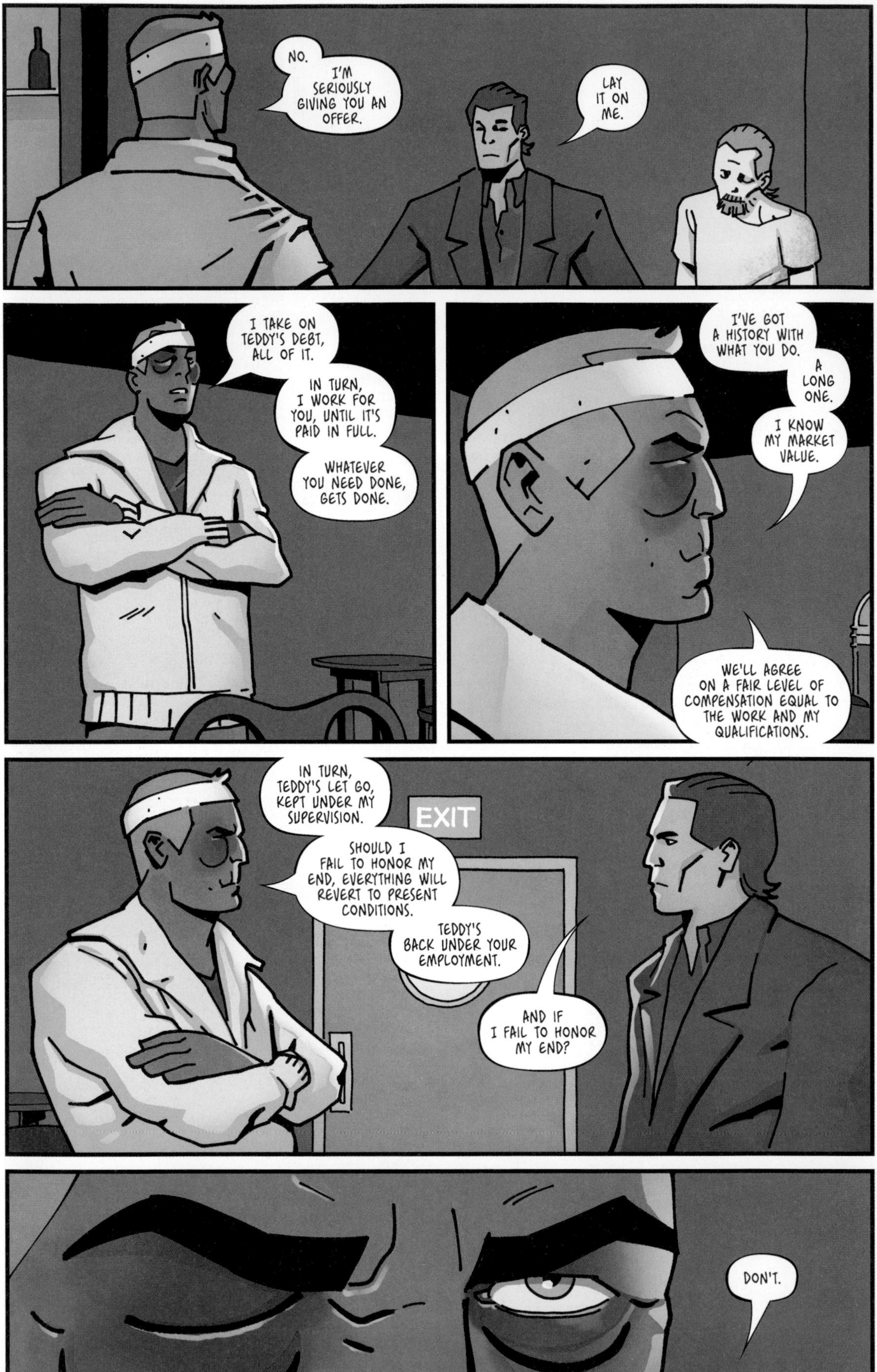
NO.
I'M SERIOUSLY GIVING YOU AN OFFER.
LAY IT ON ME.
I TAKE ON TEDDY'S DEBT, ALL OF IT.
IN TURN, I WORK FOR YOU, UNTIL IT'S PAID IN FULL.
WHATEVER YOU NEED DONE, GETS DONE.
I'VE GOT A HISTORY WITH WHAT YOU DO.
A LONG ONE.
I KNOW MY MARKET VALUE.
WE'LL AGREE ON A FAIR LEVEL OF COMPENSATION EQUAL TO THE WORK AND MY QUALIFICATIONS.
IN TURN, TEDDY'S LET GO, KEPT UNDER MY SUPERVISION.
EXIT
SHOULD I FAIL TO HONOR MY END, EVERYTHING WILL REVERT TO PRESENT CONDITIONS.
TEDDY'S BACK UNDER YOUR EMPLOYMENT.
AND IF I FAIL TO HONOR MY END?
DON'T.

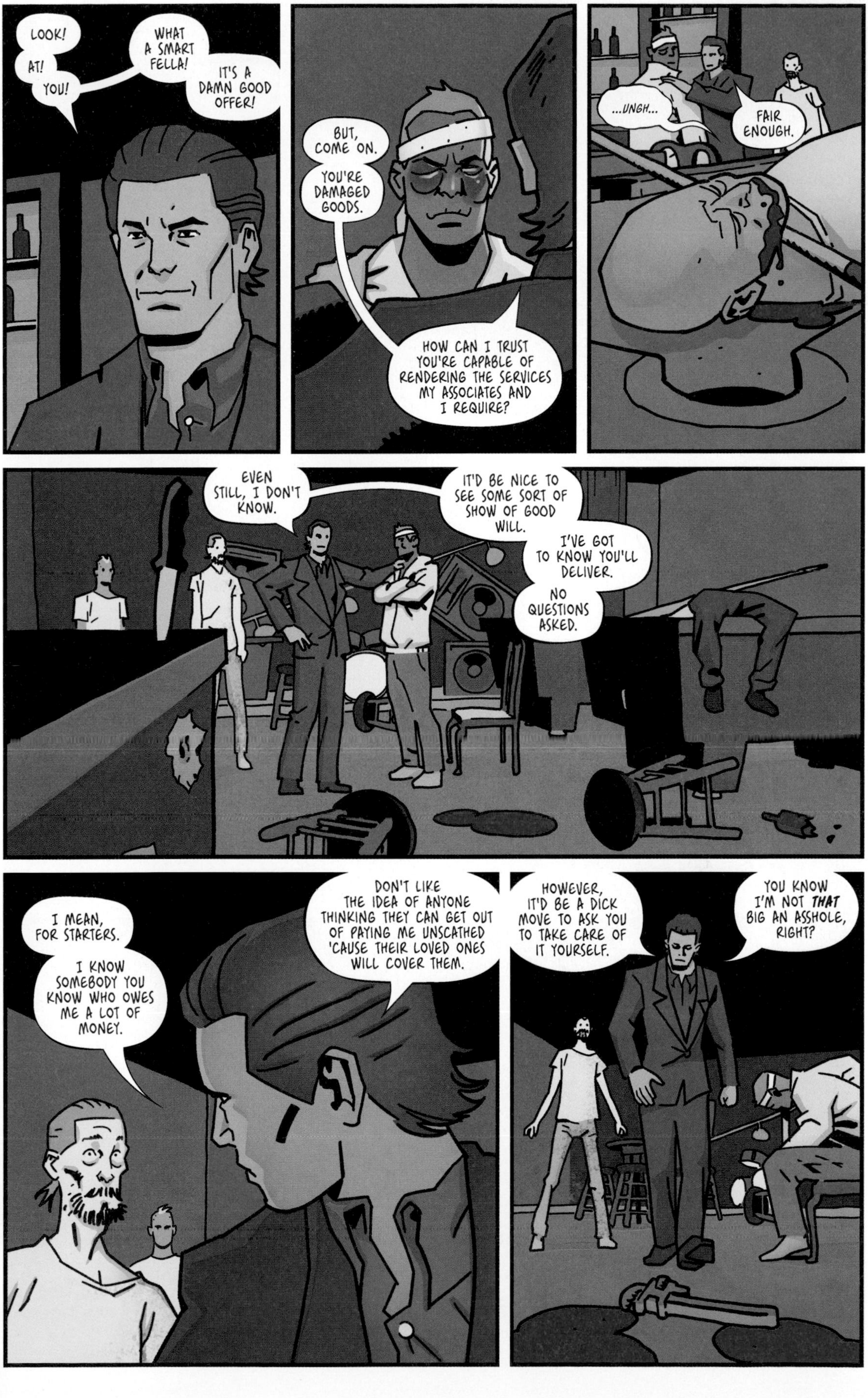
LOOK!
AT!
YOU!
WHAT A SMART FELLA!
IT'S A DAMN GOOD OFFER!
BUT, COME ON.
YOU'RE DAMAGED GOODS.
HOW CAN I TRUST YOU'RE CAPABLE OF RENDERING THE SERVICES MY ASSOCIATES AND I REQUIRE?
...UNGH...
FAIR ENOUGH.
EVEN STILL, I DON'T KNOW.
IT'D BE NICE TO SEE SOME SORT OF SHOW OF GOOD WILL.
I'VE GOT TO KNOW YOU'LL DELIVER.
NO QUESTIONS ASKED.
I MEAN, FOR STARTERS.
I KNOW SOMEBODY YOU KNOW WHO OWES ME A LOT OF MONEY.
DON'T LIKE THE IDEA OF ANYONE THINKING THEY CAN GET OUT OF PAYING ME UNSCATHED 'CAUSE THEIR LOVED ONES WILL COVER THEM.
HOWEVER, IT'D BE A DICK MOVE TO ASK YOU TO TAKE CARE OF IT YOURSELF.
YOU KNOW I'M NOT *THAT* BIG AN ASSHOLE, RIGHT?

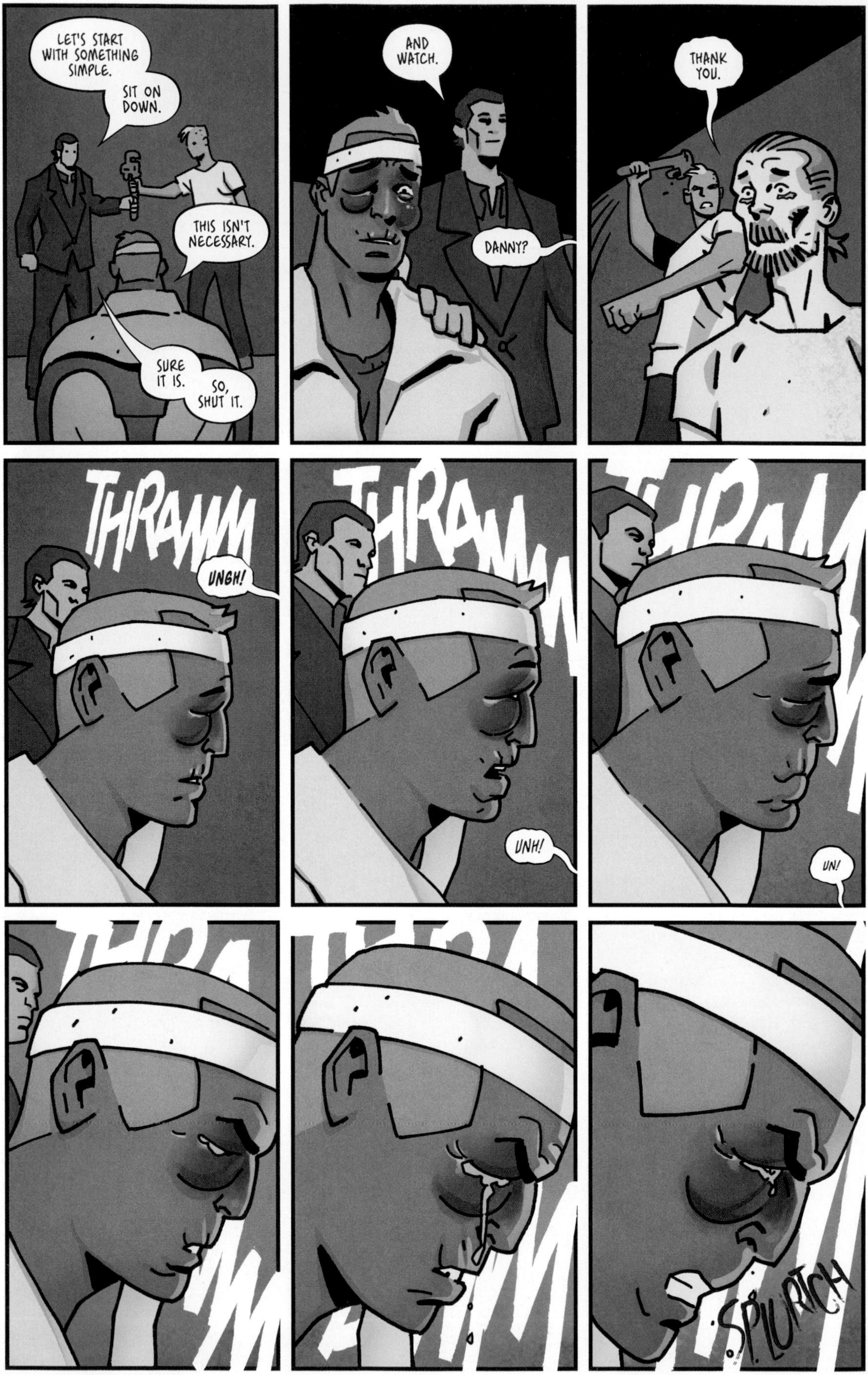
LET'S START WITH SOMETHING SIMPLE.
SIT ON DOWN.
THIS ISN'T NECESSARY.
SURE IT IS.
SO, SHUT IT.
AND WATCH.
DANNY?
THANK YOU.
THRAMM
UNGH!
THRAMM
UNH!
THRAMM
UN!
SPLURTCH

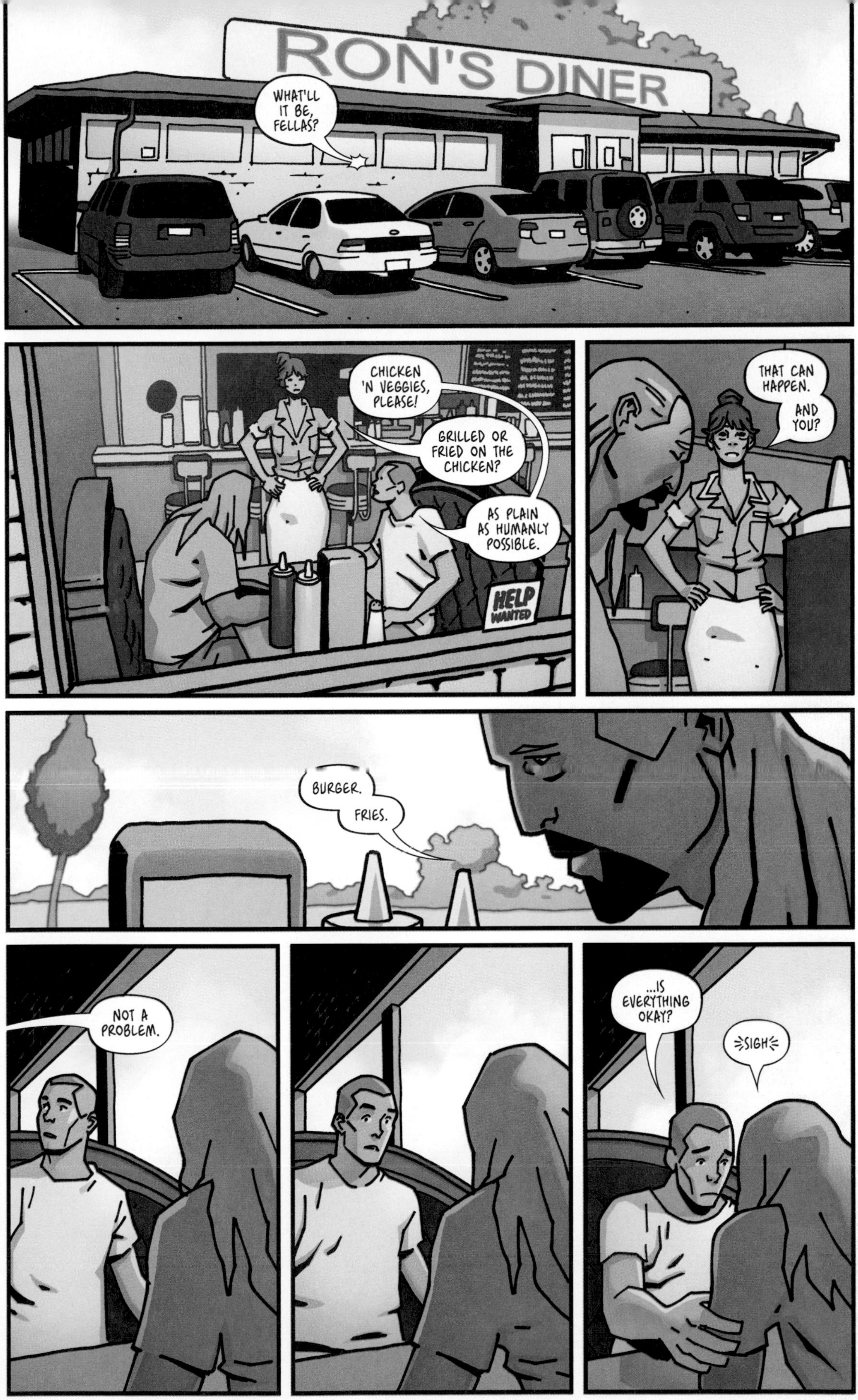
RON'S DINER
WHAT'LL IT BE, FELLAS?
CHICKEN 'N VEGGIES, PLEASE!
GRILLED OR FRIED ON THE CHICKEN?
AS PLAIN AS HUMANLY POSSIBLE.
HELP WANTED
THAT CAN HAPPEN.
AND YOU?
BURGER.
FRIES.
NOT A PROBLEM.
...IS EVERYTHING OKAY?
SIGH

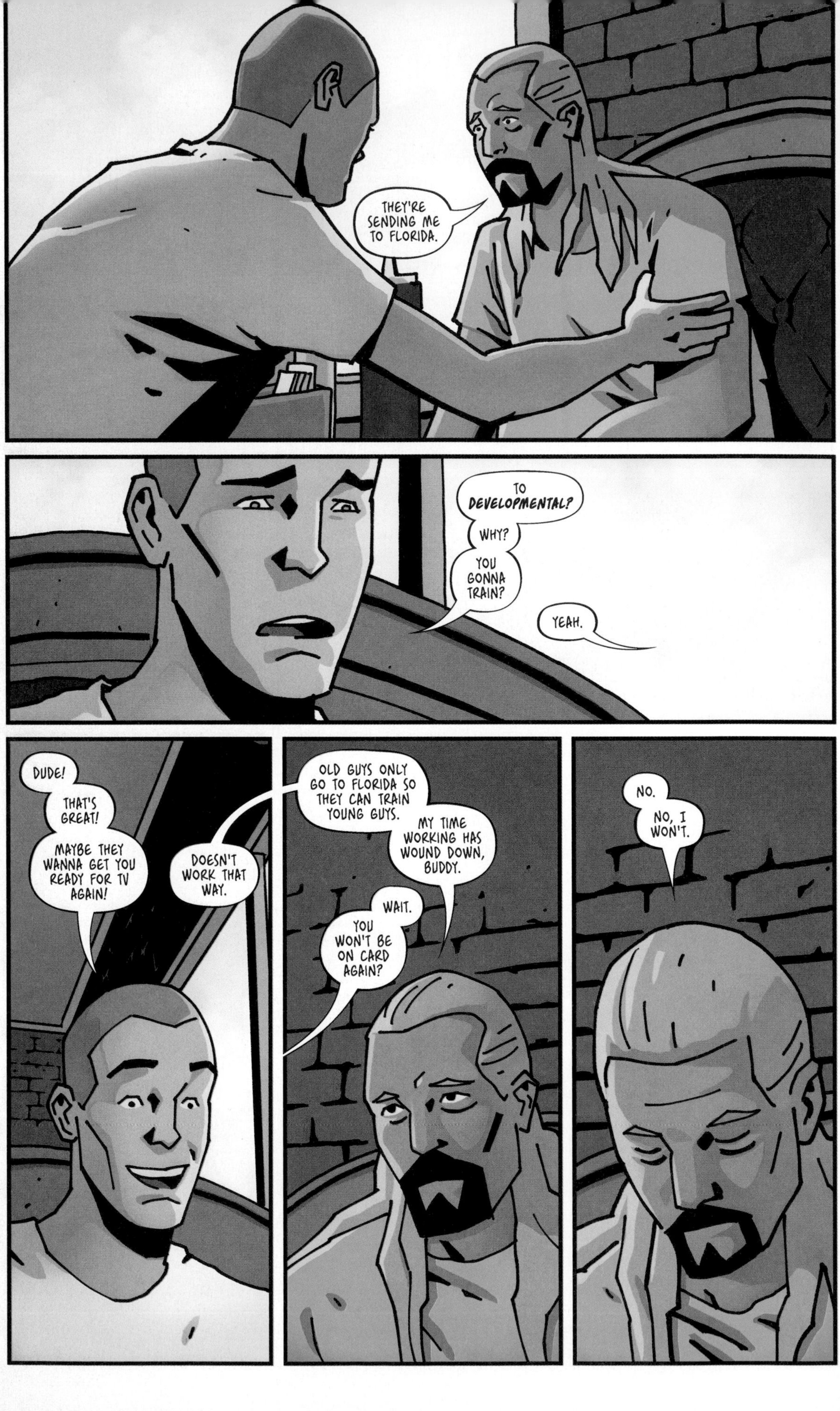
THEY'RE SENDING ME TO FLORIDA.
TO DEVELOPMENTAL?
WHY?
YOU GONNA TRAIN?
YEAH.
DUDE!
THAT'S GREAT!
MAYBE THEY WANNA GET YOU READY FOR TV AGAIN!
DOESN'T WORK THAT WAY.
OLD GUYS ONLY GO TO FLORIDA SO THEY CAN TRAIN YOUNG GUYS.
MY TIME WORKING HAS WOUND DOWN, BUDDY.
WAIT.
YOU WON'T BE ON CARD AGAIN?
NO.
NO, I WON'T.

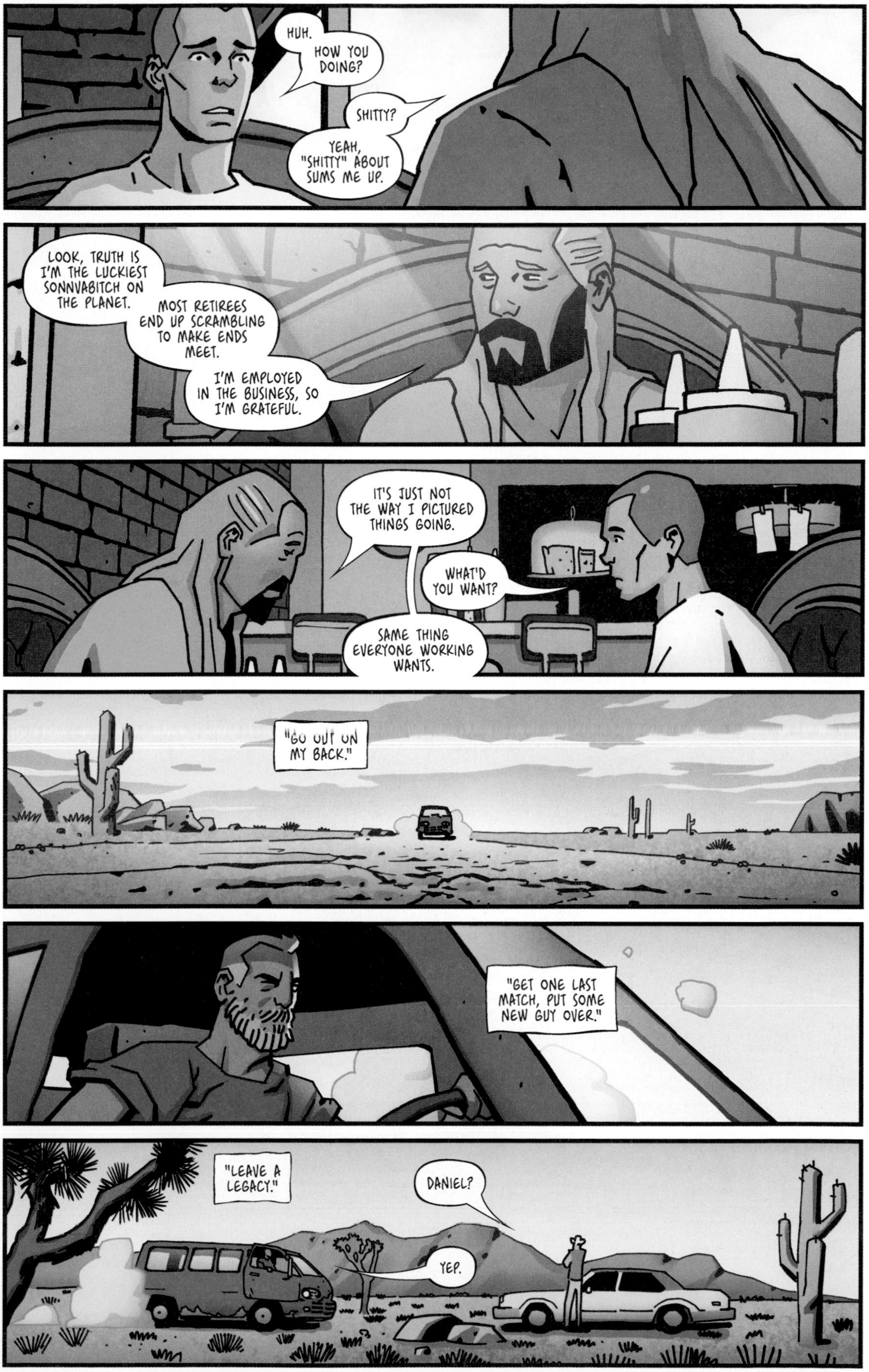

HUH.
HOW YOU DOING?
SHITTY?
YEAH, "SHITTY" ABOUT SUMS ME UP.
LOOK, TRUTH IS I'M THE LUCKIEST SONNVABITCH ON THE PLANET.
MOST RETIREES END UP SCRAMBLING TO MAKE ENDS MEET.
I'M EMPLOYED IN THE BUSINESS, SO I'M GRATEFUL.
IT'S JUST NOT THE WAY I PICTURED THINGS GOING.
WHAT'D YOU WANT?
SAME THING EVERYONE WORKING WANTS.
"GO OUT ON MY BACK."
"GET ONE LAST MATCH, PUT SOME NEW GUY OVER."
"LEAVE A LEGACY."
DANIEL?
YEP.

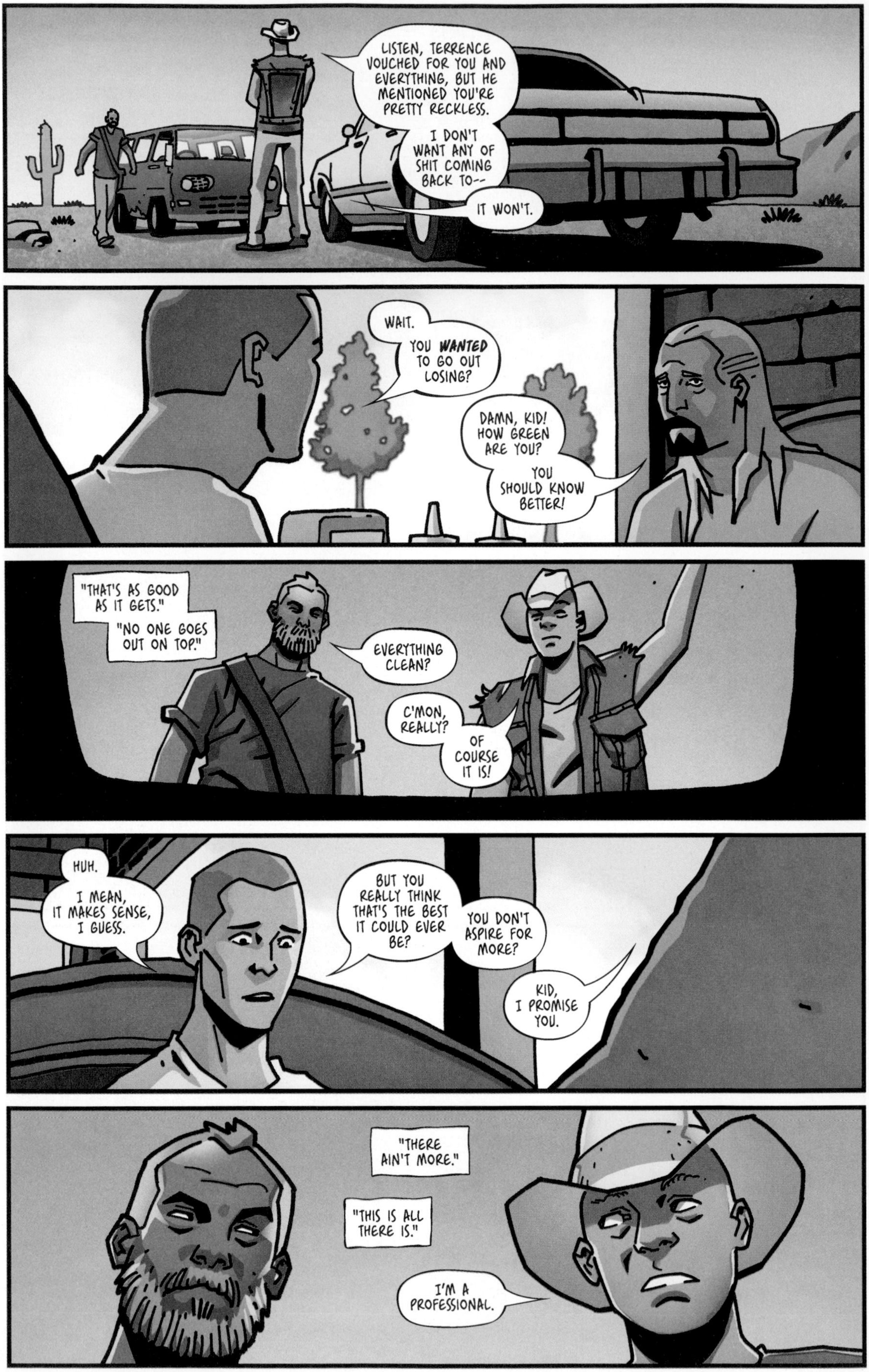
LISTEN, TERRENCE VOUCHED FOR YOU AND EVERYTHING, BUT HE MENTIONED YOU'RE PRETTY RECKLESS.
I DON'T WANT ANY OF SHIT COMING BACK TO--
IT WON'T.
WAIT.
YOU WANTED TO GO OUT LOSING?
DAMN, KID! HOW GREEN ARE YOU?
YOU SHOULD KNOW BETTER!
"THAT'S AS GOOD AS IT GETS."
"NO ONE GOES OUT ON TOP."
EVERYTHING CLEAN?
C'MON, REALLY?
OF COURSE IT IS!
HUH.
I MEAN, IT MAKES SENSE, I GUESS.
BUT YOU REALLY THINK THAT'S THE BEST IT COULD EVER BE?
YOU DON'T ASPIRE FOR MORE?
KID, I PROMISE YOU.
"THERE AIN'T MORE."
"THIS IS ALL THERE IS."
I'M A PROFESSIONAL.

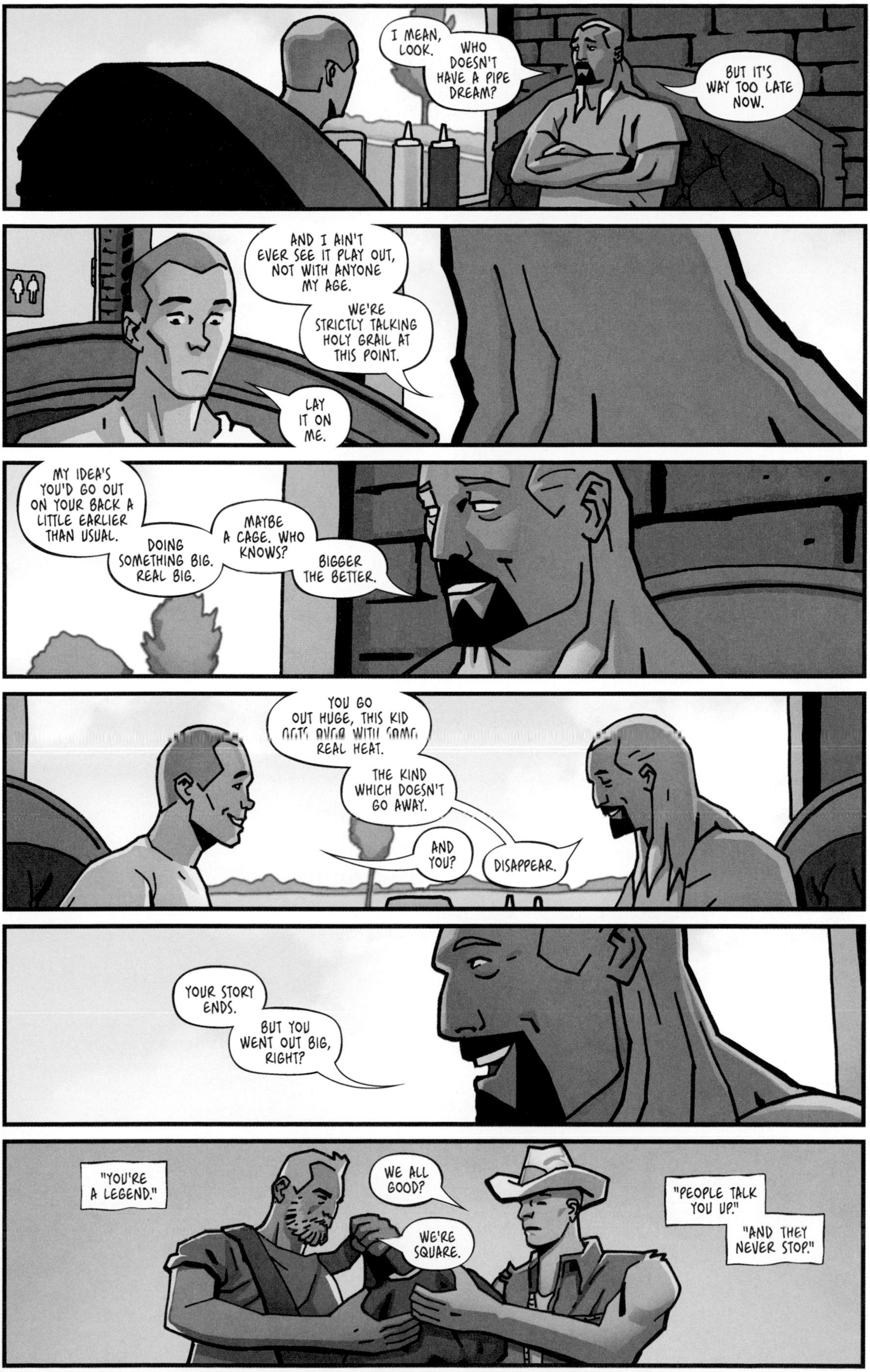
I MEAN, LOOK.
WHO DOESN'T HAVE A PIPE DREAM?
BUT IT'S WAY TOO LATE NOW.
AND I AIN'T EVER SEE IT PLAY OUT, NOT WITH ANYONE MY AGE.
WE'RE STRICTLY TALKING HOLY GRAIL AT THIS POINT.
LAY IT ON ME.
MY IDEA'S YOU'D GO OUT ON YOUR BACK A LITTLE EARLIER THAN USUAL.
DOING SOMETHING BIG. REAL BIG.
MAYBE A CAGE. WHO KNOWS?
BIGGER THE BETTER.
YOU GO OUT HUGE, THIS KID GETS OVER WITH SOME REAL HEAT.
THE KIND WHICH DOESN'T GO AWAY.
AND YOU?
DISAPPEAR.
YOUR STORY ENDS.
BUT YOU WENT OUT BIG, RIGHT?
"YOU'RE A LEGEND."
WE ALL GOOD?
WE'RE SQUARE.
"PEOPLE TALK YOU UP."
"AND THEY NEVER STOP."

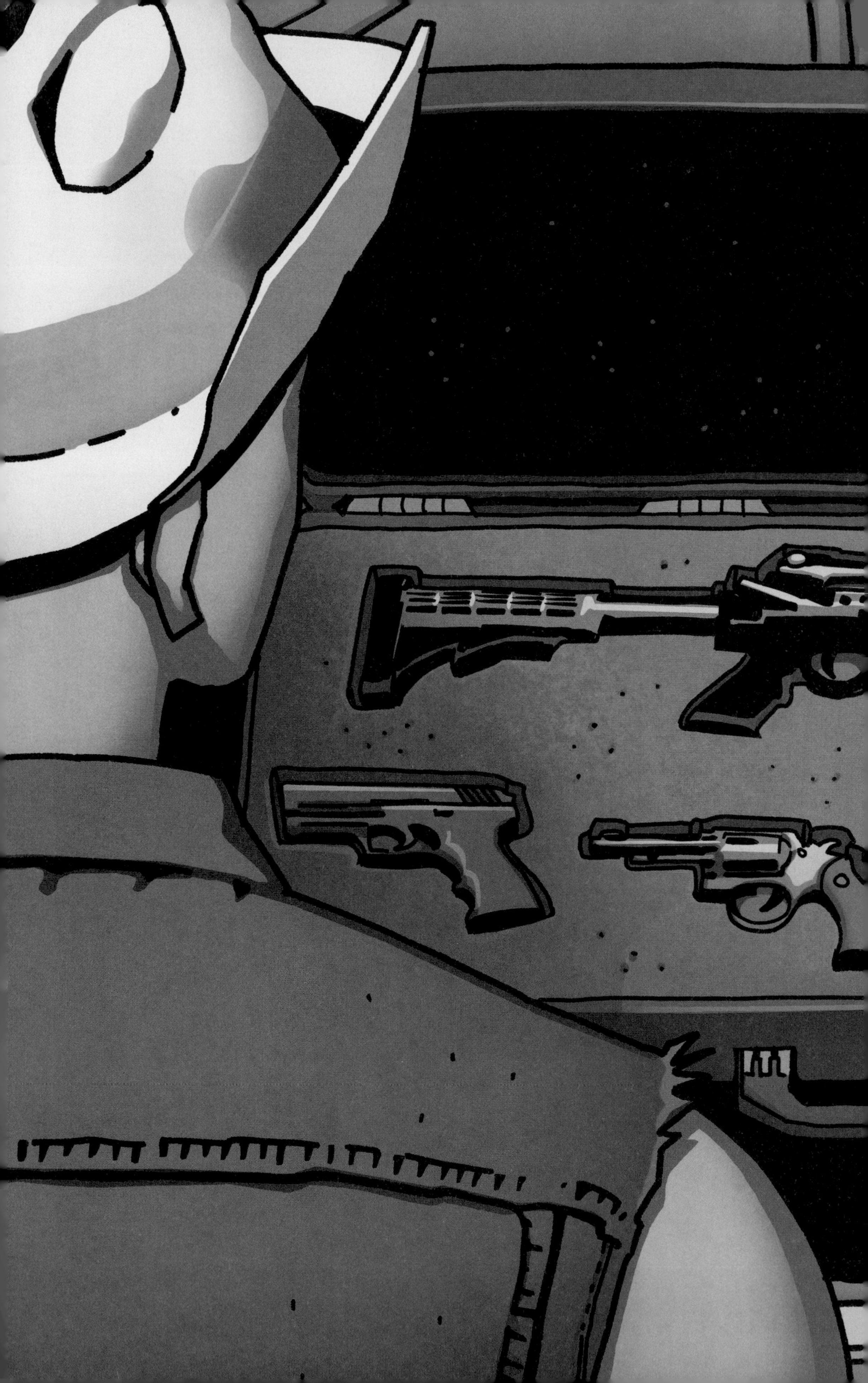

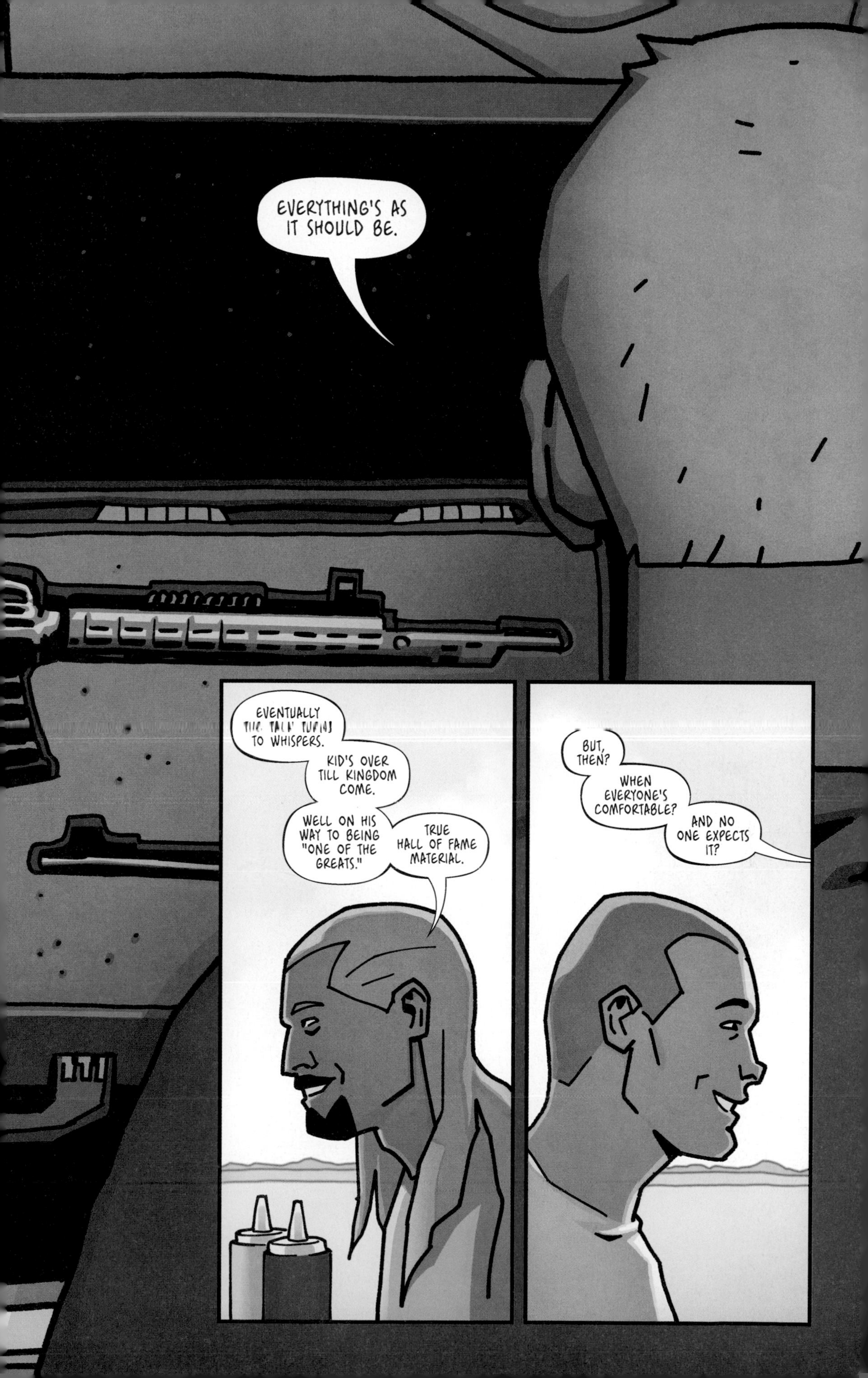
EVERYTHING'S AS IT SHOULD BE.
EVENTUALLY THE TALK TURNS TO WHISPERS.
KID'S OVER TILL KINGDOM COME.
WELL ON HIS WAY TO BEING "ONE OF THE GREATS."
TRUE HALL OF FAME MATERIAL.
BUT, THEN?
WHEN EVERYONE'S COMFORTABLE?
AND NO ONE EXPECTS IT?

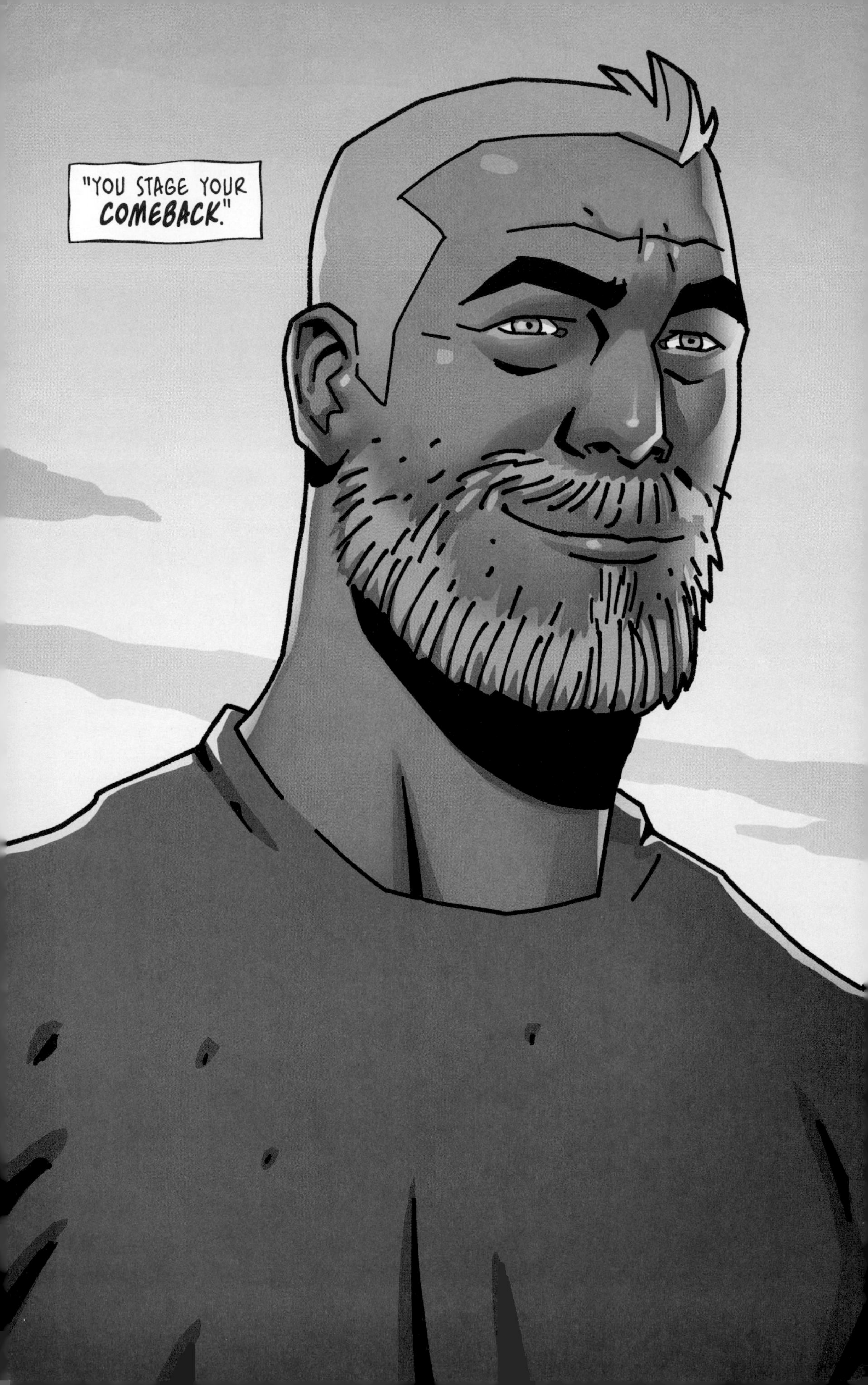
"YOU STAGE YOUR COMEBACK."

CREATOR COMMENTARY

Let's start with how it all began for you guys. What's your history with wrestling? Who kept you going as a mark and led you to making RINGSIDE?

JOE KEATINGE: I've gone through a few phases, but it all started thanks to my uncle, who saw my love of superheroes and thought he'd share his love of wrestling. Which was, especially at the time, a pretty easy transition. We're talking the early 1980s, we were seeing the very end of the transition from the territory days to the global takeover with Larger Than Life titans like Hogan, Macho Man Randy Savage, Jake "The Snake" Roberts, Undertaker, Ultimate Warrior, Andre the Giant, Million Dollar Man, Papa Shango, Sgt. Slaughter, and Iron Sheik, among a pantheon of others, taking center stage. Wrestling was everywhere at the time -- in my cartoons, in comic books, in bendy action figures, in Princess Bride. You couldn't escape it, not that I wanted to.

Years later a lot of life happened and I wasn't as in tune with the scene as I once was, but the same uncle somewhat frantically called me and said I had to start watching again Right Now. Some guy named Steve Austin had just changed the game. I watched. And I was addicted, but that was thanks to Mick Foley.

Foley was the guy who changed my perception of what wrestling was. Not just because of who he was in the ring – he was one of the best on a technical level, but he also had a cadence and honesty about why he was doing what he was doing. He was the first guy I read who wrote eloquently about the pursuit, who discussed the real world sacrifice and pain that went far beyond anything in the ring. Seeing Beyond the Mat and witnessing this guy who was falling from the roofs of steel cages be the sweetest dude on the planet with his family and putting it all on the line despite the cost to his health (and in one case, ear), because there wasn't any way he was going to give it less than his best. And that changed everything for me.

Another big love of mine is comics and it's an industry which has historically been unkind to those giants who came before. The co-creator of Batman never got any credit for essentially changing the character from the absolute most generic garbage into the icon we know today. The artist and co-creator of Superman ended up drawing porn comics to make ends meet. To this day, there are organizations like the Hero Initiative who assist those still with us with every day expenses. These people broke their backs and wrists, in the very literal sense, creating what now fuels multi-billion dollar multimedia industries. Luckily companies like Marvel and DC have since evolved with the times and were particularly generous with me and largely kind to work with, but it's hard to not see those historical parallels

Through Foley I started to see a lot of parallels between wrestling and comics along these lines, seeing what happens to the big stars when they become the old guard and, in some cases, become the forgotten. How despite them giving everything night after night, they don't all get the happy ending. Even in a more contemporary sense, seeing someone as young as Edge being forced to retire from the thing he spent his life pursuing or Shango living under such harsh condition – it's eye opening and unfortunately familiar.

There's a positive side too. A big positive side. Through getting into Foley's past, I got into early ECW, which opened my eyes to the amazing independent scene. I'm living in Oregon, which the WWE wouldn't go to for years, but in its place grew Portland Wrestling, which always brought to mind the emergence of independent publishing in want of somewhere to do what they wanted to do without restriction. Places like Image, sure, but the other parallels with the Dave Sims, Colleen Dorans, Scott McClouds, Robert Kirkmans, Kelly Sue DeConnicks, Matt Fractions, Sean Philips, Ed Brubakers and Raina Telgemeiers of the comics world. People who did their own thing by themselves either because no one else was giving them a shot on a nation wide level or the corporate companies just didn't provide the proper means of their expression anymore, much like contemporary promotions like Ring of Honor and Chikara. These people all did something new and interesting and in the case of both ECW and Image Comics, ended up radically changing how the major organizations functioned and marketed themselves.

Anyway, as a guy who makes his living writing comics, the more I'd get into the work of guys like David Shoemaker or Colt Cobana and see where the various scenes are now on a very personal and intimate level, and how it continues to evolve whether it's indie or corporate, it made me feel an element of kinship with this thing I've loved for so long.

A big part of RINGSIDE is wanting to examine a number of points which emerge from that cross pollination of both interest in and passion for comics and wrestling. Examining why people dedicate their lives to something which will likely break them. To see the conflict between art and industry. To see what it takes to be successful, and how success can radically change from person to person, then looking at how hard you can fall.

On the offset, the books does follow two wrestlers – one who's long passed his prime and is dealing with a brutal situation from the life before he ever got in the ring and a young guy who's seeing what he grew up loving be stripped away of passion and turned into market commodity – but my goal's to get at it from a number of perspectives. Corporate and independent. Wrestler

and fan, accountant or music composer, who knows? As long Nick and I feel we are serving the book well and have more to say, we'll keep growing its scope and ensemble.

NICK BARBER: When I was growing up my older brother was a WWF fanatic, so he was probably the one that fueled my interest in it. Over here in New Zealand it was on TV really late at night (which in hindsight probably wasn't that late, but really made it more desirable to us). We had wrestling magazines, action figures (even a small ring), posters, trading cards – the works. Hulk Hogan was obviously the big name back then, Macho Man etc. And of course, the local heroes The Bushwackers. Hard to pick favourites amongst such an entertaining cast. I had a pretty big crush on Miss Elizabeth.
Then later during highschool there was a big wrestling renaissance for me, with the Stone Cold 'attitude era', and WCW. We would 'wrestle' during lunch time (basically would just beat the crap out of each other). In fact, one of my friends received a broken rib from a 'doomsday device' tag-team move gone wrong. I think it led to a ban on wrestling at the school.

I'm really curious as to your inspirations, and any real-life wrestlers or instances you've drawn from. In the wrestling business, it's always hard to find something authentic - people are always playing parts, or creating these exaggerated versions of themselves, and sometimes it's hard to really know what's part of that persona and what's not. As two people outside of a business who still tries to remain heavily guarded, what do you do to bring that authenticity without sounding like a just couple of guys who know some insider terms?

NICK BARBER: Inspiration for working on this book came from the stories revolving around wrestler's lives outside of the ring. Guys like Jake the Snake, Bret Hart, Kamala (and countless others) really seemed to get chewed up and spit out by the 'business' of wrestling, or wind up going down a dark path. There's just a fascinating contrast between the in-ring theatrics, the spectacle - and the everyday repurcussions of making it in that industry.

RINGSIDE is definitely an honest look at people within the business – but doesn't assume an existing knowledge from the reader. It's accessible to anyone that likes a great story, in much the same way something like The Sopranos could be enjoyed without knowing the inner workings of the Mafia.

Not having done a lot of comics it was both freeing and terrifying to figure out how RINGSIDE would look. I didn't have a go-to 'style', again both a blessing and a curse. I wanted to come up with a look that suited the story - the art is very loose and sketchy, there's roughness to the world of RINGSIDE that I wanted to emphasise.

JOE KEATINGE: Like I mentioned, Foley was the catalyst for me having an interest in what was going on behind the curtain and not caring about rumors or gossip, but the very real cost people gave to entertain millions. In between then and now a number of people – many I mentioned already – but very much including the whole debacle CM Punk went through, both in the spotlight and reality, made it abundantly clear that the initial outline I had for RINGSIDE – which dates back to 2010, so its been in the making for a while – was even more relevant now than it was upon conception, for better or worse.

All this said, I do get I'm an outsider examining and conveying an industry and, more importantly, a community I'm not a part of. One of the big reasons its taken half a decade to get this book going was being conscious that I didn't want to risk appropriating said culture and misrepresent it despite good intention.

The biggest eye opener has been going to a lot of Portland indie shows lately and seeing these people bust ass and break backs in the ring as if they were filling seats in a massive arena even if they were in an Eagle Lodge for little financial reward has made me very conscious that we can't fuck this one up. And if I do, own up to it and improve where we fall short.

It's a tough balance, because on the one hand, I want to make this accessible to people who have never watched a match. I also want to make it feel authentic in spirit, even though we're

highly fictionalizing reality (and definitely conveying some shit I know would never happen in the real world) yet I'm also very conscious a lot of people in the business don't like it when random assholes like me start spouting off, claiming they're on the inside of this understandably guarded community, but my hope is the love and respect comes through in tone and execution.

It seems like you have a knack for finding the perfect artists for your stories. The incredible Sophie Campbell (currently doing things that make my heart sing on Jem and the Holograms), Leila de Duca, Ming Doyle - all of them worked so well in striking the right tone for each book. Now, with Nick and RINGSIDE, it seems like another perfect fit. How did the partnership come about?

NICK BARBER: I think I got on Joe's radar from posting art online. We talked about working on something together and what that might be. I said I would like to do a comic that would be kind of like a Michael Mann film, we both shared a interest in 'Thief'. Joe said he had the perfect project - and he was right.

JOE KEATINGE: Getting the right team together is one of the most important aspects of developing a series. Making sure you have the perfect collaborator can make or break a book. RINGSIDE has been an idea I've been kicking around for over half a decade, but it wasn't complete, it was never right. It wasn't until I saw Nick's art on Tumblr in the form of sketches based off movies I loved (Breathless was the big one which made me drop him an e-mail, but generally Kubrick and Kurosawa) and thought I finally found the perfect collaborator. He's perfect at nuance, perfect at getting across what the actors/directors intended in a totally different medium, his storytelling in stills was dead on so I had a good read he'd be just as good with sequentials. And he's even better. Like with Leila, Sophie and Ming before, I'm grateful we came together.

Wrestling comics have been done before, but conflating the fantasy of a comic world with the fantasy of the wrestling world has proven to be a difficult balance to strike. Both can go from a gritty, stripped down style to entire universes of high fantasy and gimmicks that take the most suspension of disbelief to follow. In RINGSIDE, you have some pretty rough and tumble 'normal' looking fellows, and then a giant-ass minotaur gimmick. How hard is it to decide how far you want to go with the freedoms that both avenues give you?

JOE KEATINGE: This is tough to answer, because I don't think it'll be evident until the series goes on for a bit, but the conflict between fantasy and reality is actually a major through line of the series. Despite it being years since our initial lead (and who the lead is will change as it goes on) was in the ring, he finds his reality struggles with the fiction his gimmick built around him.

NICK BARBER: The contrast of in-ring personas and gimmicks vs. the reality of the character's lives is definitely a big focus in the book. Daniel's 'Minotaur' persona sort of embodies everything he's trying to get away from in that industry.

Joe, one of the things that immediately made me connect with your writing, and books like Glory and Shutter is your ability to write such amazing, strong female characters. Wrestling is traditionally terribly unkind to women, though progress in that area lately has been slow but steady. RINGSIDE has a male lead with primarily male characters. Without spoiling too much, will we get to see more of that strong female presence?

JOE KEATINGE: Absolutely. RINGSIDE having such a masculine set up is methodical and as we'll see, we'll be shifting away towards something reminiscent of my other work in terms of representation once we get into the second arc. I'd rather the work speak for itself here, but I think readers of Shutter and Glory who connected with it for the same reasons as you did will end up very happy with one of the messages we'll be getting across as the series goes on.

NICK BARBER: I feel like Amy is probably the most bad-ass character in the book so far.

The overlap between wrestling fans and comic fans is pretty big, especially when it comes to the wrestlers themselves. Since the book will also attract people who may like comics but not wrestling, and vice versa, what do you hope will speak to each side of that audience?

JOE KEATINGE: My hope is the book will appeal to people whether or not they're into wrestling. If you're into it, sure, you'll likely get something different than someone who's not. Yet in the end, the most important aspect of the book are the general empathy I hope people have for the characters, the situation, and the general struggle of dreams versus money, that kind of thing.

For example, I've never watched a Texas high school football game, but I loved Friday Night Lights. I'm hoping the same happens for people who've never watched wrestling and RINGSIDE.

NICK BARBER: RINGSIDE will definitely appeal to both wrestling fans and people that don't know anything about it. It's not like El Santo or something where disputes are settled in the ring, the tone is more like 'Scalped' or 'The Sopranos' - that type of thing. It's a fairly gritty story.

And lastly, again, without giving too much away, what can expect from the future of RINGSIDE?

NICK BARBER: I've been genuinely excited to get each new script on this book to see what happens next. You learn a lot about the characters as the series progresses which makes the story even more engaging, and at times really intense.

JOE KEATINGE: RINGSIDE's a brutal book about the different relationships forming throughout industry and art form, whether people meet or not, from worker to mark to creative to anyone, really. While entirely based in fiction, our aims to respect and service those who inspired us to create our own work to the best of our ability. I love wrestling too much to aim for anything less.●

JOE KEATINGE is the writer of Image, Skybound, Marvel and DC Comics titles including SHUTTER, RINGSIDE, GLORY, TECH JACKET, MARVEL KNIGHTS: HULK and ADVENTURES OF SUPERMAN as well as the Executive Editor of the Eisner & Harvey award-winning Image Comics anthology, POPGUN, and the Courtney Taylor-Taylor penned ONE MODEL NATION.

NICK BARBER is from Auckland, New Zealand which means he has a funny accent and a penchant for second breakfast. Nick likes to tell stories and entertain people which he is now lucky enough to do for a living. RINGSIDE is Nick's first professional comic, and hopefully the first of many.

SIMON GOUGH is a 34-year-old man with a 4-year-old's job. Colouring in! Born in Birmingham, in the middle of the United Kingdom, but now living down south in the sunny seaside hamlet of Brighton. Always eager to paint from a young age, and even more eager to read comics, it seemed only natural to eventually, after all those years of exploratory art education, intertwine those two loves into one (hopefully) booming career!

ARIANA MAHER is a Brazilian-American born in New Jersey who spent her formative years in Japan and Singapore. You wouldn't think any one person could talk about comic book lettering for hours... but then you met her. By day, she is an ordinary citizen, but by night she transforms into a weird recluse obsessed with balloon tails and text placement. Her last reported sighting was the Seattle area. If spotted, approach with caution and/ or more comics for her to letter.

RINGSIDE

CREATED BY **JOE KEATINGE + NICK BARBER**

JOE KEATINGE writer

NICK BARBER artist

SIMON GOUGH colorist

ARIANA MAHER letterer

SHANNA MATSUZAK editor

design + layout by **ADDISON DUKE**
logo designed by **BRANDON GRAHAM**
special thanks to **DARREN SHAN**

SEP 0 1 2016

IMAGE COMICS, INC.
Robert Kirkman- chief operating officer
Erik Larsen- chief financial officer
Todd McFarlane- president
Marc Silvestri- chief executive officer
Jim Valentino- vice-president
www.imagecomics.com

Eric Stephenson - publisher
Corey Murphy - director of sales
Jeff Boison - director of publishing planning & book trade sales
Jeremy Sullivan - director of digital sales
Kat Salazar - director of pr & marketing
Emily Miller - director of operations
Branwyn Bigglestone - senior accounts manager
Sarah Mello - accounts manager

Drew Gill - art director
Jonathan Chan - production manager
Meredith Wallace - print manager
Briah Skelly - publicity assistant
Sasha Head - sales & marketing production designer
Randy Okamura - digital production designer
David Brothers - branding manager
Ally Power - content manager

Addison Duke - production artist
Vincent Kukua - production artist
Tricia Ramos - production artist
Jeff Stang - direct market sales representative
Emilio Bautista- digital sales associate
Leanna Caunter- accounting assistant
Chloe Ramos-Peterson - administrative assistant